I0815901

Praise for
Our Life, Our Sweetness, and Our Hope!

One of the devil's most cunning tricks is trying to lead us to despair, to believing that we are beyond God's redemptive grace. Donna-Marie Cooper O'Boyle's fine book, *Our Life, Our Sweetness, and Our Hope!* is a welcome reminder that our Blessed Mother is always there for us, and a constant source of hope, encouragement, and companionship towards a closer relationship with her Son, Jesus.

— **His Eminence, Timothy Cardinal Dolan,**
Archbishop of New York

Explore the profound journey of the Blessed Virgin Mary in *Our Life, Our Sweetness, and Our Hope!* This captivating book illustrates Mother Mary's life as the perfect example of the Christian journey of life. Discover how her unwavering faith and devotion can inspire and guide your own pilgrimage toward Eternal salvation.

— **Father Luke Fletcher, CFR,** chaplain of The World
Apostolate of Fatima, USA Shrine

Every pilgrimage is a sacred journey. In *Our Life, Our Sweetness, and Our Hope!* Donna-Marie Cooper O'Boyle takes you on a sacred journey of hope through the heart and apparitions of our Blessed Mother, Mary. No matter what trials and uncertainties you face, they will seem less daunting by the time you finish this reassuring book.

— **Marge Steinhage Fenelon,** author of
Defend Us in Battle: The Promises of St. Michael and the Heavenly Angels and *America's Mary: The Story of Our Lady of Good Help*

In reading Donna-Marie's new book, I slowed down to savor the beauty of the presentation. The author skillfully leads readers on a luminous pilgrimage with Mary and addresses our need for more hope. This is more than a book to read; it is a retreat with Mary in which we ponder the wonder of Our Lady's life, legacy, and love. Mary's Heart radiates throughout these pages. I highly recommend Donna-Marie's book and pray it graces every Catholic home!

— **Kathleen Beckman,** author of *A Family Guide to Spiritual Warfare*, evangelist, and president, Foundation of Prayer for Priests

Donna-Marie has given us a great gift for the Jubilee Year — a prayerful, guided walk through the year with Our Lady. Her grace-filled insights into Mary's walk with us on our pilgrimage to Jesus will help countless souls encounter her Son more intensely during this Year of Hope.

— **Patrick Novecosky,** author of *100 Ways John Paul II Changed the World*

In this beautiful book, Donna-Marie Cooper O'Boyle invites us on a worldwide pilgrimage through biblical scenes, apparitions, images, and miracles to enrich our hope. Truly the Blessed Virgin Mary is "our life, our sweetness, and our hope," our prayerful intercessor and exemplar, causing our life to be filled with purpose, abundant with sweet consolation, and sealed with hope for eternal joy. As we follow the author's prompts to reflect, act, pray, and savor, our heavenly Mother will guide us in the way of her Son as we make our pilgrim journey toward the source and goal of our precious life.

— **Stephen J. Binz,** author of *The Way of Mercy: Pilgrimage in Catholic Poland* and *Threshold Bible Study* at Bridge-B.com

If St. Paul could say "Hope does not disappoint" (Romans 5:5), we can say in tandem that Donna-Marie Cooper O'Boyle's newest book about "Hope" does not disappoint! This book offers a spiritual roadmap with Mother Mary as our guide. Regaling us with fascinating tidbits, anecdotes, well-documented citations, and brilliant reflections, the author grounds our steps in sound Catholic tradition. After presenting a foundational understanding of the Blessed Virgin Mary in the Sacred Scriptures, the author portrays Mother Mary in action. She gives us a panorama of Church-approved apparitions and mystical intuitions, bursting at the seams with the theme of hope. Hope is this book's *leitmotif.* Mary is its protagonist, the embodiment of hope. She conducts the pilgrim on a path towards union with the Divine source of hope.

— **Father James McCurry, OFM Conv,** Minister Provincial Emeritus, Franciscan Friars Conventual

Mary is an icon of hope. The people of God waited with expectant hope for the Savior's coming. Mary, through her Fiat, brought hope incarnate into the world. The people of God still wait in joyful hope of Christ's return. During our time of waiting, we are encouraged by Our Lady who has spoken messages of hope at the bleakest of times. In daily life, we still turn to Mary and her intercession for restored and renewed hope. Donna-Marie Cooper O'Boyle writes an icon of Our Lady in her latest book, unlocking her as a vessel of hope for Christians today. Find your inspiration to return to Mary, who is our life, our sweetness, and our hope.

— **Father Edward Looney, STL,** past president of the Mariological Society of America, author, and podcaster

Since the first century, Mary has appeared to Christians to give them hope. That the Church has survived the ordeals of 2,000 years is in part due to her ongoing maternal mission. This book is a record of her visitations in modern times, and so it is a vessel of hope.

— **Mike Aquilina,** author of *History's Queen* and *Keeping Mary Close*

As you journey through this expressive and relevant book *Our Life, Our Sweetness, and Our Hope!* Jubilee Pilgrims of Hope with Mary, you'll find that through the recounting of Marian apparitions, historical events, and true compelling modern life stories, author Donna-Marie Cooper O'Boyle reminds us that in the example and inspiration of Mary we have the perfect guide on our pilgrimage of hope towards Heaven.

— **Michael O'Neill,** "The Miracle Hunter,"
award-winning author and EWTN host.

Our Life, Our Sweetness, *and* Our HOPE!

Jubilee Pilgrims of Hope with Mary

By Donna-Marie Cooper O'Boyle

© 2024 Donna-Marie Cooper O'Boyle. All rights reserved.

Available from:
Marian Helpers Center
Stockbridge, MA 01263
Prayerline: 1-800-804-3823
Orderline: 1-800-462-7426

Websites:
ShopMercy.org
TheDivineMercy.org
DivineMercyPlus.org

Library of Congress Catalog Number: 2024946581
ISBN: 978-1-59614-632-7

Imprimi Potest:
Very Rev. Chris Alar, MIC, Provincial Superior
The Blessed Virgin Mary, Mother of Mercy Province
October 7, 2024
Feast of Our Lady of the Rosary

Nihil Obstat:
Robert A. Stackpole, STD, Censor Deputatus
October 7, 2024

Note: The *Nihil Obstat* and corresponding *Imprimi Potest* are not a certification that those granting it agree with the contents, opinions, or statements expressed in the work. Instead, they merely confirm that the work contains nothing contrary to faith and morals.

All illustrations are public domain, Adobe Stock, Metropolitan Museum of Art/Open Access, or provided. Page 80 is courtesy Wikimedia Commons/ Sailko, and page 144 is from championshrine.org.

Cover design and layout by Kathy Szpak

Scripture quotations are taken from the New Revised Standard Version Bible: Catholic Edition, copyright © 1989, 1993 the Division of Christian Education of the National Council of the Churches of Christ in the United States of America. Used by permission. All rights reserved.

Excerpts from the English translation of the *Catechism of the Catholic Church* for use in the United States of America Copyright © 1994, United States Catholic Conference, Inc. — Libreria Editrice Vaticana. Used with Permission. English translation of the *Catechism of the Catholic Church: Modifications from the Editio Typica* copyright © 1997, United States Conference of Catholic Bishops — Libreria Editrice Vaticana.

Lovingly for my children:
Justin, Chaldea, Jessica, Joseph,
and Mary-Catherine.

And much love for my grandchildren:
Shepherd and Leo.

For my brother, Dr. Eugene J. Cooper,
in loving memory.

And especially for my dear Mother Mary,
my life, my sweetness, and my hope!

CONTENTS

"The Immaculate Conception of Aranjuez" by Bartolome Esteban Murillo, c. 1675.

PREFACE

Hail, Holy Queen, Mother of Mercy,
our life, our sweetness, and our hope ...

In spite of being held at gunpoint and kept captive by a deranged ex-Marine, I still have hope.

In spite of being abandoned by my husband at the side of the road with small children and one due to be born any day, I still have hope.

In spite of my many miscarriages, I still have hope.

In spite of chronic illness, Lyme disease, and daily headaches, I still have hope.

In spite of losing three siblings, I still have hope.

In spite of being sexually assaulted, I still have hope.

In spite of losing my family home and being put out on the street, I still have hope.

In spite of being falsely accused, I still have hope.

In spite of physical and emotional abuse, I still have hope.

In spite of struggling as a single mother for many years, I still have hope.

In spite of endless court battles for my children, I still have hope.

In spite of living in poverty, I still have hope.

I certainly do not wish to compare myself to St. Paul when he spoke of his severe hardships and experiences, including "imprisonments, with countless floggings, and often near death ... in toil and hardship, through many a sleepless night, hungry and thirsty, often without food, cold and naked" (2 Cor 11:23, 27). But if I can be like St. Paul at all, I would also choose to speak of my weakness as he did.

You can read about the traumas and terrible hardships in my life in my memoir *The Kiss of Jesus*. But this book is all about hope.

Let's talk about that wondrous, miraculous, and essential virtue of HOPE! We all need it, and even crave additional hope to fill our lives. We would be fooling ourselves if we said we were happy and at peace (perhaps filling our lives with things to fill the void or mask the pain) but did not have hope dwelling in our hearts.

Yes, no doubt as we traverse this seemingly mysterious pilgrimage through life with all of its twists and turns, we will get wounded, tears will be shed, and we might even lose our way at times. We experience misery — we can feel miserable! We certainly acutely feel the torturous stabbing pains of hardship. We might have questions about unanswered prayers or harbor bitterness towards God.

Nevertheless — there is hope!

With God's grace and our cooperation, even in just opening the door of our hearts a little bit, we will begin to recognize that there is always the sure existence of holy hope. The hope to get better, the hope to go on — but not just simply by dragging our feet. I mean real hope for real miracles in our life! Yes! It happens! It will continue to happen! When it does, we won't be dragging our feet, but we will be running forward with *Supercalifragilesticexpealadocious* hope! (Sorry! I couldn't help myself.) But I think you know what I mean! Our heart will be brimming, even overflowing, with hope! We will become crusaders of hope! All the while, we will be a radiant example of hope in a world in desperate need of hope.

Jesus' beautiful Sacred Heart goes out to the hurting, the weak, and the weary, to the downtrodden, helpless, and forgotten. He seeks to impart His great love and mercy upon us. Wow! Talk about hope!

When St. Faustina felt she had given herself entirely to Jesus and that there was nothing more she could possibly offer to Him, Jesus kindly corrected her. She *did* have something. She could offer Him her very misery.

Specifically, He told her, **"My daughter, you have not offered Me that which is really yours."**[1]

Saint Faustina tried to understand. Jesus explained, **"Daughter, give Me your misery, because it is your exclusive property."** A holy light immediately illuminated the young mystic's soul. She nestled in against Jesus' Sacred Heart with complete trust in His mercy.

Another time, Jesus told His "Secretary of Mercy," **"For you, I am mercy itself; therefore I ask you to offer Me your misery**

and this very helplessness of yours and, in this way, you will delight My Heart."[2]

Along my crooked path in life, I have learned to offer my misery to Jesus — to strive to give everything to Him! To trust Him with all of my heart — not only when things are peachy keen, but especially during the times when I have no idea about what might be or actually is lurking around the corner — and so far, it's looking pretty terrible. At those times, I prayerfully hung on to hope! With God's grace, I hoped against all hope.

I have great hope because of the amazing gift of faith. I have hope in my heart because of Jesus' glorious love and mercy. I have hope because I have a beautiful Mother in Heaven, who loves me and guides me ever closer to her Son Jesus! She is my tremendous anchor of hope.

I have abundant hope in my heart because I have seen God's grace move so powerfully in my own life and in the lives of others too. I possess real hope because I have witnessed miracles. Yes! I have seen major miraculous transformations occur. Yes, I have lived miracles as well as trauma.

I hope because I have known saints personally. Through them, I have seen God's grace radically change the world. I don't deserve the blessings of having saints like St. Mother Teresa and Servant of God Fr. John Hardon, SJ, in my life, as well as Fr. Andrew Apostoli, CFR. But I truly believe that God allowed me to experience those blessings to not only help me but, perhaps more importantly, so that I can share these amazing saints and their teachings with the world to help others!

Speaking of the wisdom from the saints in my life, I'll impart one of the teachings right now. Dear Mother Teresa taught me to lovingly offer my sufferings to Jesus, and, further, she told me He would bring good out of them. Really! He does! He unites them to His Passion, death, and Resurrection and redeems the suffering for our own good and the good of others.

In one of her letters to me, typed on an old typewriter (in the night when her other duties were fulfilled), Mother Teresa wrote:

> I am sorry to hear the suffering you have to undergo. Jesus loves you and though He is the Lord of all — He

> cannot interfere with the gift of free will He has given to man. Jesus shares His love with you and shares His suffering and pain. He is a God of love and does not want His children to suffer, but when you accept your pain, suffering, death and resurrection, your pain becomes redemptive for yourself and for others.[3]

Miracles are waiting around the corner. We have to have hope!

Our Life's Journey

That said, let's get down to some brass tacks, shall we? Truth be told, we are all wayfarers on a mysterious pilgrimage through life, hoping to one day arrive at our Eternal Reward, the bliss of Heaven. Every journey is perfectly unique, and there's much to be done, lived, and shared before finally reaching that pivotal day. Along the way, we become increasingly aware that we surely have need of a great big dose of hope in a seemingly hopeless world. Some of the time, it's because of the absolute craziness of the world. Other times, it's because of the scuffles and wounds we endure and experience.

We learn in Scripture, "For in hope we were saved" (Rom 8:24). But where and how can we discover this yearned-for, genuine hope amid the confusion, despair, suffering, and discord of our present world? How is it that we can become a more hopeful person? Perhaps even able to offer a measure of our own hope to others we meet who are struggling? It's what we are meant to do, after all.

Truth be told, at times the world can appear to be a pretty scary place, and we might begin to feel utterly hopeless. That beautiful virtue of hope we were gifted at our Baptism might be forgotten, just a vague and distant memory. Or if not, it is a bit rusty or even buried too deep in our hearts to matter to us right now.

There's got to be a way to resurrect that precious hope in our hearts.

If we study psychological journals, we see that HOPE is very important, if not essential, to living a stable and happy life. When there's an abundance of depression, people do not know how to rejoice. Perhaps they are, at times, unable to do so. Lack of hope cripples us. Lack of hope robs our JOY!

We are blessed because our Catholic Church sees a great need for hope and has set aside the year 2025 as a special Jubilee Year of Hope, a holy year of grace and pilgrimage! We are blessed to live in these times.

In his papal bull *Spes Non Confundit*, Pope Francis reminds us of St. Paul's encouraging words to the Christian community of Rome: "Hope does not disappoint" (Rom 5:5). "Hope is also the central message of the coming Jubilee," the Holy Father continued. "My thoughts turn to all those *Pilgrims of Hope* who will travel to Rome in order to experience the Holy Year and to all those others who, though unable to visit the City of the Apostles Peter and Paul, will celebrate it in their local Churches."

Our pontiff wishes us to all encounter our Lord, Who is "our hope." Specifically, he expressed, "For everyone, may the Jubilee be a moment of genuine, personal encounter with the Lord Jesus, the 'door' (cf. Jn 10:7.9) of our salvation, whom the Church is charged to proclaim always, everywhere, and to all as 'our hope' (1 Tim 1:1)."[4]

Indeed, we long for great hope. For survival, we absolutely need hope in our lives. Pope Francis enlightens us, saying, "Hope finds its supreme witness in the *Mother of God*. In the Blessed Virgin, we see that hope is not naive optimism but a gift of grace amid the realities of life."[5]

What did Mary do? How can she teach us to persevere in hope — no matter what? Pope Francis tells us:

> Like every mother, whenever Mary looked at her Son, she thought of his future. Surely she kept pondering in her heart the words spoken to her in the Temple by the elderly Simeon: "This child is destined for the falling and rising of many in Israel, and to be a sign that will be opposed, so that the inner thoughts of many will be revealed — and a sword will pierce your own soul too" (Lk 2:34–35).

Mary knew. And Mary rose to the occasion with grace. She shows us how hope and grace were all wrapped up and interwoven with great suffering, grief, and sadness. Her hope never stopped. Her trust in God did not waiver.

Pope Francis points out, "At the foot of the cross, she witnessed the passion and death of Jesus, her innocent Son. Overwhelmed with grief, she nonetheless renewed her 'fiat,' never abandoning her hope and trust in God."

He elaborates, "In this way, Mary cooperated for our sake in the fulfillment of all that her Son had foretold in announcing that he would have to 'undergo great suffering, and be rejected by the elders, the chief priests, and the scribes, and be killed, and after three days rise again' (Mk 8:31)."[6]

Mary is our true Mother. How profoundly blessed we are that her Divine Son, despite His unspeakable suffering, made sure that we are not left orphans — that we have a Mother who will usher us to Heaven with our cooperation. Jesus made a point of giving us the most precious gift of His own Mother before He breathed His last.

Pope Francis tells us:

> In the travail of that sorrow, offered in love, Mary became our Mother, the Mother of Hope. It is not by chance that popular piety continues to invoke the Blessed Virgin as *Stella Maris*, a title that bespeaks the sure hope that, amid the tempests of this life, the Mother of God comes to our aid, sustains us, and encourages us to persevere in hope and trust.[7]

Holy Mary cooperated with every grace and moved her will to follow God's holy will. Looking back to Our Lady's courageous and exceedingly hopeful Fiat, we recognize that the Holy Family came into being with Mary's wholehearted yes. It's true! Jesus, Mary, and Joseph were Pilgrims of Hope in our world.

We learn from the *Catechism of the Catholic Church* that, down through the ages, as people were converted and became believers, "they desired that 'their whole household' should also be saved. These families who became believers were islands of Christian life in an unbelieving world."[8] Learning from the virtuous examples of the Holy Family and those who followed in their footsteps, we too can become more hopeful and strive to become a radiant example to others.

Hope is truly a lifesaver! Whether we have struggled through a world-wide pandemic, are dealing with seemingly hopeless diagnoses, losses, family troubles, or whatever else that might have caused us to become tempted to give up on hope, we should realize that God is certainly the foundation of our every hope. He will forever be. We need to continue to hope in His loving promises. He will never leave us! Again, He gifted us with the most eminent gift ever — His own Mother!

We know without doubt that salvation comes through Jesus. Still, many of the saints have preached the necessity of getting to know Mary so that she can more readily bring us to her Son. Saint Louis de Montfort, for instance, tells us that Mary, "is the most sure, the most easy, the most short, and the most perfect means by which to go to Jesus Christ."[9] God has designed it this way — that we go to His Mother and she lovingly brings us to Him.

To some people, God can seem scary. But a loving Mother is much less scary — even exceedingly welcoming. Remember, Mary knows our needs better than we know ourselves. We see this clearly in the account of the Wedding at Cana.

We are in excellent company with the saints. Saint Louis de Montfort quoted St. Augustine in his book *True Devotion to Mary*. He said, "The world being unworthy to receive the Son of God directly from the hands of the Father, he gave his Son to Mary for the world to receive him from her."

Saint Louis expanded upon St. Augustine's words: "The Son of God has made Himself Man; but it was in Mary and by Mary. God the Holy [Spirit] has formed Jesus Christ in Mary; but it was only after having asked her consent by one of the first ministers of His court."[10]

Saint Padre Pio used to say, "All graces given by God pass through the Blessed Mother." He encouraged the faithful to "love the Madonna and pray the Rosary, for her Rosary is the weapon against the evils of the world today."[11] Indeed, let us remember to pray for the graces from Mary and pray the Rosary often.

Saint John Paul II tells us:

> This woman of faith, Mary of Nazareth, the Mother of God, has been given to us as a model in our pilgrimage of faith. From Mary we learn to surrender to God's will in all things. From Mary, we learn to trust even when all hope seems gone. From Mary, we learn to love Christ, her Son and the Son of God. For Mary is not only the Mother of God, she is Mother of the Church as well. In every stage of the march through history, the Church has benefited from the prayer and protection of the Virgin Mary.[12]

With God's amazing grace and our Queen of Heaven's help, we can indeed discover great hope, allow it to grow in our hearts, and move forward in loving faith, blessing others with the medicine of hope. Even an unimposing glimmer of holy hope shining from our eyes can help someone who has lost hope.

Reasons for Hope

This book will present many reasons for hope in our world today through the lens of the Queen of Heaven and Earth. Our Mother Mary has many titles and has visited our world through many apparitions. This book is not a complete telling of all the approved Marian apparitions, nor does it include all of Mary's many titles. That would take many volumes. (Perhaps I'll discuss more in a future book!)

Through intriguing true stories, Marian apparitions, and meaningful prayers, I pray that the reader will be encouraged and guided by Jesus, Mary, and Joseph, as well as many saintly Pilgrims of Hope.

As Pope Benedict XVI called to mind in his encyclical *Spe Salvi* ("On Christian Hope"), "Paul reminds the Ephesians that before their encounter with Christ they were 'without hope and without God in the world' (*Eph* 2:12). … It is important to know that I can always continue to hope, even if in my own life, or the historical period in which I am living, there seems to be nothing left to hope for."[13]

Let's learn from and become inspired by the great Pilgrims of Hope who have gone before us (and those still with us): Jesus,

Mary, St. Joseph, and the saints! Let us pray to encounter our Lord Jesus Christ in a more profound way, becoming Pilgrims of Hope in our weary world!

Pope Francis encourages us in this time of jubilee:

> Let us lift up our hearts to Christ and become *singers of hope* in a world marked by too much despair. By our actions, our words, the decisions we make each day, our patient efforts to sow seeds of beauty and kindness wherever we find ourselves, we want to sing of hope, so that its melody can touch the heartstrings of humanity and reawaken in every heart the joy and the courage to embrace life to the full.[14]

Yes, we can do this — during the Jubilee Year and beyond! Mother Mary will help us! Our world thirsts for hope. Let us carry the torch!

Totus Tuus! Totally Yours!

United in prayerful, fervent hope,
Your fellow pilgrim,
Donna-Marie Cooper O'Boyle
Solemnity of the Annunciation of the Lord,
April 8, 2024

"Our Lady, Immaculately Conceived" by Francis Smuglewicz, 1782.

PRACTICAL DETAILS

Just a few short words to help guide you in using this book. First of all, please enjoy it!

Right from the beginning of this book, we see that our Mother Mary gives us great hope. She is the foundation of all hope. I have positioned the key moments of Mary's life in the first four chapters, and then we move on to some of her apparitions, which show us how Mary has appeared to us over the centuries for one intrinsic reason: to renew our hope. She has, in effect, been on a pilgrimage of her own to us, always imparting her marvelous wisdom and holy instruction — unceasingly leading us to her Son Jesus, through Whom our salvation comes.

I think it's important to share a quick explanation on Marian apparitions, since I cover some in this book. I have only included Church-approved apparitions.[15]

The *Catechism of the Catholic Church* instructs us that Marian apparitions are considered private revelations and do not belong to the deposit of faith:

> It is not their role to improve or complete Christ's definitive Revelation, but to help live more fully by it in a certain period of history. Guided by the magisterium of the Church, the *sensus fidelium* knows how to discern and welcome in these revelations whatever constitutes an authentic call of Christ or his saints to the Church.[16]

In other words, we are not bound to accept the messages of private revelations, but in many cases — such as the ones in this book — they are a source of inspiration and hope!

Use this book and read it as you wish — whether chronologically or picking and choosing chapters as you will. You can certainly read it any way you desire. I do recommend that you read at least the first four chapters in a row. I suggest bringing it with you at times to your visits in Adoration of our Lord Jesus, Who is truly present in the Blessed Sacrament. Read the reflections while there with Jesus, and don't forget to make use of the many hopeful prayers in the back of the book.

In addition to your own personal reflection, you can also gather together with your fellow parishioners and friends to use this book in a group study setting or book club. All of the elements at the end of the chapters will help to guide your discussions. You can meet in-person or virtually.

The "Act" and "Pray" sections are simply suggestions for you based on the reflection. The Holy Spirit might guide you to other actions or prayers as well. The "Savor" section is all your own. Don't be afraid to write your personal prayers, thoughts, or resolutions in the spaces provided. You might look back at the pages at a later time and be reminded of an experience in prayer, a resolution not yet carried out, a special prayer, and so forth. If you run out of space, use a notebook along with this book.

Finally, after reading the stories in the "Reflect" sections, consider meditating upon them for a while and put yourself into the scene so that you can, in a sense, experience what you are reading — kind of like a *Lectio Divina* method of prayer in which you pause to really take it in.

To give you a simple analogy, it's similar to watching sports — an instant replay is used at times. Sometimes, it's in slow motion so you can get a much closer look at just how high that basketball player jumped to make a basket. Or, it's like when taking a video of a hummingbird, for instance. If you slow down the video or get a screenshot afterwards, you might actually see the marvelous details of fluttering wings, iridescent feathers, and glorious vibrant colors.

Some chapters might cause you to go a little slower and really take it in. There's more than meets the eye. In addition, when you take time to prayerfully meditate upon the stories and teachings, you are also giving our dear Lord and His Holy Mother a chance to whisper to your heart and soul. Be quiet and listen with the ear of your heart.

Remember also to call on Mary often as you read through this book. She distributes graces and helps to perfect your prayers. She will surely help you. The great Marian preacher St. Louis de Montfort assures us:

To Mary, His faithful Spouse, God the Holy [Spirit] has communicated His unspeakable gifts; and He has chosen her to be the dispensatrix of all He possesses, in such sort that she distributes to whom she wills, as much as she wills, as she wills, and when she wills, all His gifts and graces. The Holy [Spirit] gives no heavenly gift to men which He does not pass through her virginal hands. Such has been the Will of God, who has willed that we should have every thing in Mary; so that she who impoverished, humbled, and hid herself even to the abyss of nothingness by her profound humility her whole life long, should now be enriched, and exalted by the Most High. Such are the sentiments of the Church and the Holy Fathers.[17]

“The Annunciation,” artist unknown.

1

The Hope of Mary's Fiat: "Behold, I am the Handmaid of the Lord"

"Here am I, the servant of the Lord;
let it be with me according to your word."
— Lk 1:38

The opening of Mary's heart in accepting her mission would deliver boundless and abiding hope to our world, for our Lord Jesus Christ's Incarnation is the source of all of our hope. Pope Benedict XVI stated that, through Mary's Fiat, "The hope of the ages became reality, entering this world and its history."[18] *Let's now reflect upon Mary's amazing and courageous Fiat.*

REFLECT

God has made Mary "full of grace," and Mary was addressed in this precise way by the Angel Gabriel. In his teachings on the Blessed Virgin Mary, St. John Paul II said that "full of grace" is "the name Mary possesses in the eyes of God." The pontiff explained that her new title points to her mission. He said, "The title 'full of grace' shows the deepest dimension of the young woman of Nazareth's personality: fashioned by grace and the object of divine favor to the point that she can be defined by this special predilection."[19]

Saint Stanislaus Papczyński (1631–1701), founder of the Marian Fathers of the Immaculate Conception of the Blessed Virgin Mary, had a deep devotion to Mary, the Immaculate Conception. He wrote, "Therefore, it ought to surprise no one, that the one who was predestined to be the Mother of God was she, who was adorned by God with so many virtues, that it is simply [too] hard to count them all, and surely no one among men could possess them all at once. No celestial body shines with such radiance to compare with the brightest light of the sun."[20]

Saint Ambrose tells us, "And who could be more perfect than the Mother of God? Who can shine more than she, whom Light itself chose? Who could be more pure than her, who gave birth to a body without contact with a body? ... Mary was such a one, that her life can be a school for all."[21]

Let's now step back in time to a well-known, yet humble, cottage to ponder a specific moment, when seemingly without so much as a whisper of warning, the Angel Gabriel appeared in a burst of heavenly light before the young Mary of Nazareth. Gabriel had been sent by God to deliver the astonishing news that the pure and prayerful teen would become the Mother of the Messiah. That is, once she accepted the mammoth mission. This amazing moment would be forever remembered and contemplated throughout the following 20 centuries, especially when the Joyful Mysteries of the Rosary are prayed.

Mary had fervently hoped for this very day. Enveloped in blinding, radiant light before the praying virgin, the Angel said, "Do not be afraid, Mary" (Lk 1:30).

Mary Could Have Feared

Certainly, there could have been much for Mary to fear given her circumstances. After all, she was a young teenaged Jewish girl, betrothed to Joseph of the house of David. Being betrothed to Joseph meant that the couple was already married, but not yet living together. Mary was a virgin. If she said "yes" to the holy creature, her entire world as she knew it could suddenly become in complete disarray — and even worse than that! After all, what would Joseph say? Would his heart be broken? Would she be stoned to death? This was the very real consequence at the time for women found guilty of adultery. And Mary's consent to Gabriel would certainly cause her to look as if she had committed adultery.

Surely, Mary knew that her pregnancy would raise every single eyebrow in town if she consented to the Angel's message. Perhaps more importantly, this teenage peasant girl might have been afraid of the overwhelming vocation being offered to her — to be the mother of the long-awaited Messiah, and thereby also the Queen Mother of His everlasting Kingdom!

In addition, the deep impact of the Angel's words "Blessed are you among women," and that her son would be "The Son of the Most High" and occupy the promised "throne" of his father,

King David, forever, might have caused Mary to shudder in her shoes at the immense holy weight of it all. After all, though Mary was pure and holy, she must have felt completely inadequate for such a monumental role in life.

Yes, Gabriel told Mary that she shouldn't be afraid. No doubt, his words comforted and calmed the young visionary's heart at least a bit, knowing that the Holy Spirit was going to be deeply involved in working all this out. In addition, we might assume that Mary would have been completely unsuspecting — having no advance warning of this exalted invitation prior to Gabriel's visit.

Most likely, she did not know the precise time this grand invitation would take place. Yet, biographers and mystics tell us that there was some sort of pre-announcement to Mary's heart and soul to enable her to prayerfully prepare for Gabriel's visit.

For instance, Venerable Mary of Ágreda (a Spanish Conceptionist Poor Clare nun who lived from 1602–1665) tells us from her private revelations that Mary prayed a novena for nine days ahead of that momentous visit. Imbued with the hopeful Sacred Scriptures of Israel, Mary had been prayerfully and patiently waiting with great hope.

Mary's Life was a Pilgrimage of Hope

Knowing in her heart that cooperating with God's grace in that moment was indeed her holy mission, Mary, who had pilgrimaged in great hope all through her life, steeped in expectant prayer, consented by giving her most wondrous and faith-filled Fiat. Mary completely abandoned herself to the holy will of God — to "the obedience of faith."[22]

The most pure Mary was then overshadowed by the Holy Spirit. Gabriel had told her, "The Holy Spirit will come upon you, and the power of the Most High will overshadow you; therefore the child to be born will be holy; he will be called Son of God" (Lk 1:35).

Soon after Mary's yes, Joseph would become confounded about the absolutely mysterious, yet perplexing, situation when learning of Mary's pregnancy, which he had not been a part of. However, loving Joseph decided to divorce Mary quietly in order to save her from a cruel and certain death.

Can we even imagine the sadness that might have entered St. Joseph's heart? Or the unworthiness he might have felt when learning that Mary's pregnancy was from the Holy Spirit (see Mt 1:18-25)?

Mary's life was always impregnated in humble and contrite prayer. She had been trained by the masters in the Temple. Her parents Joachim and Anne had fulfilled their holy promise to thank God for gifting a child to them by selflessly giving their 3-year-old daughter back to Him — to ascend the steps of the Temple. There, inside plaster walls and amid wafting incense and profound prayer, Mary's heart was abundantly blessed by God and profusely guided and prepared by the Holy Spirit.

Mary's Fiat was the Beginning of Our Salvation

So, when the time came for that fateful, holy visit in the town of Nazareth, Mary listened carefully, and, within mere moments after his greeting, without hesitation and with complete faith, Mary answered Gabriel, saying, "Here am I, the servant of the Lord; let it be with me according to your word" (Lk 1:38).

Mary's humble "yes" was overflowing with abundant hope which would change our world forever. Mary's Fiat was the beginning of her holy, faith-filled pilgrimage of hope, as well as the beginning of our own salvation.

ACT

Carve out some time to prayerfully ponder teenage Mary's faithful life, particularly at the moment of the Annunciation. Consider how humble Mary, who was human like us, chose to move her will to answer yes to the Angel Gabriel, and, ultimately, to the God of the Universe that she would indeed consent to Heaven's plan for her and the world.

Close your eyes and stay there with Mary and the Angel Gabriel in your imagination. Pray and listen. Consider how you can learn from Mary, Gabriel, and our Lord. Think about how Mary's Fiat connects to your own life and gives you hope. Certainly, Mary's courageous Fiat can inspire us all on our own journeys through life. Meditating upon her beautiful virtues and how she courageously moved her will to accept the will of God is awe-inspiring and can motivate us to move our wills to follow God's holy will.

Can you plan to make a nine-day novena of prayer to Mary soon? Can you personally thank Mother Mary for her Fiat?

Finally, ask Mary for an increase in faith.

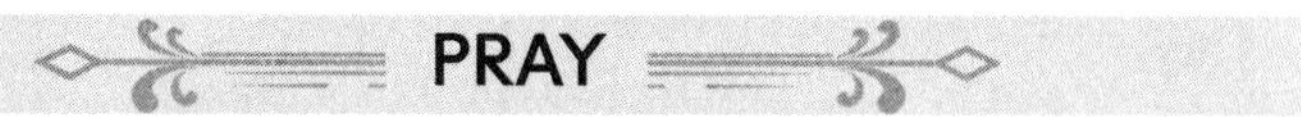

Dear Holy Family, Jesus, Mary, and Joseph,
please bless me and pray for me.
Dear Holy Mary, Mother of the Redeemer, Mother of Mercy
and of hope, thank you for being my Mother.
Stella Maris, please help me.
Gate of Heaven, strengthen my virtues of faith, hope, and love.
Seat of Wisdom, please grant to me your graces.
Mirror of Perfection, mold my heart and teach me to believe,
to hope, and to love right along with you.
Mary, my Mother, I need your help. Please perfect my simple prayers.
Please guide my steps today and always closer to your Son Jesus.
Star of Hope, Star of the Sea, please shine upon me
and guide me ever closer to your Son's Kingdom!
Amen.

Recite the Our Father, Hail Mary, Glory Be,
Hail Holy Queen, Memorare.

Today or soon, choose an additional prayer to pray to Mary
(found in the Appendix).

SAVOR

A prayer, a thought, a resolution:

“The Visitation,” stained-glass panel, Germany, 1444.

2

The Hope of Mary's Visit: "My Soul Proclaims the Greatness of the Lord"

"Who more than Mary could be a star of hope for us?"[23]

— Pope Benedict XVI

How very extraordinary to comprehend that Mary actually carried the holy HOPE of the world nestled in her own womb as she hastened across the hills of Judea to be of service to her elderly cousin Elizabeth. Let's take a close look as we reflect on this holy journey, which continues to resound through the ages.

When the Angel Gabriel informed Mary about her elderly cousin Elizabeth's miraculous pregnancy, which occurred after she had been barren, generous Mary chose to put her own needs aside to help her elderly cousin Elizabeth.

Mary had just heard the amazing news of her own pregnancy. She could have stayed home with concerns for herself, since she was newly pregnant and might have been trying to grasp the full meaning of carrying the Savior of the world in her womb.

She might have been wondering how her husband, St. Joseph, would accept this sudden, mysterious miracle. Still, Mary set out in haste and with great faith and love.

After traveling her 100-mile or so journey, Mary joyfully entered Zechariah and Elizabeth's home. We can imagine that Mary greeted Elizabeth with a warm embrace. How does Elizabeth react? We read in Scripture:

> When Elizabeth heard Mary's greeting, the child leaped in her womb. And Elizabeth was filled with the Holy Spirit and exclaimed with a loud cry, "Blessed are you among women, and blessed is the fruit of your womb. And why has this happened to me, that the mother of my Lord comes to me? For as soon as I heard the sound

> of your greeting, the child in my womb leaped for joy. And blessed is she who believed that there would be a fulfillment of what was spoken to her by the Lord" (Lk 1:41–45).

Mary's Faith was a "Life-Giving Flame of the Spirit"

Saint John Paul II stated, "In her greeting, Elizabeth first called Mary 'blessed' because of 'the fruit of her womb,' and then she called her 'blessed' because of her faith." The pontiff shared that both blessings refer to the Annunciation.

"Now, at the Visitation, when Elizabeth's greeting bears witness to that culminating moment," St. John Paul II continued, "Mary's faith acquires a new consciousness and a new expression. That which remained hidden in the depths of the 'obedience of faith' at the Annunciation can now be said to spring forth like a clear and life-giving flame of the spirit."[24]

Mary was not looking for praise from Elizabeth. Filled with the deepest of humility, Mary chose to speak of her "lowliness" and gave unsurpassed glory to God instead. The young virgin then gives her profession of faith, her "Song of Praise":

> My soul magnifies the Lord, and my spirit rejoices in God my Savior,
> for he has looked with favor on the lowliness of his servant.
> Surely, from now on all generations will call me blessed; for the Mighty One has done great things for me, and holy is his name.
> His mercy is for those who fear him from generation to generation.
> He has shown strength with his arm; he has scattered the proud in the thoughts of their hearts.
> He has brought down the powerful from their thrones, and lifted up the lowly;
> he has filled the hungry with good things, and sent the rich away empty.
> He has helped his servant Israel, in remembrance of his mercy,
> according to the promise he made to our ancestors, to Abraham and to his descendants forever (Lk 1:46–55).

Mary's sublime piercing words, or profession of her faith, wouldn't be uttered just that one momentous time. Her holy words have continued through generations. Mary's Magnificat is recited daily in the Liturgy of Vespers and during personal and communal devotions.

Mary Teaches Us to Be Generous in Service

Mary teaches us to serve. In pondering that beautiful visit between Mary and Elizabeth, we can learn something more. Even though Mary is the Mother of God and the Queen of Heaven and earth, she always comported herself and acted in deep humility during her life on earth. She consistently sought to be of generous service to others.

Our Blessed Mother gives us a beautiful example of providing service to others with the deepest humility. It's important to note that the devil hates humility and does not know how to deal with it. Humility thwarts the evil one's tricks.

The Mother of God chooses the lowly tasks and always operates through humility in order to praise, honor, and glorify her Son's unequaled humility. Mary's thoughts, words, and actions and her entire being seek to glorify God.

Mary also teaches us to have a generous heart like hers. We meditate upon Mary's loving heart when we pray the Second Joyful Mystery — the Visitation.

Saint John Paul II stated, "Mary also anticipated, in the mystery of the Incarnation, the Church's Eucharistic faith. When, at the Visitation, she bore in her womb the Word made flesh, she became ... the first 'tabernacle' in history — in which the Son of God, still invisible to our human gaze, allowed himself to be adored by Elizabeth, radiating his light as it were through the eyes and the voice of Mary."[25]

ACT

Let's take a quick look at something very hopeful and also soul-stirring. Pope Benedict XVI spoke of Mary's joyful journey as well as the "Hope" residing in her womb. He also spoke of suffering. He stated:

> When you hastened with holy joy across the mountains of Judea to see your cousin Elizabeth, you became the image of the Church to come, which carries the hope of the world in her womb across the mountains of history. But alongside the joy which, with your Magnificat, you proclaimed in word and song for all the centuries to hear, you also knew the dark sayings of the prophets about the suffering of the servant of God in this world.[26]

Take time to prayerfully ponder dear Mother Mary's generous, loving heart in service to Elizabeth, her choice to move her will to be obedient to God's holy will in her life, as well as the reality of suffering involved.

A few things to ponder: How do Mary's choices and actions affect your own life? What can you personally learn from Mary? How can you open your heart to holy hope today?

We know that we can never be exactly like the Mother of God, but we can certainly pray to emulate her virtues and ask her for many graces. When we push beyond our comfort zone, not anxious about our own needs, we can be a beacon of hope to others when we visit, call, or write to them.

Sometimes, we just need to make a greater effort to get up and out of ourselves in order to aid someone who is dire need of our help. Our little works of love — the seemingly littlest things (albeit, with some effort!), with God's grace and Mother Mary's help, can be utterly transforming to the person in need and ourselves too. Holy hope will jump into our hearts!

Think about it. Pray about it. Write your thoughts down below in the "Savor" section.

Finally, ask Mary to give you a greater awareness of God's grace in your life.

PRAY

Dear Holy Family, Jesus, Mary, and Joseph,
please bless me and pray for me.
Dear Holy Mary, Mother of the Redeemer, Mother of Mercy
and of hope, thank you for being my Mother.
Gate of Heaven, strengthen my virtues of faith, hope, and love.
Seat of Wisdom, please grant me your graces.
Mirror of Perfection, mold my heart and teach me to believe,
to hope, and to love right along with you.
Mary, my Mother, I need your help.
Please perfect my simple prayers. Please guide my steps
today and always closer to your Son Jesus.
Star of Hope, Star of the Sea, please shine upon me
and guide me ever closer to your Son's Kingdom!
Amen.

Recite the Our Father, Hail Mary, Glory Be,
Hail Holy Queen, Memorare *(pages 201-202).*

Pray the "Litany of Loreto" *(page 219).*

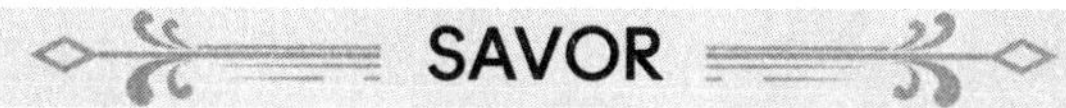

SAVOR

A prayer, a thought, a resolution:

____

____

____

____

____

____

____

“The Marriage Feast at Cana” (detail) by Juan de Flandes, c. 1497.

3

The Hope of Mary's Instruction:
"Do Whatever He Tells You."

"When the wine gave out, the mother of Jesus said to him, 'They have no wine.'"

— Jn 2:3

How blessed we are to have such a loving Mother, who is always advocating for us and knows our hearts better than we do ourselves! She is acutely aware of what we need before we do — always desiring the absolute best for us — forever pointing us to her Divine Son Jesus. Let's now reflect upon Mary's attentiveness and love, as well as how she saved the day and helped to bring about her Son's first public miracle and thus brought hope to an unbelieving world.

REFLECT

Our Blessed Mother Mary is generous and also attentive and insightful! Mary's quick sizing up of a young, newly-married couple's predicament — having run out of wine for their guests — certainly saved the day and revealed to us Mary's loving, generous heart. In addition, it set the stage, if you will, for Jesus' first public miracle, which revealed His glory.

Stepping back 2,000 years, to a small town called Cana in Galilee, Jesus, His Mother Mary, and the first disciples were guests at a Jewish wedding feast. At that time, these Jewish feasts were steeped in rich tradition and rituals, typically lasting for about a week, while an elaborate banquet of food and wine was continuously lavished upon guests throughout every day of celebration. These people were very keen on hospitality and traditions!

Because a great feast of food and a bountiful pouring of wine were expected, it would be completely shameful and a deep dishonor to the bride and groom should they run out of wine for their honored guests and family.

Mary is the First to Notice

At what might be considered the most famous wedding in history, Mary is the first to notice this dilemma which could quickly turn into a disaster. The wine stewards, charged with the task of serving the wine, did not realize the shortage. But Mary knew. Mary also knew her Son's heart. She wanted compassion to be shown to the couple, and ultimately to their guests.

She tells Jesus, "They have no wine" (Jn 2:3). In just a few words, Mary informed her Son of what looked to become a very embarrassing situation for the newly married couple. Jesus was quick to tell His Mother that the time had not yet come for Him to begin His public ministry. Specifically, He said, "My hour has not yet come" (Jn 2:4).

Was Mary suggesting that Jesus should begin His messianic mission — publicly announce His identity? Could we say that Mary had interceded for this miracle?

Loving and Holy Mary did not miss a beat. As soon as Jesus stated that it was not the time, Mary succinctly instructed the wine stewards, "Do whatever he tells you" (Jn 2:5).

Mary never draws attention to herself. She pointed to Jesus. She always points to Jesus. She will always lead us to Jesus. She desires that all mankind "do whatever He tells you."

We know that Jesus came to do the will of His Father. And we see that Mary clearly comports herself in the deepest of humility and tells the wine stewards to do the will of Jesus. Our Mother Mary was not looking to bring attention to herself, being the one who first noticed the dilemma. No. She desired that the entire matter be turned over to her extremely capable Son. Of course, we know that Jesus was so much more than capable! He was (and is!) the Son of God! In instructing the wine stewards, Mary fully trusted that her Son Jesus would do whatever needed to be done.

Dear Jesus, on the other hand, was not being rude to His Mother. No, He simply succinctly responded with the TRUTH. His hour had not yet come. The simple and precise truth. And, as always, God had a plan!

Mary's Presence was Significant

We observe that St. John the Evangelist, who, inspired by the Holy Spirit, wrote his Gospel after a long life, made certain that we would know the significance of Mary's presence at this wedding celebration. His writings help us to recognize that the Blessed Mother's presence in the carrying out of Jesus' first public miracle was certainly worthy of our attention.

We can say that the dilemma we see on the surface here is not only about the young bride and groom. It's much deeper. It's also for Mary. If she speaks up now, she knows what will likely begin — and exactly what will be set into motion. Mary's instruction, "Do whatever he tells you," is another part of her Fiat — of letting go of her Son — of fully giving Him up. Our Mother Mary never forgot Simeon's message to her when she presented her Baby Jesus in the Temple — how the sword of sorrow will pierce her own heart, how Jesus will be hated once He begins His mission. She knew that as soon as His mission began, He would be catapulted at breakneck speed toward the most certain cruel death on the Cross.

Mary also remembered the Angel Gabriel's words to her when she gave her Fiat: "He will be great, and will be called the Son of the Most High, and the Lord God will give to him the throne of his ancestor David. He will reign over the house of Jacob forever, and of his kingdom there will be no end" (Lk 1:32–33).

We recognize, too, that Mary was always involved in her Son Jesus' ministry — she was present and participated from the very beginning, at the Annunciation when she gave her wondrous Fiat, to the very end, when she courageously stood in utter sorrow at the foot of the Cross. In addition to this, she is still working hard from Heaven now! Mary wants us all to be safe in Heaven one day. She loves us, guides us, and intercedes for us.

Mary is our loving Mother, given to us by our Savior Jesus Christ. Venerable Archbishop Fulton Sheen explains the wording we read in Sacred Scripture regarding Jesus' birth in the manger:

> Here is the answer, after all these years, to the mysterious words in the Gospel of the Incarnation which stated that Our Blessed Mother laid her "first born" in the manger. Did that mean that Our Blessed Mother was to have

> other children? It certainly did, but not according to the flesh. Our Divine Lord and Savior Jesus Christ is the only Son of Our Blessed Mother by the flesh. But Our Lady was to have other children, not according to the flesh, but according to the spirit![27]

Mary Knows Our Every Need

Archbishop Sheen adds that Mary knows our needs better than we do. He reflected on Mary's contribution at the Wedding at Cana and said, "The people at the table did not know what they needed to maintain the joy of the marriage feast, even when the Lord was in their midst. There are many of us who would not come to Our Lord, unless we had someone who knows our needs better than we know ourselves, and who will ask Our Lord for us." And he tells us that Mary was there for them and is here for us:

> This role of Mary makes her acceptable to everyone. Those at the marriage table did not need to know she was the Mother of the Son of God in order to receive the benefit of her Divine Son. But one thing is certain — no one will ever call on her without being heard, nor without being finally led to her Divine Son, Jesus Christ, for Whose Sake she alone exists — for Whose Sake she was made pure — and for Whose Sake she was given to us.[28]

This reflection gives us so much to ponder. Let us remember that Mother Mary knew before anyone else that the wine had run out. She interceded and acted on behalf of the couple to save them from shame. Mary knows what we need before we know — every single thing! We can trust her and run to her to receive her motherly and expert help.

Take time to ponder your life and make more room for Mary. Allow her to help you every step of your spiritual journey and bring you to her Son Jesus.

As you make more time for Mary in your life, allow her to mother you! You can do this daily as you meditate for just 15 minutes while praying the holy Rosary. Get into the habit of beginning your day with prayers to Mary, and you will surely be getting your day off on the right foot!

Finally, ask Mary to give to you a greater awareness of God's grace in your life and ask her to intercede for you that God will grant many graces.

PRAY

Dear Holy Family, Jesus, Mary, and Joseph,
please bless me and pray for me.
Dear Holy Mary, Mother of the Redeemer, Mother of Mercy
and of hope, thank you for being my Mother.
Gate of Heaven, strengthen my virtues of faith, hope, and love.
Seat of Wisdom, please grant me your graces.
Mirror of Perfection, mold my heart and teach me to believe,
to hope, and to love right along with you.
Mary, my Mother, I need your help.
Please perfect my simple prayers. Please guide my steps today
and always closer to your Son Jesus.
Star of Hope, Star of the Sea, please shine upon me
and guide me ever closer to your Son's Kingdom!
Amen.

Recite the Our Father, Hail Mary, Glory Be, Hail Holy Queen, Memorare *(pages 201-202).*

Pray the "Christifideles Laici" *prayer (page 214).*

SAVOR

A prayer, a thought, a resolution:

____

____

____

____

____

____

“The Thirteenth Station: Jesus is taken down from the Cross,” bronze by Timothy Schmalz at the National Shrine of The Divine Mercy in Stockbridge, Massachusetts.

4

Hope Does Not Die:
Mary's Sword of Sorrow and the Foot of the Cross

"Shining over his birth in the stable at Bethlehem, there were angels in splendor who brought the good news to the shepherds, but at the same time the lowliness of God in this world was all too palpable. The old man Simeon spoke to you of the sword which would pierce your soul (cf. *Lk* 2:35), of the sign of contradiction that your Son would be in this world."[29]

— Pope Benedict XVI

Mother Mary inspires great hope in our hearts. Through horrendous and earth-shattering sorrow, Mary courageously and unwaveringly chose hope. Even while watching every devastating moment of anguish her dear Son suffered, she clung to the hope of Jesus' Resurrection and the salvation of souls — the salvation of her beloved children. Mary is our true Mother. Let's now take a closer look at what transpired.

Even though the bitter sword of sorrow pierced the Blessed Virgin Mary's heart, hope did not die. We recall the scene at the Presentation of Jesus in the Temple. What should have been a moment overflowing with the most precious joy for Mary as she presented her beautiful newborn Jesus to Simeon was, instead, intertwined with the reality of the great suffering that would occur in both their lives. Joy and sorrow had met. However, this would be a holy sorrow imbued with profound and hopeful purpose. That is, for the salvation and sanctification of souls. Hope was not going to die. No. Gabriel's words at the Annunciation were etched upon Mary's heart: "He will reign over the house of Jacob forever, and of his kingdom there will be no end" (Lk 1:33).

In *Spe Salvi*, Pope Benedict XVI stated, "The old man Simeon spoke to you [Mary] of the sword which would pierce your soul (cf. Lk 2:35), of the sign of contradiction that your Son would be in this world." The pontiff continued, "Then, when Jesus began his public ministry, you had to step aside, so that a new family could grow, the family which it was his mission to establish and which would be made up of those who heard his word and kept it (cf. *Lk* 11:27f)."[30]

Mary's life was one of deep and humble sacrifice and filled with great suffering for the salvation of the world through her Son's mission. Pope Benedict XVI recalled Mary's experiences leading up to and while at the foot of her Son's Cross. He said that Mary "saw the growing power of hostility and rejection which built up around Jesus until the hour of the Cross." The pontiff colorfully described how she must have felt — how she must have "experienced the truth of the saying about the 'sign of contradiction.'" He noted how Mary must have experienced this, "when you had to look upon the Savior of the world, the heir of David, the Son of God dying like a failure, exposed to mockery, between criminals."[31]

Certainly, Mary experienced all the above and much more. She had always been completely united to her Son Jesus, even, and perhaps most especially, in His suffering.

Did our Mother Mary's faith ever fail or waver? No. Even under the killing shadow of the Cross that murdered her only Son, Mary's faith stood strong. Saint John Paul II explained in his encyclical letter, *Redemptoris Mater* ("The Mother of the Redeemer), "Through faith the Mother shares in the death of her Son, in his redeeming death; but in contrast with the faith of the disciples who fled, hers was far more enlightened."[32]

Mary chose to stand firm in faith. Mary's great faith gives us much hope.

Hope was Never Lost with Mary

Unquestionably, with God's grace, Mary confidently hung onto her own Son's words: "But take courage; I have conquered the world!" (Jn 16:33). And, amid the greatest of sorrows, bravely standing there at the foot of His Cross, Mary, our dear Mother received her new mission. "Woman, here is your son!" (Jn 19:26). Mary became the Mother of the Church and also our Mother.

Hope was not lost. Hope did not die. In fact, Jesus' great gift of His Mother to us lavished a flood of hope all over the world. Turning to Mary and receiving her assistance engulfs our hearts with abiding holy hope.

Switching gears for a moment, I want to mention a generous little 6-year-old girl who did not give up on hope. Our Mother of Hope, coming to us as Our Lady of Fátima, appeared in many apparitions to this little girl, Jacinta Marto (now a canonized saint in the Catholic Church), and her older brother St. Francisco, as well as their older cousin Venerable Lucia dos Santos. This occurred in 1917 in a little hamlet called Aljustrel in Fátima, Portugal.

There's so much I could tell you about these faith-filled children. However, I'll reserve that telling for another chapter.

Prayer and Penance for the Salvation of Souls

For now, I wish to express that Our Lady taught the simple peasant children very much about the need to pray and offer penance for the salvation of souls, for many were going to hell because no one prayed for them. Mary went so far as to show an eye-opening vision of hell to the young children, which frightened the children to their very core. While it was utterly devastating for them to see the reality of hell with all the gory details, it made a lasting impression on little Jacinta, who would commit to spending the rest of her life saving souls through her earnest prayers and loving penance.

What especially touches my heart is what Jacinta chose to do.

It occurred when little Jacinta was dying of a prolonged illness and the painful Spanish flu during a worldwide pandemic. She underwent several stays at hospitals, which included surgery without anesthesia. Francisco was also very ill. Our Lady of Fátima visited them both and let them know she would take Francisco to Heaven soon, but wanted to know if Jacinta would like to stay longer to suffer for sinners. Though her condition worsened and her sufferings increased, sweet Jacinta chose to suffer more. She desired that more souls be saved.

She knew she was going to die and that she would die alone. Did she lose hope? No. She offered her sufferings for the conversion of sinners. She could have chosen to go to Heaven sooner but chose to suffer longer for poor sinners and in reparation for sin. We can say that hope actually grew in her heart, as she knew she was helping souls get to Heaven! Her loving sacrifices brought about hope for dying souls and sinners.

Turn to Mary

Pope St. John Paul II said that in looking to Mary and "praying to her ... your tedium will become serenity, your anguish [will] change into hope, and your grief into love."[33] He also encourages us, "Turn your eyes incessantly to the Blessed Virgin; she who is the Mother of Sorrows and also the Mother of Consolation, can understand you completely and help you."[34]

Pope St. John Paul II's words of how anguish can change to hope remind me so much of something amazing that happened to my friend Mariola and a gathering of Ukrainian refugee women and children on Easter Sunday in 2022. It was just a few weeks after the Russian invasion of their country. The women and children had escaped, leaving their husbands and fathers behind to fight the invasions. Mariola's mother's church, Our Lady of Fatima Parish in Kraków, Poland took in 70 children and their mothers. Parishioners welcomed them into their homes.

At this time, Mariola quickly bought a plane ticket and flew to Poland with suitcases filled with clothing and supplies and stayed for a while to help in the effort. The parish organized an Easter luncheon for the displaced families. Despite the fears, trauma, anguish, and uncertainties, Ukrainian and Polish children dined together and sang songs in their native languages. The Polish parishioners tried their best to be of service and befriend their unexpected visitors.

Still, there existed a deep piercing fear and disquiet in the hearts of the Ukrainian mothers. However, Mother Mary had a plan! When Mariola visited her family in Poland at that time, she was handed a bag full of 12 newly painted Icons of Mary! They were from a poor and very talented artist Mariola knew who lived in the mountains. She had supported his work in the past. And now, suddenly she had in her hands numerous colorful Icons of Mary! She was speechless upon receiving them. She didn't know what she was supposed to do with them. She told me, "But God knew." And Mary would come to the rescue. The plan suddenly became crystal clear to Mariola.

"It was meant for the women and children — a gift for Easter," she recalled to me, "and I brought this bag to the Easter luncheon prepared for them by the parish." Mariola vividly remembers the reactions from each of the displaced mothers upon receiving the unexpected gifts of Our Lady. Mariola said, "You can't even imagine the joy!"

The women were pierced through with great joy and a beautiful gift of hope to go on. Mary was their answer!

Mariola said, "How incredible it was that Our Lady came and consoled these women in a very amazing way by people from all walks of life and geographically different places. The painter somewhere in the mountains, my family, myself from the U.S., and my Mom's parish with a priest who was incredibly busy helping and organizing everything."

Let's never hesitate in turning to our Mother in Heaven. She understands our lives and desires to help us. Getting close to her surely gives us the hope we need in this complicated and arduous journey through life.

Along these lines, I was delighted to find out that St. Stanislaus Papczyński advised, "Oh, do not procrastinate to do everything that you can to venerate the Most Blessed Virgin. If only you served her so willingly, as she did so for us, when with such great desire she bore the Passion which tormented her Son."[35]

ACT

Take time to ponder Mary's sacrificial life. If possible, sometime soon, be present with our Lord Jesus, Who is truly present in the Blessed Sacrament, in a time of Adoration.

When we think of Adoration of Our Lord, we might be concerned that we cannot commit to an entire hour to adore Our Lord, thinking it should be a "Holy Hour." That concern can cause us not to go at all. In addition, some people think that the Blessed Sacrament needs to be exposed in a Monstrance for Adoration to occur. No, not at all. Jesus is truly present in the Blessed Sacrament — Body, Blood, Soul, and Divinity — whether exposed in the Monstrance or reserved in the tabernacle in every Catholic church. He awaits our visits, no matter how long they may be.

Of course, we should strive to be with Jesus in the Blessed Sacrament whenever we are able. I often encourage people to visit Jesus on the way home or on the way to work, an event, shopping, or whatever. Make time for Him. If you're unable to spend an hour, at least make it a meaningful and sincere visit. Jesus will welcome you with open arms. Your time with Him will be time well spent. In fact, it will be some of the best moments of your life.

Certainly, endeavor to be present with our Lord wherever you are. Quiet your mind, close your eyes, and put yourself into the scene of the Presentation of Jesus in the Temple. Prayerfully ponder what was happening there in the Temple, and going forward, when Jesus was scorned and tortured by the very people He had served, leading up to His death on the Cross for our salvation.

Envision Mary standing there at the Cross of her Son as tears ran down her sorrowful face. Remember too (and never forget!) the most hopeful words from Jesus when He called down from the Cross, "Woman, here is your son" (Jn 19:26). With them Jesus gave us the most exalted gift of His own Holy Mother. Take time in quiet prayer to thank Mary for being your Mother and ask her to fill your heart with great hope. If you haven't yet asked her to be a special Mother to you, ask her now.

Pray for many graces and pause to prayerfully listen to Jesus and Mary speaking to your heart. Ask Mother Mary to open up more times for Adoration in your life.

PRAY

Dear Holy Family, Jesus, Mary, and Joseph,
please bless me and pray for me.
Dear Holy Mary, Mother of the Redeemer, Mother of Mercy
and of hope, thank you for being my Mother.
Gate of Heaven, strengthen my virtues of faith, hope, and love.
Seat of Wisdom, please grant me your graces.
Mirror of Perfection, mold my heart and teach me to believe,
to hope, and to love right along with you.
Mary, my Mother, I need your help.
Please perfect my simple prayers. Please guide my steps today
and always closer to your Son Jesus.
Star of Hope, Star of the Sea, please shine upon me
and guide me ever closer to your Son's Kingdom!
Amen.

Recite the Our Father, Hail Mary, Glory Be,
Hail Holy Queen, Memorare *(pages 201-202).*

Pray the "Star of the Sea" prayer (page 223).

SAVOR

A prayer, a thought, a resolution:

5

Hope Displayed on Cactus Cloth:

Our Lady of Guadalupe

"Am I not here, who is your Mother?"[36]

— Our Lady of Guadalupe to St. Juan Diego

Countless times throughout history our Mother Mary reassures us of her tender love and exclusive, unwavering protection. Mary did so when she appeared to the unsuspecting St. Juan Diego. Never in his wildest dreams did he think the Mother of God would ever speak to him, never mind appear to him with a history-changing mission and message.

Let's begin by taking a look at a real-life, modern-day story in which Our Lady of Guadalupe came to the rescue of a Mexican woman and her baby. Then, we will step back to the year 1531 to experience the miraculous hope which Heaven displayed upon simple cactus cloth.

REFLECT

"I was worried, but happy at the same time," she told me. At 40 years old, my friend Rosie found out she was pregnant. She and her husband had three living sons, and Rosie had suffered two miscarriages a couple of years before her new positive pregnancy discovery.

As the days rolled along, Rosie began to "feel some fear and panic." She was concerned for her unborn baby because of her age, "but surrendered to God and His holy will," she said. Still, ever on her mind was the sorrowful loss of her two previous unborn babies, both in the early weeks of the pregnancies.

Thankfully, she made it to four months along. Rosie's doctor performed a standard ultrasound to check for Down's Syndrome. The doctor discovered cysts in her baby's brain. Rosie was devastated beyond words to hear this news. The doctor informed her that they would follow up on this the next month.

Rosie left the doctor's appointment in tears. She couldn't stop crying and rushed downstairs to the hospital chapel. As she entered the chapel, Rosie couldn't miss seeing the beautiful portrait of Our Lady of Guadalupe. "As soon as I saw her, I implored her help."

Our Lady of Guadalupe Brings Hope and Healing

Being a Mexican Catholic, Rosie had a deep devotion to Our Lady of Guadalupe. She had traveled to the Shrine in Mexico City on two occasions before this new life in her womb. Our Lady of Guadalupe had always been a big part of her spiritual journey.

Seeing Our Lady's image when she needed her most brought a bit of comfort and hope to Rosie's troubled heart. After all, Our Lady of Guadalupe is the Mother of the unborn Jesus! She appeared pregnant in the miraculous image, clothed as an expectant Aztec princess. How very fitting that her image was there for Rosie to see!

Our Lady of Guadalupe is often implored for help with and protection of the unborn. She can truly sympathize with expectant mothers, walking alongside them during their pregnancies, bringing comfort and imparting tremendous peace.

Rosie knelt down before the tabernacle and poured her heart out to Jesus, her Eucharistic Lord. "You are the Doctor of Doctors. Help me!" she begged Jesus. Next, she would tell her husband and children. They were all concerned about the brain cysts and the uncertainty. Rosie's tears continued to flow.

The next day, Rosie made a decision. She wouldn't cry anymore. She wanted to be sure her unborn baby would be happy and not upset by her sorrowful tears, as well as the rest of her family. "I surrendered to God and Our Lady," Rosie said. She was certain that they would "walk with us on this journey."

Some time passed, and Rosie prayed through another ultrasound. The technician was very quiet as she moved her probe all around Rosie's abdomen. It seemed like time stood still. Rosie held her breath. So much silence — it was deafening. Finally, the technician spoke up.

"I can't see any cysts! I looked all over. I can't see them!"

Peace flooded Rosie's heart. Her prayers were answered. She was then told she was having a girl — the baby girl she had always hoped and prayed for! Rosie's heart soared! Tears flowed. This time, they were happy tears, tears of gratitude. Rosie relished in the wonderful news.

But then, something else would happen.

Her water broke at 32 weeks. It was much too early to deliver her baby. Contractions began, and Rosie was hospitalized for a few weeks so that she and her unborn baby could be monitored and in the safest place in case her little *Niña* decided to make her sudden debut to the world. Prayers to Jesus and Our Lady of Guadalupe were continuously offered. Rosie also offered her sufferings to God. "If we don't offer our sufferings, we lose the opportunity to offer them for others," she said.

"Here I Am, Lord"

Rosie would have more opportunities to offer her sufferings and pray earnestly. Her beautiful daughter was born in November. Rosie and her husband gave great thanks to our Lord and Our Lady and baptized their daughter Mariana Guadalupe on December 12, the feast of Our Lady of Guadalupe.

As exciting as this all was, soon after, Mariana's heart began to bleed. There was a perforation in her little heart. Rosie quickly turned earnestly again to Our Lady of Guadalupe.

Rosie pleaded with God, "You have shown me Your power, Your will, Your magnificence. Again, I ask You to heal my baby. I am trusting again. Here I am, Lord."

Mariana's heart was healed miraculously!

When Mariana was 5 years old, she and her family made a pilgrimage to see the Our Lady of Guadalupe Shrine and the exact spot where Our Lady appeared to St. Juan Diego at Tepeyac. They prayed together with grateful hearts. Rosie cried and offered kisses to Our Lady, giving thanks. Every December 12, Rosie is on her knees with a grateful heart, thanking Our Lady of Guadalupe, the Patroness of the Unborn, and her dear Son Jesus for all the blessings which They have given to them.

Rosie has been involved with planning an Our Lady of Guadalupe feast day celebration at her Texas parish for 20 years now. I was blessed to be at one of these celebrations and was in complete awe at the beautiful devotion of the faithful people there.

It's important for us to remember that our prayers are not demands for healing for us or for our loved ones. We cannot demand miracles from God. We pray and we hope — earnestly and endlessly. We should not turn our backs on God when He doesn't provide what we think we need or desire. I will boldly point out that if we reject God because we don't approve of His ways, we are following the evil one and not God. As I have often said, God is the Divine Physician, Who knows exactly want we need and when we need it. We have to trust Him with wholehearted surrender. It's not always easy.

At times, it could seem absolutely impossible to trust God when we see and experience devastating atrocities in our world or in our very lives. This was the case for someone I knew. I'll call her Anna. My very elderly neighbor Anna flat out told me one day that she couldn't — she actually *wouldn't* — bring herself to believe in God because she simply could not comprehend why little children suffer or die. How could a loving God allow this?

I will back up just bit to tell you that Anna lived alone after her husband's death and often felt depressed. She became very bitter because her own two daughters did not visit her. Anna's couple of friends were deeply concerned about her soul and began preaching at her. Notice I said, "at her" and not "to her." They feared she would go to her grave with ugly bitterness and un-forgiveness in her heart. Because of this, Anna was very clear and forthright to me when I first began visiting her. She wanted to prevent me from putting her through the same unease as her friends had done by badgering her.

"Do not preach at me!" she demanded.

I reassured her that I wouldn't ever do so.

Well, I certainly never profess to have all of the answers. I simply don't have them. However, in that moment when Anna explained to me that she didn't believe in God, and asked why God allows suffering and sorrow, I tried to answer her in the best way I could by telling her that I did not have every answer to all of the perplexing problems of the world.

I am a simple pilgrim just like everyone else — a work in progress. I seek the Truth and I strive to learn more about my Faith every day. Even so, I knew I might not be able to calm Anna's heavy, unsettled heart.

As I gently tried to help her, I even went so far as to tell her that God actually brings good out of sufferings. I also explained that I need to pray in order to have faith to believe in God's designs, and also to try to accept what He has allowed. I absolutely have to ask for an increase in the gift of Faith. This gift of Faith spurs me on to trust God more — no matter what is happening. The virtue of Faith residing in my heart also gives me great hope.

I truly believe that there is such a thing as Eternal Life and that we are meant to strive for that. I have seen much suffering in this crazy world. However, there will be an end to all of the suffering. I tried to explain this to Anna.

In fact, we can be comforted when reading Scripture: "He will wipe every tear from their eyes. Death will be no more; mourning and crying and pain will be no more, for the first things have passed away" (Rev. 21:4).

In addition, we can feel tremendous hope when we read, "Do not worry about anything, but in everything by prayer and supplication with thanksgiving let your requests be made known to God. And the peace of God, which surpasses all understanding, will guard your hearts and your minds in Christ Jesus" (Phil 4: 6-7).

God's peace surpasses our simple understanding. It also gives us strength for the journey ahead. It is powerful! And it is available to us. Prayer and the Sacraments immensely help us. They are essential for spiritual survival.

Trusting our Creator is the only way to navigate this unpredictable pilgrimage through life. That said, with God's grace, we can be a balm of hopeful love to those we know who feel their prayers are not answered. They might deeply suffer, believing that God is not listening to their prayers. Or, even worse — that God does not love them! We can earnestly pray for them and offer hopeful counsel when appropriate.

Maybe even with some chicken soup! I say this because that was the way to my elderly neighbor's bitter heart. I never forced my beliefs upon Anna. I was never pushy. I simply befriended her and tried to love her with God's love. I visited her, I called her on the phone, and I made her some good old fashioned (and healthy!) chicken soup! And, you know what? An amazing thing happened.

One day, when I was visiting, Anna, sitting in her wheelchair, suddenly grabbed a hold of both of my hands and looked straight up into my eyes. She begged me to never stop praying for her. This atheist was acknowledging my prayers (though I had not mentioned them) and went further to ask for additional prayers! She knew she needed them, and she desired them. Anna felt a good deal of hope from my prayers and my visits. It helped her through her doubts and uncertainties.

God works powerfully through our works of love and mercy towards those who are struggling. We must never forget this, and we should do our best to do all we can to bring comfort to those God puts in our midst.

Humble Juan Diego

Now, let's switch gears to learn a bit more about the devotion to Our Lady of Guadalupe. Let's step way back to the year 1531, when a mysterious glowing visitor suddenly showed up on the Mexican hill of Tepeyac (in the outskirts of Mexico City) to an unsuspecting and humble Native American on his way to Holy Mass.

It was early on a Saturday morning. The sun had not yet risen when Juan Diego, with his *tilma* (cloak) wrapped tightly around him to stave off the bitter chill in the Mexican mountains, left his abode and began his trek. It was a six-mile hike from his home in Tolpetlac to the neighboring village of Tlatelolco, a suburb of Tenochtitlan. Though it was a long journey to complete on foot two days in a row, 57-year-old Juan Diego was faithful to going to Mass every Saturday and Sunday since his conversion to the Catholic Faith six years prior. He had been hoofing it alone for two years now since his beloved wife and traveling partner, Maria Lucia, had died.

This particular Saturday morning, a day dedicated to the Blessed Virgin, would turn out to unfold into something unbelievably miraculous — something Juan Diego could never have imagined, not in a million years — *something* which would change the world forever.

What was that charming music? Juan Diego had never heard such heavenly music — ever! *Where was it coming from? Could it be birds singing these exquisite melodies?* Juan Diego wondered as he approached Tepeyac Hill, while the enchanting music filled the air. It seemed to enrapture his heart and soul. He almost felt like he was dreaming. *Could he be in Heaven?*

As he got closer, the music stopped. There was complete silence. And a voice called to him: "*Juanito, Juan Dieguito.*" He drew closer. He was unafraid. Suddenly, a glowing white cloud appeared above the crest of the hill. The earth around the apparition seemed to display glowing rainbow colors, and the surrounding foliage radiated shades of jade, gold, and turquoise. Beautiful flowers exuded an enchanting fragrance.[37]

Our Lady of Guadalupe Revealed Herself

It was the 9th of December, and the heavenly visitor identified herself. She told Juan, "I want you to know for certain, my dear son, that I am the perfect and always Virgin Mary, Mother of the True God from Whom all life comes, the Lord of all things, Creator of Heaven and Earth."[38] The visitor is otherwise known as Our Lady of Guadalupe or the Virgin of Guadalupe.

His Eminence, Raymond Leo Cardinal Burke commented on Our Lady's words to Juan Diego:

> Her words declare her vocation and mission as Mother of God, Mother of God the Son, the Second Person of the Most Holy Trinity, who took a human heart under her Immaculate Heart. ... She also refers to the mystery of her Immaculate Conception by which she was chosen from the beginning of time to be the privileged instrument of the redemptive Incarnation and partner with God the Son in carrying out the work of our Redemption, the sole reason for His taking of our human flesh and becoming one of us.[39]

He continued, "The Coming of the Son of God into the world is the true and lasting remedy of our spiritual poverty, God the Father's perfect act of love for us as His sons and daughters. The Mother of God, Our Lady of Guadalupe, is constantly directing us to the mystery of the Incarnation which gives us unfailing hope and sound direction for our lives."[40]

Let's take a deeper look at how Our Lady of Guadalupe directs us to the unfailing hope of Jesus.

We first notice that the Blessed Virgin did not choose to deliver her message to a high-ranking person, a bishop, a pope.

No. She chose a lowly and simple but faithful Catholic, Juan Diego. She entrusted him with a mission to communicate with the Bishop of Mexico. Mary could have gone straight to the Bishop himself with her saving mission. Yet, she desired that simple and unqualified Juan carry out the heavenly mission. I believe she calls upon us too, as unqualified as we may be. God uses the humble and faithful!

Our Lady of Guadalupe appeared to Juan Diego on the exact spot where the evil one had inspired the worship of pagan gods. The Mother of God desired to save these souls and future generations. And she requested that a chapel be built on that very spot in her honor so that she could show her love and compassion and, most of all, glorify her Divine Son Jesus. The very nature of her mission was to manifest Divine Mercy. She desired that it be a place of pilgrimage, where she would make known her maternal love to pilgrims who come.

The Virgin of Guadalupe told her little Juanito, "I will give Him to the people in all my personal love, in my compassion, in my help, in my protection: because I am truly your merciful Mother, yours and all the other people of different ancestries, my lovers, who love me, those who seek me, those who trust me. Here I will hear their weeping, their complaints and heal all their sorrows, hardships, and sufferings."[41]

Mary sent Juan Diego to the Bishop with her request, and the disbelieving Bishop demanded proof of the vision. He wanted a sure sign that the message was from "the Lady from Heaven."

The Bishop indeed received his sign, and it came about in such a glorious way! This should not come as a surprise, however, because everything Our Lady does is glorious! She asked her little Juanito to collect some flowers and bring them to the Bishop as a holy sign. Sounded simple enough. But, then again, it was December. Additionally, Juan Diego's uncle was sick, and Juan was troubled about getting to him to care for him, and now Our Lady's requests were lovingly lying upon his shoulders.

Our Lady Allays Our Fears

Mary told St. Juan Diego, "Let not your heart be disturbed. Do not fear that sickness, nor any other sickness or anguish. Am I not here, who is your Mother? Are you not under my protection? Am

I not your health? Are you not happily within my fold? What else do you wish? Do not grieve nor be disturbed by anything."[42]

Mary takes care of everything. She wanted her Juanito to understand this and not be troubled. Our Lady speaks these words to our hearts as well. She allays our fears. Our Lady of Guadalupe offers great hope to us. She is our true Mother!

Our Lady told Juan Diego just where he could find the flowers. Despite the December frost, he discovered beautiful roses miraculously growing atop a high hill. Our Lady then lovingly arranged them with her own hands in his *tilma* before he headed off to the Bishop's residence. Can we even imagine this beautiful attention to detail on Mary's part? We shall soon see why she arranged them with her own holy hands.

When Juan opened his *tilma* to reveal the luscious, beautiful roses, including Castilian roses (which did not grow in Mexico), tucked tightly against his body, *something* else was also revealed. That is, the colorful and vibrant miraculous image of Our Lady of Guadalupe on Juan's *tilma*!

Our Lady of Guadalupe's Miraculous Image

Needless to say, the Bishop was exceedingly pleased and completely enraptured by Our Lady's miraculous image in her native features and dress displayed on the peasant's clothing. As I noted in my book, *30 Marian Eucharistic Visits: Adoring Jesus with His Mother*:

> This tilma, which was a poor-quality cactus cloth, should have deteriorated within about twenty years. However, 476 years later, it still shows no sign of decay, and the image on it completely defies all scientific explanations of its origin. Studies show that reflected in Our Lady's eyes in the image is what was in front of her when she appeared in 1531.[43]

The miraculous image was placed in the chapel for veneration. Juan Diego lived the remaining 17 years of his life as a hermit in a tiny abode near the chapel and cared for the church and the first pilgrims who came to pray to Our Lady of Guadalupe. We can only imagine the countless number of pilgrims with whom he spoke — telling every detail of the miraculous story again and again, no doubt, with a twinkle in his eyes.

Juan Diego died in 1548 and was buried in the first chapel dedicated to the Virgin of Guadalupe.

All in all, there were five apparitions of Our Lady of Guadalupe to St. Juan Diego. The first was the initial meeting with Our Lady. At the second apparition, Juan asked Mary to choose someone else since he felt he failed with the Bishop. Mary reassured Juan that he was her appointed messenger and asked him to remind the Bishop of her identity.

In the third apparition, Mary agreed to provide the sign the following day, December 11. But, alas, dear Juanito didn't meet with Mary on December 11 due to taking care of his uncle, whom he feared was dying. The fourth apparition occurred in the early morning of December 12, when Juan was trying to avoid his Holy Mother while on his way to seek a priest to hear his dying uncle's confession. Our Lady met him and then gave Juan the heartfelt and powerful words we ponder today. I mentioned them briefly earlier. However, here they are now in full. Let them sink in:

> Listen, put it into your heart, my youngest and dearest son, that the thing that disturbs you, the thing that afflicts you, is nothing. Do not let your countenance, your heart be disturbed. Do not fear this sickness of your uncle or any other sickness, nor anything that is sharp or hurtful. Am I not here, I, who am your Mother? Are you not under my shadow and protection? Am I not the source of your joy? Are you not in the hollow of my mantle, in the crossing of my arms? Do you need anything more? Let nothing else worry you, disturb you. Do not let your uncle's illness worry you, because he will not die now. You may be certain that he is already well.[44]

Within the first 10 years after Our Lady of Guadalupe's apparitions, in which Our Lady manifested herself to the native peoples of Mexico as a sign of her motherly care, it is said that 10 million people were converted from paganism and accepted the Catholic Faith. Conversions continue. This is the largest mass conversion in history.

Venerable Pope Pius XII declared the Virgin of Guadalupe the Empress of all the Americas. In a prayer he composed in 1945 to commemorate the 50th anniversary of her first crowning, he said, "For we are certain that as long as you are recognized as Queen and Mother, Mexico and America will be safe."

In 1990, St. John Paul II visited Mexico and beatified Juan Diego. In 2002, this same pontiff canonized him. In 1999, St. John Paul II declared Our Lady of Guadalupe the Patroness of the Americas. The feast of Our Lady for Guadalupe is December 12.

It's been almost 500 years since Our Lady of Guadalupe appeared to the humble St. Juan Diego. Her message is the same for us now: Mother Mary loves us and desires that we turn away from sin, turn to her Son Jesus, and call upon her as our protective and loving Mother. As Cardinal Burke has stated:

> It was during an age much like our own when Our Lady first appeared to St. Juan Diego some 500 years ago. Again, we are contending with disease, war, and deep spiritual confusion. Again, many poor souls are tempted to fear that all hope is lost. But Our Lord has not called us to fear. No matter the darkness of our age, men and women of faith are not without the truth and love of Christ, nor the faithful care of His mother. Through St. Juan Diego's humble and courageous cooperation with grace, Our Lady's intercession transformed the world and brought millions of souls to Christ. It is this same maternal care and protection that we seek today — a care and protection that she will grant us, should we earnestly ask for it.[45]

ACT

Our Lady's loving words to St. Juan Diego were a certain comfort to him and can be for us too. Similar to what Our Lady of Guadalupe had said to Juan, "Do you need anything more?" Our Lady answered Lucia, one of the Fátima visionaries, "Are you suffering a great deal? Don't lose heart. I will never forsake you. My Immaculate Heart will be your refuge and the way that will lead you to God."[46]

Our Lady always consoles our hearts and promises to remain with us to strengthen us on our pilgrimage of hope.

Take time to ponder the story of Our Lady of Guadalupe. What does she mean to you? As I wrote about Our Lady of Guadalupe above, at one point, my eyes brimmed with unexpected tears. Though I already knew the story, I was suddenly very overcome with the absolute reality of the miraculous image on Juan's *tilma*. How utterly amazing!

You know, having great fear in our hearts because of the state of our world or because of situations in our own lives can cause us to panic at times. We may not realize that we can get all wrapped up in the chains of fear. We might then have trouble praying as we should, becoming crippled in fear. The sooner we turn our fears over to God, the better! Ask our Lord to remove the shackles of fear that have been stifling you and holding you back from the life you are meant to live. Ask Mary to help you to surrender your fears to God.

Mary, our Mother, has much to give us. Ask her. Stay quiet and listen to her. Remember, she says, "Let not your heart be disturbed." Allow her to console you. Give her everything in prayer. Ask her to allay your fears so that you can breathe again and hope again! This will also allow you to lovingly serve God and your neighbor.

Also, pray about how you can tell someone about Mother Mary — how she can be their Mother too. This can be accomplished in simple ways and through sharing your heart with others.

PRAY

Dear Holy Family, Jesus, Mary, and Joseph,
please bless me and pray for me.
Dear Holy Mary, Our Lady of Guadalupe,
Mother of the Redeemer, Mother of Mercy and of hope,
thank you for being my Mother. Help me to have hope
when my prayers seem unanswered.
Gate of Heaven, strengthen my virtues of faith, hope, and love.
Seat of Wisdom, please grant me your graces.
Mirror of Perfection, mold my heart and teach me to believe,
to hope, and to love right along with you.
Mary, my Mother, I need your help.
Please perfect my simple prayers.
Please guide my steps today and always closer to your Son Jesus.
Star of Hope, Star of the Sea, please shine upon me
and guide me ever closer to your Son's Kingdom!
Amen.

Recite the Our Father, Hail Mary, Glory Be,
Hail Holy Queen, Memorare *(pages 201-202).*

Pray a prayer to Our Lady of Guadalupe (page 236).

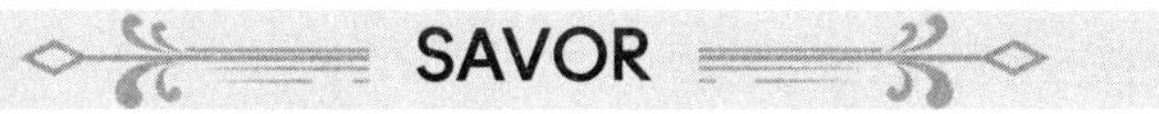

SAVOR

A prayer, a thought, a resolution:

____

____

____

____

____

____

____

O MARY CONCEIVED WITHOUT SIN PRAY FOR US WHO HAVE RECOURSE TO THEE
1830

6

The Hope of the Miraculous Medal: "Graces Will Be Shed Upon All"

"Have a medal struck after this model. All who wear it will receive great graces; they should wear it around the neck. Graces will abound for persons who wear it with confidence."[47]

— The Blessed Virgin Mary to St. Catherine Labouré

What is the significance and meaning of a Miraculous Medal? Is the Miraculous Medal a prayer in metal form? Did the Blessed Mother really design this medal? We will begin our reflection with a lot of questions, including, "Why is the Miraculous Medal one of the most popular sacramental among Catholics?" We will discover answers as we delve into the fascinating and rich history of the Miraculous Medal, as well as learn about some modern-day Miraculous Medal miracles.

REFLECT

We have more questions! What causes a permanently brain-injured child with a fractured skull to come out of a coma completely cured after a blessed Miraculous Medal was placed around his neck? Or miraculously secures a property deal for a convent when Mother Teresa tosses a blessed Miraculous Medal onto the property? Or how does that little oval-shaped piece of metal cause a murderous gang member to collapse into my arms as soon as I place one in his open hand?

What caused an adamant Catholic hater to fall to his knees and tearfully pray to the Blessed Mother? Or a man named Tim, not expected to survive his intubation and coma, which was necessary due to his dire condition caused by COVID-19, to pull through with flying colors? His daughter was told at one point that he would soon pass away peacefully within two days. If he survived, they said he would have severe organ damage. Yet, he came out of a coma and healed miraculously, growing stronger with each passing day. A Miraculous Medal I had sent to him became part of his healing journey.

We will get into all of this. For now, we will step back to the summer of 1830.

Heaven Sends Our Lady to Paris

When God decided to send Holy Mary to appear in Paris, France, in 1830 to deliver a great mission, He chose humble and faithful Sr. Catherine Labouré, a new novice of the Daughters of Charity, to be the recipient of the heavenly and history-changing visits. Sister Catherine would be given the amazing mission of seeing that Mary's medal, designed exclusively by Mary herself, would be cast and propagated throughout the world.

A very tall task for a young novice just getting her feet wet in religious life!

Let's go back a bit further — to the very beginning.

It was at the ringing of the *Angelus*[48] bell at 6:00 p.m. on May 2, 1806, in the charming village of Fain-lès-Moutiers in Burgundy, France, when Catherine Labouré came into the world. Perhaps, due to a holy intuition, just moments after her birth, as Catherine was nestled against her mother, Madeleine Louise requested that her daughter's name be entered right away into the civil register. So, within a quarter of an hour after her birth, Catherine was registered: "Catherine, daughter of Pierre Labouré and Madeleine Gontard his wife, was born this same day (May 2, 1806) at six o'clock in the evening."[49]

Catherine was the only one of the 17 children to be registered so quickly. She was baptized into the Catholic Church the very next day.

A Saint in the Making is Born

Catherine was affectionately called Zoe by her loving, tight-knit family, and eventually by others too. She grew up as a simple farm girl. Her family lived comfortably in a spacious house set on a picturesque farm. As Catherine grew, she loved helping her father Pierre take care of their hundreds of pigeons. Raising pigeons was a native French industry. Pierre was a good man and a hard worker, but ruled the household with a somewhat iron hand.

Catherine also helped her mother, Madeleine Louise, with chores around the house and with her younger sister, Tonine, and her disabled brother, Auguste. Her mother's gentle warmth made up for her father's gruffness.

Catherine and her mother spent much time together. They were very close and shared a spiritual bond as well. However, that togetherness would abruptly change on October 9, 1815, when Catherine was 9 years old. The rug of her peaceful, ordinary life was yanked out from under her. Her Mama had died at only 42 years of age. The family was shaken to the core — the heart of their home had been summoned to Heaven.

What's a little girl like Catherine to do without a mother? Well, she did precisely what came to her mind and heart. When no one was looking, or so she thought, she quietly meandered into her parents' bedroom. Since she thought she was alone, she pushed a chair over to a shelf, got up on it, reached up high, took the statue of the Blessed Mother down, and drew it against her heart.

Saint Catherine Labouré Adopts Mother Mary

"Now, dear Blessed Mother," Catherine expressed, "now you will be my Mother!"[50] And that was that. Her simple, yet earnest, childlike desires were communicated to her Mother in Heaven.

Unbeknownst to Catherine, Mary already had a careful eye on her daughter. After all, Mary had big plans for her.

You might recall that St. Teresa of Avila, when praying before a statue of Mary, also chose Mary as her Mother after her own mother died. That was a few centuries before Catherine's request of Mary. She wouldn't have known about St. Teresa's pronouncement, but we see that Catherine was in good company. Holy minds think alike!

Indeed, Mary would become even more significant to Catherine during her life and mission. Catherine grew to be happy and obedient. At 18 years old, she had a transforming dream about a priest. It wouldn't be the last time she saw him. She would see his image later on in a picture on a convent wall. Still later, he was her spiritual director (from Heaven!).

His name is St. Vincent de Paul. I'll get back to him. First, we'll continue with Catherine planning her future. Or shall we say that it was our Lord and Our Lady doing the planning?

Destined to Enter Religious Life

Catherine was so certain that she was called to religious life that she turned down at least three marriage proposals. The only problem was that her dear father tried to put his foot down and on more than one occasion! He was not going to allow his daughter to leave him for the convent. Well, it took a while to happen, due to his resistance, his refusal to provide a dowry, her lack of enough formal education, and more. However, the Mother of God paved the way. And she opened the door!

Finally, at 22 years of age, in God's Divine Providence, Catherine entered the religious congregation of the Daughters of Charity (or Sisters of Charity), established by St. Vincent de Paul and St. Louise de Marillac. These religious were known for their cheerful presence all over Paris and their love for the poor and needy.

God must have been in a big hurry because things started happening very fast in religious life for Catherine. As soon as she entered the convent, Catherine began having mystical experiences. These involved visions of the founder's heart and of Jesus, and eventually the great apparitions with Our Lady in the chapel regarding the Miraculous Medal, which we will get to shortly.

When these mystical experiences were occurring, Sr. Catherine had to tell her priest director. What did he tell her to do? "Forget about it!" But how could she forget about it? She did her best to follow his advice, but these continued, and got even more intense.

You see, on the eve of the Feast of St. Vincent de Paul, July 18, 1830,[51] Catherine would be woken by her Guardian Angel and summoned by the Blessed Virgin Mary to meet her in the chapel.

Mary Reveals Herself and Her Medal Design

There in the chapel, Mother Mary told Catherine many things as Catherine knelt before her, resting her arms on Mary's lap while Our Lady sat in a chair (which you can see today!). Can we even imagine this? Mary told Catherine that she was chosen for a great mission. She spoke to her about great graces that would be bestowed at the foot of the altar.

Later, on November 27, 1830, Mary came back and displayed a remarkable vision to Catherine in the chapel. The Blessed Mother showed her daughter the exact model of the medal that she herself had designed — front and back. Catherine was to have the medal struck. Of course, there was a lot more to this than simply carrying out that request. She would need others to believe about this grand visit and mission.

"Have a medal struck after this model. All who wear it will receive great graces; they should wear it around the neck. Graces will abound for persons who wear it with confidence," Mary told Catherine. The Mother of God also told her the prayer to be etched on the front of the medal: "O Mary, conceived without sin, pray for us who have recourse to thee."[52]

It's a powerful prayer we should pray throughout the day.

Sister Catherine was so humble that she would keep secret her identity as the Miraculous Medal visionary her entire life. Only her spiritual director, Fr. Aladel, would know, and her Mother Superior, who learned of it towards the very end of Sr. Catherine's life. The Blessed Mother would continue to speak to Sr. Catherine for the next 46 years (in what are called "locutions"). They had daily conversations!

It took a while for the authenticity of the vision to be fully discerned and investigated before medals were made, but eventually the first 20,000 medals were struck and distributed quickly. It turned out that the medals couldn't be passed out quickly enough! They brought countless miracles of mind, heart, body, and soul.

The medal was originally called the Medal of the Immaculate Conception. But soon, it was called the Miraculous Medal, as people would hand them to someone and say, "Here, take this! It's miraculous! It's a Miraculous Medal!" And the name stuck!

Countless cures and miracles through the Miraculous Medal have continued all over the world. Back in the day, the Sisters of the Daughters of Charity gave blessed Miraculous Medals to all of their patients. They also secretly slipped the medals under stubborn atheists' pillows! Many experienced miraculous changes of heart and asked to see a priest so they could repent of their sins. Others were baptized into the Catholic Faith.

It's important for us to recognize that it is not a good luck charm or anything superstitious. Our Lady created it and asked us to wear it with faith. She promised miracles of grace bestowed on those who believe.

Sister Catherine's body was exhumed 57 years after her death and was found to be completely incorrupt (as some saints are) with her eyes as blue as ever. She was beatified on May 28, 1933 and canonized on July 27, 1947 by Ven. Pope Pius XII. Her feast day is November 28. It's important to mention that St. Catherine Labouré's sanctity was not based on the fact that she witnessed apparitions or that she was entrusted with a huge holy mission. No. It was in her obedience to her state of life — her vocation. Catherine had always immersed her heart and soul into everything she did — her humble and dirty farm work in Fain-lès-Moutiers, caring for her family, ministering to the poor and sick, or her hidden life and custodial work in the convent. Catherine remained faithful and obedient to her daily duties of prayer and work, striving to perform everything as well as she could in order to please God, and ultimately to become a living example of holiness.

We have much to learn from her beautiful example!

Hundreds of Millions of Medals and Miraculous Conversions

Hundreds of millions of medals were distributed in the first 40 years after the apparitions. The Archbishop was very involved. And the skeptical Fr. Aladel, who initially told Catherine to "forget about it!" ended up writing a large book about the Miraculous Medal. (I have read his book! And I have derived pertinent information from him.)

Associations and an Archconfraternity were formed, and the number of devotees continually increased throughout the years. The chapel where Mary appeared to Sr. Catherine at 140 Rue du Bac in Paris would eventually become a pilgrimage site: "Chapel of the Apparitions." Originally built in 1913, and expanded later on, the chapel is at the heart of Paris, but you can easily miss this amazing sacred place if you're not careful. It is hidden down a little lane and tucked inside a modern building.

I must mention the miraculous conversion of Alphonse Ratisbonne, said to be the greatest miracle of conversion since

St. Paul. It occurred in 1841 and brought much attention to the Miraculous Medal in the secular world.

Alphonse was a well-connected 28-year-old Jew who vehemently hated Catholicism. He was not happy about the fact that his older brother Theodore had left Judaism to become a Catholic priest. Well, it's a long story, but it's important that I at least give some highlights because Alphonse's amazing transformation really stirred things up!

Suffice it to say that he was challenged by his brother's friend to wear a Miraculous Medal and to pray the *Memorare*. It all led to him walking into a Catholic Church and seeing a resplendent heavenly vision: first, a cross, then an aggressive black dog getting in the way, who then disappeared.[53] Then, the Blessed Mother appeared in a surge of resplendent light in the exact pose as in the Miraculous Medal! Brilliant rays of grace streamed from Mary's hands. Alphonse fell to his knees. His soul was pummeled with holy love.

News of Alphonse's conversion from Judaism to Catholicism reverberated around Rome, then throughout Europe. Because of this, Rome instituted an official inquiry and rendered their decision, which fully recognized this occurrence to be a signal grace from the Miraculous Medal.

By the way, after Alphonse's experience with Our Lady of the Miraculous Medal, he immediately studied the Catholic Faith, came into the Church, received the Sacraments, became a priest, and joined his brother in the Congregation of Our Lady of Sion, which he founded in order to evangelize the Jews. Alphonse went on to spend over 30 years evangelizing his own people in the Holy Land.

Miraculous Medal Miracles

Many saints and holy people are associated with the Miraculous Medal: St. Catherine Labouré, of course; St. Maximilian Kolbe, who established the Knights of the Immaculata and who would call the Miraculous Medal the "silver bullet"; Frank Duff, who established the Legion of Mary, helped the poor, and saved the family in Ireland; and Mother Teresa, who deeply loved the Blessed Mother and continuously gave out Miraculous Medals, to name a few.

I have worn a Miraculous Medal most of my life, and it became an unmistakable conduit to my 10-year friendship with

Mother Teresa, which started out with the first medal she gave to me. It's another long story, but I mention it because, by the grace of God, I have ended up, for years now, giving out Miraculous Medals all around the world — something I learned from my spiritual mother, Mother Teresa, but never intended to do. To this date, I have given out tens of thousands of blessed Miraculous Medals and have written a book, *The Miraculous Medal: Stories, Prayers, and Devotions.*

Mother Teresa depended upon Mother Mary's help. She wisely and earnestly put the special medal designed by Mary herself to use to bring about hope and healing for those in need. She often rubbed a blessed Miraculous Medal on a sick or injured person, invoking the Blessed Virgin Mary to come to his or her aid. She even tossed blessed Miraculous Medals onto properties which she wanted to purchase as convents for her sisters. Suddenly, miraculously, the funds became available.

Incidentally, our friend Tim, whom I mentioned earlier, was astounded as he read my book about the Miraculous Medal. He said, "The book really shook me up, because my church is called St. Vincent de Paul, so that was God speaking to me."

Tim is the man who was dying of the COVID-19 virus. He explained, "[At] my follow-up visit with my heart doctor, [the doctor] said I am only the second person after being intubated to make their after-hospital appointment. The rest passed away." He added, "My doctor said I made a 100 percent recovery. A true miracle."

Fully recovered, Tim added, "I am surrounded by a lot of daily Bible readers who are convinced that Satan is in charge of the world. After reading your book, it showed me that you just need to ask Mary, and she will protect you from Satan. I pray to Mary way more than I ever did."

I have witnessed numerous amazing transformations during encounters with people in my life — most of them complete strangers — wealthy and homeless alike. As Mother Teresa often preached, the Western world is starved for love. And I believe they are starved for a Mother's love — loving hope from Our Lady.

One such encounter was with a murderous gang member, whom I met in a family restaurant. When I offered a blessed Miraculous Medal to him and told him that Mary was his Mother and would take care of him, he wrapped his arms around me and collapsed into my arms like a little boy clinging to his mother. He sobbed on my shoulder — right in front of his peers at the restaurant! It was a profound experience. I have no doubt that it changed his life forever. Mine too!

Weeks after giving a blessed Miraculous Medal to a woman at a book signing, she got in touch with me to tell me that her breast cancer was completely cured. May God be praised!

"Those Medals are Powerful"

Life is always a fascinating adventure. I often tell my audiences when I am out presenting that they shouldn't worry at all if they can't get out of the house to do their ministry work or evangelizing because God will certainly bring the people to them! I live way back in the woods, yet pretty interesting conversations unfold here in the "quiet." Sometimes, it happens unexpectedly with delivery people, repairmen, or technicians.

One morning, my elderly neighbor's health aide knocked on my door to tell me that my neighbor's phone was not working and asked if I could kindly make a couple of calls for her. I checked and found my landline was not working either. But I could use my cellphone to make the calls. One call was to alert the phone company about the outages. Thankfully, after some time, the technician was able to fix everything over the phone on my neighbor's line and mine.

After her intervention, the phones seemed to be working fine, but she said she would leave the order for a repairman to come to the houses that day just in case they went out again. I thought it sounded like a good idea, but I was very busy with work and didn't have time to be dealing with a visit and all it entailed. The phones did go out again, but they came back on shortly after.

Soon after, my elderly neighbor called to thank me for helping. I loved the opportunity to help and also to speak with her. We arranged to have tea together soon.

I got back to my work, and then another phone call came in. It was the phone company repairman. I told him that the phones had been fixed by the phone company woman during the call. He told me that he would check it out by going to the telephone pole down the road and then would stop by the house. He warned me that the phones might go out again, but I shouldn't be alarmed because it might just be him tinkering with the connections and wires.

"It's a good thing I don't have a radio show today," I said. "I do regular radio shows from my telephone," I explained.

The technician then asked, "Do you mind if I ask you a personal question?"

"Not at all," I reassured him.

"Did you write a book?" he inquired.

"Is your name Dave?" I fired right back.

I instantly recalled the entire scenario, which had transpired years prior, when a phone man showed up at my house, but my phone was completely fine. During that visit, he ended up telling me all about his life-changing experience, and after a while, he left with one of my books in one hand and a couple of blessed Miraculous Medals in the other.

"Yes!" he said.

Wow. His name was Dave! He added that he would see me within the hour. I could tell that he was so surprised that we had mysteriously reconnected after an interesting encounter years ago. Truth be told, I was very surprised too!

Wait a minute!

I asked myself. *Isn't he IN my Miraculous Medal book? He is. I know he is!*

I hurried up to my office to get a copy of the book to check. Yes, indeed, he was there right under the subtitle, "The Phone Man." I took the book downstairs because I planned to give it to Dave when I saw him. *Wow. God never ceases to amaze me!*

Dave arrived at my front door, and we heartily shook hands, smiling, happy to see one another again.

"Wow, you know those Mir-a-cle Medals you gave me?" Dave asked.

"The Miraculous Medals?" I asked him. I couldn't help smiling at his slight change of the word. "Yes, I remember. I gave you two — one for you and one for your son."

"Well, those medals sure are powerful! My son keeps his in his wallet. I keep circulating the one you gave me to each person in the family who needs it. It really works!" he explained.

"I'll need to give you more blessed medals before you leave so you won't have to keep passing the one around."

I also explained that it is best to wear the medal around the neck if possible. The Blessed Mother actually said that great graces will be received when it is worn around the neck. I gave Dave a little more history while we both stood on the walkway outside my front door.

I told Dave that he was actually in my Miraculous Medal book. He was so surprised! He couldn't believe it.

"Wow, I am really blown away to know that I am in your book."

"Yes, your story is inspiring people all over the world," I told him.

"I can't believe it — wow!" he said.

"Maybe I shouldn't tell you where you are in the book," I teased, "so that you will read the whole thing and learn the history of the Miraculous Medal and about St. Catherine Labouré."

I handed the book to Dave, and he expressed his gratitude. I did point out the location of his story. He read it and smiled. I ran to grab a copy of my memoir, *The Kiss of Jesus*, too, as well as five blessed Miraculous Medals and a bunch of blessed St. Benedict medals. I told him about the power in a blessed St. Benedict Medal (when blessed with the full exorcism blessing), also explaining that there is nothing superstitious about it. I gave him a few leaflets that explained the origin.

Dave told me that every night he thanks God for his life. When we first met, he shared with me about a harrowing experience when out on the job. He is extremely grateful to be alive. By God's grace, during a sudden and severe thunderstorm, he was able to quickly get out of the bucket truck and then jump out of the way of a falling killer tree — right in the nick of time!

I reminded him that God is always in control and that it was very interesting that both times that he came to my house there was really no problem with the phone. But I believe that God wanted Dave to receive the blessed Miraculous Medals as well as the books, and that is why God brought him here to my house.

Dave made a point to mention that it had been four or five years since he came to my house the first time, and he said that day was the only other time that he worked in this area.

Just then, Dave gazed down at both books and the blessed medals he held in his hands and said, "I didn't come here to help you with the phones. It is very clear to me now that I came here for you to help me. God is in charge!"

Yes, He sure is, I thought. *And Mother Mary always helps!*

Father Hardon and the Boy at the Hospital

There's so much more I could tell you about transformations and holy experiences with Mary's medal. But I'll stop here on my own experiences because it's absolutely vital that I tell you what my friend and spiritual director of happy memory, Servant of God Fr. John A. Hardon, SJ, shared with me.

When he was a young priest, a Vincentian priest visited him and his fellow Jesuits to tell them about Our Lady's Miraculous Medal. Father Hardon admitted that he wasn't too impressed because he was not "the medal-wearing kind of guy." That sentiment would dramatically change one ordinary day when he was serving as a chaplain at a Catholic hospital.

Making his rounds one day, Fr. Hardon came upon an entirely hopeless situation. Or so he thought. It was a 9-year-old boy who had been in a coma for 10 days due to a sledding accident. He had a fractured skull and inoperable severe and permanent brain damage. Father felt his purpose was to console the parents and bless the boy. That's all he could do.

Just as he was about to leave the hospital room, an idea fiercely struck him. Father Hardon vividly remembered the Vincentian priest's words: "The Miraculous Medal works." And so, the search began to find a Miraculous Medal. Father would put it to the test. One was finally found, and Father blessed the medal and read the prayers of investiture. A chain of some sort was needed because Father wanted the boy to have the medal around his neck. After all, Mary said great graces come through the medal, especially when it is worn around the neck.

I'll let Fr. Hardon tell you what happened!

"No sooner did I finish the prayer of enrolling the boy in the Confraternity of the Miraculous Medal than he opened his eyes for the first time in almost two weeks. He saw his mother and said, 'Ma, I want some ice cream.'"[54]

Everyone in the room was astonished beyond words, and the doctor was called. The boy had his ice cream! He stayed for three more days, undergoing a battery of tests. Then, he was released from the hospital, declared completely cured of all brain damage. An absolute miracle!

Father Hardon was never the same since that fateful day. "This experience so changed my life that I have not been the same since," he said. "My faith in God, faith in His power to work miracles, was strengthened beyond description." From then on, he passionately promoted the Miraculous Medal. He added, "The wonders the Blessed Mother performs, provided we believe, are extraordinary."[55]

Let's remember those key words: "provided we believe."

As I am closing this chapter, I just remembered that I gave a blessed Miraculous Medal to a former classmate at a high school reunion last year. He was suffering with cancer, and I felt inspired to gift a tangible sign of hope to him — a beautiful sacramental from our Mother. I had no idea what his religion was or if he had one. I simply wanted to help him in some way. He received my little gift with great appreciation and hugged me.

Since then, I have kept Lee in my prayers. Recently, I found out that he died. As sad as that is, I am grateful to have had that opportunity to show love to Lee and give him a gift from our Mother. I'm sure she helped him.

Incidentally, part of a consecration prayer to Our Lady of the Miraculous Medal pertains to a happy death: "O most powerful Virgin, Mother of our Savior, keep us close to you every moment of our lives. Obtain for us, your children, the grace of a happy death; so that, in union with you, we may enjoy the bliss of heaven forever. Amen." You can read the entire prayer, "An Act of Consecration to Our Lady of the Miraculous Medal," on page 234.

I continually wear one of the blessed Miraculous Medals that Mother Teresa gave me. It's the one she gave me during the pregnancy of my daughter Mary-Catherine at the time my doctor told me flat out that I was losing my baby and that my life was in danger too. The medal got so worn from years of use that the top part broke off completely. I now wear my cherished medal in a locket for safe keeping.

That unborn baby is a young adult now. Thanks be to God.

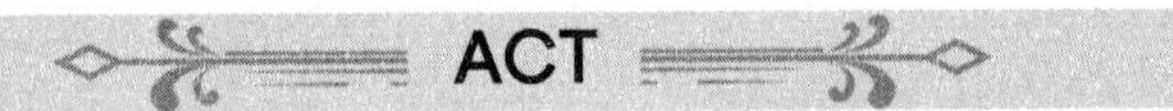

ACT

Do you wear a Miraculous Medal? Do you believe that Our Lady works miracles? Father Hardon was once very skeptical. It took an undeniable miracle in front of his very eyes before he believed in God's power, which is so often manifested through Holy Mary.

Take time to ponder the history and the devotion to Our Lady of the Miraculous Medal in the reflection above. Consider sharing one of the Miraculous Medal stories from this chapter with someone you know.

If you do not already wear a Miraculous Medal, I hope you decide to do so. Mother Mary imparts so many amazing graces through her special medal.

Take another look at the quotation that begins this chapter. Spend time with Mother Mary. Ask Mary to grant you many graces. She will! Take a look at the Appendix for special prayers for extra inspiration.

PRAY

Dear Holy Family, Jesus, Mary, and Joseph,
please bless me and pray for me.
Saint Catherine Labouré, please pray for me.
Dear Holy Mary, Our Lady of the Miraculous Medal,
Mother of the Redeemer, Mother of Mercy and of hope,
thank you for being my Mother.
Gate of Heaven, strengthen my virtues of faith, hope, and love.
Seat of Wisdom, please grant me your graces.
Mirror of Perfection, mold my heart and teach me
to believe, to hope, and to love right along with you.
Mary, my Mother, I need your help.
Please perfect my simple prayers.
Please guide my steps today and always closer
to your Son Jesus.
Star of Hope, Star of the Sea, please shine upon me
and guide me ever closer to your Son's Kingdom!
Amen.

O Mary, conceived without sin, pray for us who
have recourse to thee (*repeat three times*).

Recite the Our Father, Hail Mary, Glory Be,
Hail Holy Queen, Memorare *(pages 201-202).*

Pray the Novena Prayer to Our Lady of the Miraculous Medal
or "An Act of Consecration to Our Lady of
the Miraculous Medal," pages 233-234.

SAVOR

A prayer, a thought, a resolution:

"Apparition of Our Lady of Lourdes to Bernadette" by Antonio Ciseri, 1879.

7

The Hope of Lourdes:
"I am the Immaculate Conception"

"In Lourdes, the Holy Virgin invites all to
regard earth as a place of pilgrimage toward
our final homeland, which is heaven.
In reality, we are all pilgrims, we need Mary
to guide us; and in Lourdes, her smile invites us
to go forward with great confidence
in the awareness that God is good, God is love."[56]

— Pope Benedict XVI

Once again, we will see that Mary chooses the very simple, humble, and faithful pilgrim through which to carry out her plans. Mary also seems to choose hidden hamlets and grottos, transforming them with her graces and putting them on the map, so to speak. Let's delve into the beautiful history of Our Lady of Lourdes and the unassuming young Bernadette Soubirous.

On February 11, 1858, Bernadette Soubirous, a shy and sickly 14-year-old French peasant girl, was visited by a mysterious, yet beautiful, woman dressed in a dazzling white dress with a blue sash wrapped around her waist. Yellow roses were on this radiant visitor's feet.

It was in the foothills of the Pyrenees in southern France, where Bernadette had been doing her best to gather firewood with her younger sister Toinette and their friend Baloum. That February day brought an uninvited chill to the region, and Mama had been a bit reluctant to allow Bernadette to go out with the girls. But not a stick of firewood was left to keep the modest Soubirous abode warm. She told Bernadette to make certain she wrapped herself up well.

Due to her weakness from asthma, Bernadette was slower than the others. She hadn't yet caught up with them when suddenly, there by the river and at the bottom of a mountain, Bernadette experienced something she never could have imagined would happen in her quiet, secluded life! In that tranquil grotto, she was dazzled by a bright light and then completely mesmerized by the sudden unexpected appearance of a beautiful young Lady who appeared within the supernatural light.

The Lady Suddenly Appeared

Just seconds before, Bernadette had heard a gust of wind. As her eyes took in the mysterious image before her, she observed that the Lady was wearing a long white veil which covered her head, shoulders, and arms, almost reaching her feet. The beautiful yellow roses at the Lady's feet captured Bernadette's attention. Even so, it was all so strange — and a bit scary too.

"I was afraid. I stepped back," Bernadette recalled. "I wanted to call the younger ones, but I wasn't brave enough." She rubbed her eyes to wipe away the illusion, "but to no avail, I kept seeing the same Lady."[57] And the Lady smiled at Bernadette.

Still, the young visionary was not quite sure if this creature, though very beautiful, was "coming from God" or perhaps "sent by the Evil Spirit."[58] She decided to pull out her Rosary, thinking that if what she saw was not holy in origin, the prayers of the holy Rosary would drive evil away.

The uninvited visitor made the Sign of the Cross in a very solemn way, and Bernadette's fears immediately vanished. Bernadette felt prompted to pray the Rosary and knelt down on the damp ground. The Lady seemed to pray her Rosary too, as the Rosary beads moved through her fingers. Soon, the apparition completely disappeared.

Just then, Toinette and Baloum came back to the place Bernadette was kneeling in prayer, carrying their baskets half-filled with the sticks they had collected. They noticed that Bernadette's face was completely washed out, as if all the blood had drained from it. She was still on her knees, gazing at the niche in the grotto of Massabielle. The girls were irritated that Bernadette hadn't helped much, but Toinette quickly became concerned that her sister might be dead since she was motionless! She looked like a statue! However, Baloum allayed Toinette's fears, telling her that since she was not laying on the ground, she was indeed still alive.

Bernadette quickly came back to herself and began to put her stockings and clogs back on. She stooped to pick up a few dry sticks, and then it was time to head back home before Mama would worry. After all, the *Angelus* bell had just started to ring. It was midday. Bernadette, who was always on the quiet side, was now completely silent as she walked along with the girls. However, her curiosity got the best of her. She had to know. Did they see the Lady too? She ventured to ask them. They said they hadn't seen anything. So, Bernadette said she hadn't seen anything either! However, she had opened a can of worms, and the interrogation was instant. Well, the girls swore up and down that they would keep a secret if she would tell them what she saw. Bernadette spilled the beans.

Despite her earnest promise, Toinette did not keep Bernadette's secret. She blurted it all out to their mother when they walked through the door. Mama was not happy about this. She had a few forthright words to express to Bernadette and said it must have been a white stone, not a lady! Bernadette calmly insisted and described the Lady's pretty countenance. Mama concluded that they must pray. The apparition must have been that of a family member in Purgatory who was in need of prayer.

Bernadette was Entrusted with a Mission

Well, that bitter cold day, February 11, 1858, would be the first of 18 visits from the beautiful and mysterious Lady. Humble and faithful Bernadette was entrusted with a holy mission of penance and hope and would suffer much to carry it out. This is so often the case of saints-in-the-making entrusted with big missions. On February 18, the Queen of Heaven would tell Bernadette that she promised to make her happy in Heaven, not in this life, but in the other.

On February 25, the Lady instructed Bernadette to dig in the dirt and drink the water that would come forth. Word about the mysterious, hopefully heavenly, visitor had gotten out in that little hamlet. At that point, hundreds of people had heard, and they made their way to the grotto to see the mysterious occurrences for themselves. They watched in bewilderment as Bernadette drank the muddy water. The water that sprang forth because of the Lady's request and Bernadette's obedience became miraculous healing water. It miraculously continues to flow to this day.

On March 2, 1858, Mary told Bernadette, "Go and tell the priests that people should come here in procession, and that a chapel should be built here." Well, it wasn't going to be an easy task. Later, the Lady would finally identify herself. On March 25, 1858, she told Bernadette, "I am the Immaculate Conception." Just four years prior, in 1854, Bl. Pope Pius IX had declared the doctrine of the Immaculate Conception (Mary being born without original sin) to be an essential element of the Catholic Faith.

Thankfully, now that the Lady's identity was revealed, progress was made towards Mary's plans for the grotto, and, importantly, the parish priest then knew that the apparitions were authentic — indeed from Heaven.

A lot would unfold in Bernadette's short life. She bravely carried out her hopeful mission with great love. She eventually joined the Sisters of Charity of Nevers at their convent in Nevers, France, in 1866. She lived the remainder of her life there.

Towards the end of her life, Bernadette's physical suffering was almost unbearable. She offered her agony to Jesus — to His Sacred and merciful Heart. She asked Mary for help, to remain with her at the foot of the Cross. She accepted the "Last Rites" (as the Sacrament of the Anointing of the Sick was called at that time) for the fifth time specifically to gain strength to die well. On Holy Thursday, she told her priest that in her suffering, she was consoled with the thoughts of Eternal Life. This was after the chaplain lovingly suggested that she should sacrifice her life. Bernadette did not miss a beat. She replied, "But, my Father, there is no sacrifice in leaving this life where it is a struggle not to offend God, and where we encounter so many pathways for doing so."

Father acknowledged her words and added, "And you, my Sister, without ever having contemplated the face of the Most High, yet you know something of what is divine goodness?"

Bernadette paused a moment before replying. "Yes," she said. "And it is that memory which consoles me and turns my heart towards hope."[59]

On Easter Wednesday, April 16, 1879, two large tears rolled down Bernadette's cheeks. She softly cried out for help from her Lady of the Grotto, her Holy Mother in Heaven. The visionary's final words before leaving this earthly pilgrimage were "Holy Mary, Mother of God, pray for me, poor sinner … poor sinner."[60] At 3:15 p.m., during the Hour of Great Mercy, she breathed her last.

A large Basilica was built at the grotto at the site of the apparitions. Today, 5 to 6 million pilgrims go to Lourdes each year, seeking peace, healing, hope, and perhaps answers to their perplexing questions. They bathe in the healing waters, originally dug up by Bernadette and still flowing. Thousands have received inner healing and physical healing too.

Since 1860, more than 200 million people have visited the Sanctuary of Our Lady of Lourdes. I am blessed to have pilgrimaged there myself and have seen the ever-flowing holy water. I was also very moved to have visited St. Bernadette's incorrupt body in Nevers.

Mary Revealed God's Love in Lourdes

Pope Benedict XVI pointed out that the Blessed Mother began the encounter with Bernadette with the Sign of the Cross. He said the Cross "tells us that there is a love in this world that is stronger than death, stronger than our weaknesses and sins. The power of love is stronger than the evil which threatens us." He continued, "It is this mystery of the universality of God's love for men that Mary came to reveal here, in Lourdes."

The pontiff added that Mary "invites all people of good will, all those who suffer in heart or body, to raise their eyes towards the Cross of Jesus, so as to discover there the source of life, the source of salvation."[61] Assisted by a sister, in her last moments, Bernadette held her crucifix in her weak hands and kissed the five wounds of Jesus. Bernadette's mission began with the Sign of the Cross from Our Lady in the grotto, and her life on earth ended with the Cross.

Saint Bernadette was beatified on June 14, 1925, and canonized on December 8, 1933. Her feast day is observed in some places on April 16, the date of her death. Others celebrate the feast day on February 18 (in France). The Feast of Our Lady of Lourdes is February 11.

ACT

Take time to ponder the story of Bernadette Soubirous and Our Lady's visits with her. It might not be possible to make a pilgrimage to Lourdes or any other Marian Shrine to experience holiness or healing. Yet, each and every one of us is already on a pilgrimage during our lifetime. Our Lord and our Holy Mother will grant every grace we need. The graces are all available for the asking.

Take time to consider your life thus far. Do you consider your life to be a pilgrimage towards Heaven? Right where you are, ask the Blessed Virgin to touch your heart and grant graces of healing according to God's holy will. Can you also kiss your crucifix and strive to accept God's holy will for your life?

Stay close to Mother Mary. She is eager to help you. Ask her to give to you a greater awareness of God's abundant blessings in your life. Ask Mary to increase your faith.

PRAY

Dear Holy Family, Jesus, Mary, and Joseph,
please bless me and pray for me.
Saint Bernadette, please teach me and pray for me.
Dear Holy Mary, Our Lady of Lourdes,
Mother of the Redeemer, Mother of Mercy
and of hope, thank you for being my Mother.
Gate of Heaven, strengthen my virtues of faith, hope, and love.
Seat of Wisdom, please grant me your graces.
Mirror of Perfection, mold my heart and teach me to believe,
to hope, and to love right along with you.
Mary, my Mother, I need your help.
Please perfect my simple prayers.
Please guide my steps today and always
closer to your Son Jesus.
Star of Hope, Star of the Sea, please shine upon me
and guide me ever closer to your Son's Kingdom!
Amen.

Recite the Our Father, Hail Mary, Glory Be,
Hail Holy Queen, Memorare *(pages 201-202).*

Pray a "Prayer to Our Lady of Lourdes" (page 237).

SAVOR

A prayer, a thought, a resolution:

The statue of Our Lady of Kibeho in Rwanda, Africa.

8

The Hope of Kibeho: "Mother of the Word"

"I have come to calm you because I have heard your prayers. I would like your friends to have faith, because they do not believe strongly enough."[62]

— Our Lady of Kibeho to Alphonsine Mumureke

Mary is always concerned about saving her children from the snares of the devil and getting them onto the road that leads to Everlasting Life. She desires for us to be in Heaven with her one day. Throughout her apparitions, our Blessed Mother continues to emphasize the call to pray the Rosary and offer penance and fasting. In her apparitions at Kibeho, Mary, who suffered along with her Son for our salvation, also asks us to meditate upon her sorrows. Let's now reflect upon the history and message of Our Lady of Kibeho.

REFLECT

In November 1981, six young girls and one boy in a village in Rwanda in Africa claimed to see the Blessed Virgin Mary and Jesus. The visions of the first three girls — 17-year-old Alphonsine, 20-year-old Nathalie, and 21-year-old Marie-Claire — have received the local Bishop's solemn approval, but those of the other four alleged visionaries have not.

November 28, 1981, was an ordinary day in many respects for Alphonsine Mumureke; it was lunch time, and she was in her boarding school's dining room. Suddenly, the Blessed Virgin Mary appeared to her. Alphonsine heard a voice say, "My daughter." Alphonsine dropped to her knees and ventured to ask the Lady who she was. The mysterious being gave her name: "*Nyina wa Jambo*" or "Mother of the Word," which is synonymous with "*Umubyeyl W'iamna*" or "Mother of God," as she herself explained.

Alphonsine told her, "I love God and His Mother who has given us Their Son who has saved us." Mary proceeded to tell her daughter, "It is true. I have come to calm you because I have heard your prayers. I would like your friends to have faith, because they do not believe strongly enough."

Could this really be the Mother of God? We can only imagine what Alphonsine was thinking when she heard such unexpected and hopeful words spoken by the mystical visitor. She was a prayerful girl and well aware of the Blessed Mother. She attended a school run by nuns, after all.

Alphonsine tried to describe Our Lady's appearance, saying, "She had a seamless white dress and also a white veil on her head. Her hands were clasped together on her breast, and her fingers pointed to the sky … I could not determine the color of her skin, but she was of incomparable beauty."

Mother Mary Calls Us to Pray the Rosary

Over the years, throughout her apparitions, the Blessed Mother emphasized the call to pray the Rosary. She also asked for penance and fasting to prepare the world for her Son's return. We see this in the Marian apparitions.

The Blessed Virgin Mary also told St. Faustina to prepare the world for her Son's Second Coming. What a huge instruction! However, we should take note of it. Jesus also made this known to His Secretary of Divine Mercy. Specifically, He told the young nun, **"You will prepare the world for My final coming,"**[63] and He told her many other times as well.

Mother Mary, who always sustained St. Faustina in her mission, delivered sobering words to her, after some very comforting ones. Mary first said, *"Oh, how pleasing to God is the soul that follows faithfully the inspirations of His grace!"* This is indeed what St. Faustina had always aimed to do. Mary then informed her daughter, *"I gave the Savior to the world; as for you, you have to speak to the world about His great mercy and prepare the world for the Second Coming of Him who will come, not as a merciful Savior, but as a just Judge. Oh, how terrible is that day!"*[64]

Mary calls us to repentance, to turn away from sin, to turn to God, to pray — especially the Rosary — and to do penance and make sacrifices for sinners. In addition, she instructs us to be prepared for the Last Judgment, as well as to do our part to prepare others for it. In other words, we are to get our spiritual lives — our very souls — in order. Now! We should never wait until the last minute. All we have is right now. Tomorrow may never come. In addition, we are to help others too — by praying and offering penances for them. Remember too, Mary will help us! Just as she aided and sustained St. Faustina in her vocation and monumental mission of propagating Divine Mercy to the world.

On March 27, 1982, the Blessed Mother told these sobering facts to Marie-Claire: "The world is in rebellion against GOD. Many sins are being committed. There is no love and no peace. If you do not repent and convert your hearts, you will all fall into an abyss."[65]

After Mary began to appear in Kibeho in southern Rwanda, people started changing for the better. They gathered together for special times of prayer. There were lots of conversions, healings, and mystical phenomena during the public apparitions. People began to make pilgrimages there. They wanted to be part of what they had heard was happening. In addition, people witnessed a miracle with the sun in which it appeared to spin, pulsate, or seemed to split in two. This is reminiscent of the great Miracle of the Sun in Fátima, Portugal, which occurred on October 13, 1917.

All three girl visionaries received a most frightening and gruesome vision which would become a pivotal apparition, leading to the official acceptance and approval of Kibeho. Alphonsine, Nathalie, and Marie-Claire reported seeing clearly people killing one another, a river of blood, bodies left abandoned with no one to bury them, a tree on fire, an open chasm, a monster, and also severed heads. Their vision is now considered a prophecy of the ethnic genocide that took place in the country in the 1990s.

At that time, Rwanda consisted mainly of two tribes: the Hutus and the Tutsis who were at conflict for many years. Close to 20,000 deaths occurred in the 1990 uprising between the two tribes. Sadly, visionary Marie-Claire was one of its victims.

The Apparitions Were Investigated

To examine the visions and phenomenon, two study commissions were put into place by the local Bishop, beginning in April 1982. One consisted of doctors and the other of theologians. The Bishop decided to approve public devotion linked to the apparitions of Kibeho. Recognizing the legitimacy of this devotion, on August 15, 1988, he deliberately put forward two questions whose answers were of capital importance for the future:

> Did the Virgin Mary and Jesus appear in Kibeho as some alleged visionaries affirm?
>
> If so, what visionary, man or woman, can be believed, in view of the large number of people who in those days began to talk about visions and messages from Heaven?[66]

The commissions researched thoroughly. The declaration stated, "Alphonsine, Nathalie, and Marie-Claire corresponded satisfactorily to all the criteria established by the Church in the matter of private apparitions and revelations."

Yes, it was indeed the Mother of God who appeared to Alphonsine. She would receive visions from her for the next eight years, the last apparition on November 28, 1989. Her two friends, Nathalie and Marie-Claire, also received visions.

"Yes, the Virgin Mary appeared in Kibeho on 28 November 1981," Bishop Augustine Misago of Gikongoro, Rwanda, proclaimed, and "in the following months that followed," when he announced his official approval of the apparitions. "There are more reasons to believe in the apparitions than to deny them."[67]

In 1992, construction began for a Marian sanctuary called the "Shrine of Our Lady of Sorrows."

Of course, each Christian is free to believe or not. As stated in the 2001 declaration, "A recognized apparition, that strengthens the life of faith and prayer, is certainly a powerful help for Shepherds of souls, but the message linked to this apparition is not a new revelation; it is rather a way of recalling the ordinary teaching of the Church, which has been forgotten."

And that is good news. As with every alleged apparition, the message should never profess to reveal any new doctrine to be believed by all the faithful — that is, anything not already a teaching of the Church. However, Our Lady does reveal some new things in her apparitions, such as prophesies about the future.

The pastoral directives for the Shrine of Our Lady of Sorrows and public devotion state "that Kibeho become a place of pilgrimage and of encounter for all who seek Christ and who come there to pray, a fundamental centre of conversion, of reparation for the sins of the world and of reconciliation, a point of meeting for 'all who were dispersed' as for those who aspire to the values of compassion and fraternity without borders, a fundamental centre that recalls the Gospel of the Cross."[68]

Turn to the Blessed Virgin

In 1990, Pope St. John Paul II visited Rwanda and exhorted the faithful to turn to the Blessed Virgin as a simple and sure guide for the spiritual path — our pilgrimage to Heaven. He beseeched the faithful to pray for a greater commitment to unite against local divisions, both political and ethnic.

In 2006, to mark the 25th anniversary of the Blessed Virgin Mary's first apparition in Kibeho, the Catholic bishops of Rwanda and Burundi led the celebrations, which were attended by thousands of priests, men and women religious, and lay people from Rwanda, Burundi, the Democratic Republic of Congo, Tanzania, Uganda, and Europe. Apostolic Nuncio Archbishop Anselmo Guido Pecorari read a letter from Pope Benedict XVI during the Mass, announcing that a plenary indulgence had been granted by the Apostolic Penitentiary to pilgrims who would visit Kibeho during the Jubilee Year.

On November 29, 2006, Bishop Misago said, "Our Lady of Kibeho is a beacon of hope, a light for all Africa and the world. This was demonstrated by the fact that 10,000 people braved torrential rain to take part in the ceremony to open the Kibeho jubilee year." He continued, "I was deeply moved at the devotion of the people taking part in the procession and the Mass which followed."[69]

On April 3, 2014, Pope Francis met with Rwandan bishops and urged them to be agents of reconciliation, commending them to the Marian apparition at Kibeho. He said:

> I entrust you all to the maternal protection of the Virgin Mary. … I sincerely hope that you can make the Shrine of Kibeho radiate even more the love of Mary for her all children, especially the poorest and most wounded, and that there may be for the Church in Rwanda, and beyond, a call to turn with confidence to "Notre Dame

> des Douleurs" [Our Lady of Sorrows], that she may accompany each one in his or her path and obtain for us the gift of reconciliation and peace.[70]

Our Lady of Sorrows Devotion

The devotion to Our Lady of Sorrows, which dates back to the Middle Ages, has acquired a new popularity ever since Our Lady appeared at Kibeho and asked us to pray the Seven Sorrows Rosary (or Chaplet). Each decade consists of seven beads for seven Hail Mary's. Each of the seven decades corresponds with one of Our Lady's Seven Sorrows. These sorrows are:

1. The prophecy of Simeon
2. The flight into Egypt
3. The Child Jesus Lost in the Temple
4. Mary meets Jesus carrying the Cross to Calvary
5. Mary stands at the foot of the Cross
6. Mary receives the Body of Jesus in her arms
7. The Body of Jesus is placed in the tomb.

According to Immaculée Ilibagiza, a well-known survivor of the genocide:

> During Mary's apparitions to Marie-Claire Mukangango, she assigned the young visionary a mission to reintroduce this special Rosary to the world. ... Before her untimely death, Marie-Claire did just that, traveling widely to teach it to thousands of people, who then taught it to thousands of others. (Marie-Claire was killed in the genocide of over a million people in Rwanda, a tragedy that was foretold through visions of rivers of blood that the young people in Kibeho received several years before the killings.)[71]

Father Leszek Czelusniak, MIC, director of the Marian Evangelization Center of Kibeho, said the Seven Sorrows devotion "reminds us that Mary plays a key role in our Redemption and that she suffered along with her Son Jesus to save us." He gave a summary of Our Lady's messages in which she mentions the devotion to her Seven Sorrows:

> The Holy Virgin insisted on the need for prayer. She said that the world is bad. It is necessary to pray, to pray, to pray a lot for this world that is bad, to pray for sinners, to pray for their conversion. She insisted a lot on the need for conversion: Convert to God! Convert to God! Convert to God! While saying that people don't respect God's commands, that people have a hard heart, she also asked us to meditate on the mysteries of the Rosary and to recite it every day.
>
> She also taught us the Rosary of the Seven Sorrows. She asked us to pray it every Tuesday and Friday. She asked us to obey the Church, to love God in truth, and to love our neighbor in humility and simplicity. She spoke of the need for mortification, a spirit of penitence and sacrifice. She also spoke of the need for suffering, to bear our sufferings every day. She said that no one enters heaven without suffering. She also told us that acts of charity for the poor make us beautiful flowers that God likes.[72]

Our Lady clearly calls to us to pray more and to sacrifice for the salvation of souls. Not many people these days like to hear much about sacrificing in a world that focuses on pleasures at just about any cost. However, we need to heed Our Lady's messages, which are not gloom and doom. They are hopeful instructions to help us gain Heaven, assist others get there too, and also avoid disaster or even the loss of our souls! Shouldn't we be running towards Mary's help and not away from it?

On a personal note, I love to pray the Seven Sorrows of Mary and feel very close to the Mother of God each time I pray it. Many a time, praying to her while meditating upon her Seven Sorrows has brought unexpected tears, as I feel in union with Mother Mary in her sufferings. I highly encourage you to try this beautiful devotion. It will change you.

The feast of Our Lady of Kibeho is November 28.

ACT

Take time to meditate upon Mary's messages and appearances at Kibeho. Consider praying the Seven Sorrows Rosary, acknowledging Mary's sorrows. Ask for her help and for graces for yourself and your loved ones.

Also, very importantly, pray for those who have harmed you in any way. Forgiveness is essential in our lives. If we don't forgive, we are lost. We become bound in chains of unforgiveness. Pray for the graces to truly forgive those who need to be forgiven and to fully accept forgiveness from others. It can be very difficult, but it is so very freeing. I am living proof!

Give all of your grudges to God. When they come to mind (even after you have forgiven), give them to God through prayer and then move on. Don't dwell on them. The evil one attempts to get us to focus on past hurts so that we will be tempted in some way to turn from God.

In addition, we must remember that we are not above our Lord who has told St. Faustina that His Divine Mercy is especially for the most hardened sinner: **"The greater the sinner, the greater the right he has to My mercy."**[73]

We should always keep in mind that God supplies every grace we need. Forgiveness is the only way to authentic peace of heart. Ask your Mother Mary to help you accept God's abundant and available grace to forgive and also accept someone's apology.

PRAY

Dear Holy Family, Jesus, Mary, and Joseph,
please bless me and pray for me.
Dear Holy Mary, Our Lady of Kibeho, Mother of the Redeemer,
Mother of Mercy and of hope, thank you for being my Mother.
Gate of Heaven, strengthen my virtues of faith, hope, and love.
Seat of Wisdom, please grant to me your graces.
Mirror of Perfection, mold my heart and teach me to believe,
to hope, and to love right along with you.
Mary, my Mother, I need your help.
Please perfect my simple prayers.
Please guide my steps today and always closer to your Son Jesus.
Star of Hope, Star of the Sea, please shine upon me
and guide me ever closer to your Son's Kingdom!
Amen.

Recite the Our Father, Hail Mary, Glory Be,
Hail Holy Queen, Memorare *(pages 201-202).*

Pray the Prayer to Our Lady of Kibeho
(page 230).

SAVOR

A prayer, a thought, a resolution:

____

____

____

____

____

____

____

“May your Immaculate Heart reveal for all the light of hope!” — Pope St. John Paul II

9

The Hope of the Human Race:
"Mary, Mother of Mercy"

"Mary is also the one who obtained mercy in a particular and exceptional way, as no other person has."[74]

— Saint John Paul II

Our Mother Mary has always been united with her Son Jesus, Who is the Divine Mercy. Mary's Immaculate Heart opened wide to mercy throughout her life. She chose to be obedient to Heaven's designs through the workings of the Holy Spirit. In doing so, Mary's loving, merciful heart embraces the whole human race and offers HOPE. Let's now delve into Mary's sacrificial life of profound holy mercy as God's masterpiece of mercy to the world.

REFLECT

When we pray the "Hail Holy Queen," we refer to Mary as "Mother of Mercy." We love Mary, and we place ourselves under her beautiful and protective mantle of mercy.

When we read the Gospels, we can clearly see Mary's merciful life. According to St. John Paul II, Mary "obtained mercy in a particular and exceptional way as no other person has. At the same time, still in an exceptional way, she made possible with the sacrifice of her heart her own sharing in revealing God's mercy."[75]

Moving through the Gospels, we observe Mary's loving, wholehearted consent to be the Mother of God at the Annunciation. Soon after, we see her setting out quickly to take an arduous trip to help her elderly cousin Elizabeth. We must not forget that when Mary presented her beautiful newborn Son Jesus in the Temple, she had to interiorly cooperate with the reality of what was to come. A sword of sorrow pieced her heart — not exactly what one would expect at a celebratory time like that. Yet, Mary's merciful life was not her own. She lived to cooperate with Our Lord's holy will.

We notice Mary working mercifully in bringing to the attention of her Son a young married couple's dilemma in having run out of wine at their wedding feast. Mary's merciful heart is clearly evident through her prayerful presence at the foot of her Son's Cross, in which she united her sufferings to that of her Son and wholeheartedly accepted her new role, lovingly bestowed upon her by the Son of God, to become the Mother of the Church and of us all.

Her tenderhearted mercy does not stop there. Mary's merciful actions and prayers played an active role in the beginning of the early Church. After Jesus ascended into Heaven, Mary kept company with the disciples of Jesus who were hunkered down in the Upper Room in Jerusalem, waiting for the coming of the Holy Spirit. We can surmise that the holy and merciful Mary helped to allay their fears and that her presence among them was an amazing comfort to the faint-hearted disciples.

Our Mother of Mercy Aids Our Salvation

After her Assumption into Heaven at the end of her earthly life, exhausted Mary did not pause to flop down on a comfy cloud or take a nap after all of her hard work! Nor did she give up being merciful. No. Merciful and loving Mary continues to work hard for us in her heavenly Reward.

Our Mother of Mercy would like all her children to be with her in Heaven one day. We learn in *Lumen Gentium*, Vatican II's Dogmatic Constitution on the Church:

> Taken up to Heaven, she did not lay aside this salvific duty but by her constant intercession continued to bring us the gifts of eternal salvation. By her maternal charity, she cares for the brethren of her Son, who still journey on earth surrounded by danger and troubles, until they are led into the happiness of their true home.[76]

Mother Mary draws us ever closer to Jesus' merciful love. She always leads the way to her Son. She is the Mother of Mercy because her Son, Jesus Christ, was sent by the Father as the revelation of God's mercy (cf. Jn 3:16–18), said St. John Paul II in his encyclical *Veritatis Splendor*:

> Christ came not to condemn but to forgive, to show mercy (cf. Mt 9:13). ... And the greatest mercy of all is found in His being in our midst and calling us to meet Him and to confess, with Peter, that He is "the Son of the living God" (Mt 16:16). No human sin can erase the mercy of God, or prevent Him from unleashing all His triumphant power, if we only call upon Him.[77]

In *Dives in Misericordia,* the future saint added, "No one has received into his heart, as much as Mary did, that mystery, that truly divine dimension of the redemption effected on Calvary by means of the death of the Son, together with the sacrifice of her maternal heart, together with her definitive 'fiat.'"[78] And St. Stanislaus Papczyński said about our Blessed Mother:

> She was the unshakable rock placed before all the beatings of the violent storm; pierced by sharp pains, and she did not give up; drowned by the waves of unspeakable sadness, she did not plunge herself in it; crushed by the weight of bitterness, she did not submit to it. For even though [her] heart suffered, it was comforted by the courage drawn from the awaited joy of the foretold Resurrection of the Son.[79]

I think it would take a lifetime of meditation to fully comprehend all that Mary has received into her heart and all her sacrificial love. Still, we can take time to pray and ponder, as well as learn from the amazing Pilgrims of Hope who have gone before us.

Let's step back in time to a world-changing event. So much happened at the foot of the Cross of Jesus as He gave His very life for our salvation. We won't know or understand all of it until we pass through to Eternal Life. Thank God for wonderful saints who help us to understand more and who steadily guide us on our pilgrimage to Heaven.

Saint John Paul II profoundly pointed out, "Mary is also Mother of Mercy because it is to her that Jesus entrusts his Church and all humanity."[80] The Great Mercy Pope tells us exactly where this happened and brilliantly explains that Mary actually took part in asking the Father to forgive "those who do not know what they do." What a pure and merciful Heart!

In addition, through St. John Paul II's words, we come to understand that our Mother in Heaven, through God's grace, opened wide her humble and loving Heart to embrace the entire human race.

Wow! She is profoundly merciful as our loving Mother.

Our Merciful Mother Embraces Her Children

"At the foot of the Cross, when she accepts John as her son, when she asks, together with Christ, forgiveness from the Father for those who do not know what they do (cf. *Lk* 23:34), Mary experiences, in perfect docility to the Spirit, the richness and the universality of God's love, which opens her heart and enables it to embrace the entire human race," said St. John Paul II. "Thus Mary becomes Mother of each and every one of us, the Mother who obtains for us divine mercy."[81]

Did you get that? Mary, in union with her Son asked forgiveness from the Father. Incredible. Saint John Paul II's words show us this beautiful holy union of Son and Mother.

Speaking of Divine Mercy, the Blessed Mother informed St. Faustina, the Apostle of Divine Mercy, "*I am not only the Queen of Heaven, but also the Mother of Mercy and your Mother.*"[82] Saint Faustina heard these holy words during a novena she made for her confessor to the Mother of God. The humble mystic noted in her *Diary*, "This novena consisted in the prayer 'Hail, Holy Queen' recited nine times. Toward the end of the novena I saw the Mother of God with the Infant Jesus in her arms. … I could not stop wondering at His beauty."[83]

That is precisely when Mary revealed her title of "Mother of Mercy" to her daughter Faustina. Saint Faustina would carry this truth in her heart. She turned to the Mother of Mercy constantly, seeking her guidance, especially in the mission of spreading devotion to Divine Mercy, which was entrusted to her. Mary, the Mother of Mercy, continually strengthened and accompanied St. Faustina in her work and mission of propagating the message of Divine Mercy.

In answering the question "Why do we call Mary 'Mother of Mercy'?" Dr. Robert Stackpole aptly explains:

> In short, the first reason we can rightfully call Mary our "Mother of Mercy" is that by God's special, prevenient grace, He created her soul to be the masterpiece of His Mercy in the world, and this special gift of grace within her was the foundation of His whole work of mercy in the world through Christ. Everything about Mary was fashioned by Divine Mercy and for the work of Divine Mercy. No other creature, therefore, so completely manifests God's mercy as does Mary Immaculate.[84]

ACT

God calls us to repent from sin, turn to His Divine Mercy, and prayerfully become merciful people. Mary, the Mother of Mercy, can and will help us with this. We need to turn to her often. We see her life of mercy as we read Scripture and study our Faith.

Read a passage from St. Faustina's *Diary* each day. I like to keep my copy handy to pick up often and read and prayerfully ponder. It's such a treasure trove of spiritual guidance. I, for one, am so thankful that St. Faustina was obedient in writing the *Diary*. We are blessed beyond measure to contemplate Jesus' very words, recorded by the humble mystic St. Faustina. In addition, we have the wondrous spiritual lessons St. Faustina received from Mary, the Mother of God, right at our fingertips when we keep the *Diary* close by. Right from the start, Mary strengthened St. Faustina in her mission of Divine Mercy.

We can also pray to imitate Mary's beautiful virtues so that we can become more merciful to others — those who are good to us and those who have harmed us in some way. Mary, Mother of Mercy, explained to her daughter Faustina that she desired that she "*practice the three virtues that are dearest to me — and most pleasing to God. The first is humility, humility, and once again humility; the second virtue, purity; the third virtue, love of God.*" She continued, "*As my daughter, you must especially radiate with these virtues.*"[85]

Can we guess why it was so important to Mary that her daughter practice these virtues? Mary herself was all about humility, purity, and the love of God as I have been mentioning throughout this book. And, of course, we can't help but notice that Mary makes a prodigious point to emphasize the virtue of humility to her daughter. To be a merciful soul first requires the deepest humility.

Take time to ponder this and jot down five ways that you can imitate Our Lady in her mercy. Put them into practice soon.

PRAY

Dear Holy Family, Jesus, Mary, and Joseph,
please bless me and pray for me.
Saint Faustina, please pray for me.
Dear Holy Mary, Mother of the Redeemer, Mother of Mercy
and of hope, thank you for being my Mother.
Gate of Heaven, strengthen my virtues of faith, hope, and love.
Seat of Wisdom, please grant me your graces.
Mirror of Perfection, mold my heart and teach me to believe,
to hope, and to love right along with you.
Mary, my Mother, I need your help.
Please perfect my simple prayers.
Please guide my steps today and always closer to your Son Jesus.
Star of Hope, Star of the Sea, please shine upon me
and guide me ever closer to your Son's Kingdom!
Amen.

Recite the Our Father, Hail Mary, Glory Be,
Hail Holy Queen, Memorare *(pages 201-202).*

Pray the "Prayer to Our Mother of Mercy"
(page 234).

Or pray St. Faustina's Consecration to the Blessed Mother
(page 213).

SAVOR

A prayer, a thought, a resolution:

Saint Thérèse of Lisieux, the Little Flower.

10

Hope and Healing:
The "Virgin of the Smile"

"Everything is a grace!"

— Saint Thérèse of Lisieux

In this chapter, we get to know a bit about a beloved 19th-century saint, dear St. Thérèse of Lisieux, the Little Flower, as well as her family, and her profound discovery of her "elevator" in the spiritual life. But, more than that, we ourselves can discover the miraculous smile of our dear Mother Mary, who always brings great comfort, hope, and healing to us all.

What is it about a smile that warms our hearts, makes hope jump into our hearts, changes our glum attitudes, heals our deepest wounds, and maybe even helps us get to Heaven? But let's be clear. Smiles are amazing and transforming.

Yet, for right now, we are not talking about any ol' smile. Let's imagine Our Lady's smile, if that's possible! We will learn just how Mary's smile was received by a young French girl.

To tell this reflection properly, let's go back to 1873 in Alençon, France, to learn about the recipient of Mary's smile. That would be St. Thérèse! She is a most beloved saint, who in her simple, loving way made a profound impact on the life of the Church. She would say, "What matters in life … is not great deeds, but great love."[86]

Thérèse of Lisieux, otherwise known as the Little Flower or the Child of Jesus, is perhaps best known for her "little way of love." Yet, we must not think her so-called simple message is soft, easy, or romantic. It's about the arduous staircase of holiness. Great suffering and intense purification of faith are woven throughout the little way of love.

Saint Thérèse aspired to great holiness. She was not a theologian nor a great scholar. In fact, she felt extremely imperfect and incompetent. All the while, she desired a way in which she could ascend to Jesus' loving arms — a sort of pathway to Heaven — by what she called, a "little way." She wanted some sort of an "elevator" to Heaven! She expressed this desire:

> Instead of becoming discouraged, I said to myself: God cannot inspire unrealizable desires. I can, then, in spite of my littleness, aspire to holiness. It is impossible for me to grow up, and so I must bear with myself such as I am with all my imperfections. But I want to seek out a means of going to heaven by a little way, a way that is very straight, very short, and totally new.[87]

She pondered deeply and researched the Scriptures to fully understand this:

> I searched, then, in the Scriptures for some sign of this elevator, the object of my desires, and I read these words coming from the mouth of Eternal Wisdom: "Whoever is a little one, let him come to me" (Prov 9:4). And so I succeeded. I felt I had found what I was looking for. But wanting to know, O my God, what you would do to the very little one who answered your call, I continued my search, and this is what I discovered: "As one whom a mother caresses, so will I comfort you; you shall be carried at the breasts, and upon the knees they shall caress you" (Is 66:12–13). Ah! Never did words more tender and more melodious come to give joy to my soul. The elevator which must raise me to heaven is your arms, O Jesus! And for this I had no need to grow up, but rather I had to remain little and become this more and more.[88]

Saint Thérèse's Great Discovery

The Little Flower discovered that Jesus makes up for her weaknesses. She learned that her littleness could actually become the means to become holy! She became profoundly aware of the merciful love overflowing from Jesus' Sacred Heart. She learned that our dear Lord Jesus Christ comes to save sinners — those in need of redemption. And she wholeheartedly trusted Him with her life.

Now, let's step back a bit to learn about the beginning of this beloved saint's life. Thérèse, the youngest of nine children, was born in Alençon on January 2, 1873, and baptized the following day as Marie-Francoise-Thérèse Martin. She grew up in a tight-knit Catholic family, surrounded by boundless love. Her family endured a good deal of sorrow, too. Four of Thérèse's siblings died of enteritis at a young age. Three were just infants. One was just 5-and-a-half years old. The pain of their losses was untold.

By outside appearances, the family might have seemed quite ordinary for that place and time. However, after their sad losses, the remaining five girls — every one of them — aspired to religious life. And every one of them crossed the threshold of convent doors. They made it! Their parents, Louis and Zelie Martin (now both saints), embraced the Catholic Faith and raised their children well, with much emphasis on family prayer, practicing virtues, visiting the sick, and attending daily Mass. Four daughters became contemplative Carmelites at the Lisieux Carmel, and the other became a Visitation Sister.

But we are getting a bit ahead of ourselves!

Back to Thérèse coming into the world. Well, her life started off with a huge and frightening challenge. She had to be separated from her family — even from her mother — because the same illness that had taken the lives of her siblings was threatening to take hers, too. To save her life, doctor's orders sent her away to live in the forests of Bocage at Semalle, with Rose Taille as her wet nurse. When the danger passed, she returned home at the age of 15 months.

Saint Thérèse and Her Loving Family

Thérèse grew, surrounded by the love of her family. At the tender age of 4, she watched in pain as uncontrollable tears rolled down her father's face as he knelt beside the bed. Thérèse's beloved mother was receiving the last Sacraments. Her mother's death deeply changed her. "Every detail of my mother's illness is still with me," she later wrote, "especially her last weeks on earth."[89] Thérèse was heartbroken but managed to get by with the love of her family.

Thérèse was very mature for her age and longed to receive Jesus in Holy Communion from the time she was very young. She prepared her heart at an early age to receive our Lord Jesus Christ, truly present in the Eucharist.

On May 8, 1884, after receiving her First Holy Communion, Thérèse consecrated herself to the Blessed Virgin Mary. She recalled:

> I pronounced the Act of Consecration to the Blessed Virgin in the name of my companions. Doubtless I was chosen for this because I was left without my mother on earth … In consecrating myself to the Virgin Mary, I asked her to watch over me, placing into the act all the devotion of my soul, and it seemed to me, I saw her once again looking down and smiling on her "*petite fleur*."[90]

We will soon reflect upon what Thérèse meant about the Virgin Mary smiling on her "little flower". Notice, she said, "once again." We also notice yet another saint-in-the-making who chose and depended upon the Blessed Mother to be her Mother after the loss of an earthly mother.

In time, Thérèse would fervently cling to the Blessed Virgin Mary as her true Mother. Thérèse recognized the Blessed Virgin as "more Mother than Queen." In a poem she wrote to Mary, she said, "Waiting for Heaven, O my dear Mother, / I want to live with you, follow you each day. / Mother, contemplating you, I immerse myself delighted, / discovering in your heart abysses of love."[91]

She would also rely on her sisters and their motherly influences. She felt a strong calling to become a nun. Soon enough, Thérèse would grow older and would one day walk through the convent doors of Carmel like her older sisters. This would be a dream come true — one she had desired since she was 3 years old — and one upon which she embarked at only 15 years of age! Before that could happen, however, there would be many obstacles to overcome first, including a very devastating one.

The Strange Uninvited Visitor

In order to understand why sweet Thérèse received a miraculous smile from the Blessed Mother, we must talk about the strange uninvited visitor who had come to darken Thérèse's doorway. It was actually a peculiar illness straight out of hell, it seemed, that suddenly showed up to afflict innocent Thérèse. It made her body tremble uncontrollably.

Her frightened family called the doctor to come promptly. Everyone was puzzled as to why she would be ill in this way and at such a young age. They were very much troubled too. What would happen to their beloved Thérèse? This particular day was worse than ever.

Later on, St. Thérèse tried to describe the devastating illness when she wrote her autobiography, *Story of A Soul*, which, by the way, she wrote under the orders of the Superiors. I will tell you more about her writings later on.

For now, let's allow Thérèse to explain what she went through. She said she was "absolutely terrified by everything: my bed seemed to be surrounded by frightful precipices; some nails in the wall of the room took on the appearance of black charred fingers, making me cry out in fear." One time her father had to leave the room sobbing because he didn't want to hurt his daughter further because of his tears. Thérèse, without warning, had become extremely frightened and agitated upon seeing the hat in her Papa's hand, which "was suddenly transformed into some indescribably dreadful shape."[92] Poor Thérèse almost always appeared to be delirious, and she was affected in many strange ways. And, once, for a long period, she didn't have the power to even open her eyes.

Her Fear was a Holy Martyrdom

As if this was not enough suffering, Thérèse became desperately afraid that she might somehow be making it all up. Later on, she explained that this fear "was a real martyrdom"[93] for her soul. Her doctor assured her that she wasn't making anything up at all. Her confessor confirmed that truth as well, telling her it was impossible for her to bring on such an illness.

Yet her heart was sorely troubled. She often turned her gaze towards the statue of the Blessed Virgin, praying for her help. Thérèse was also anxious about her dear family, who were out of their minds in their concern for her. She thought she brought an abundance of trouble to them.

Papa was beyond distressed. He had never seen his "little Queen" suffer in this way. He wanted the best remedy ever for his sweet daughter. Holy Mass is indeed the most powerful prayer, and he requested that Masses be said for her at the Shrine of Our Lady of Victories in Paris to cure his poor little girl. Thérèse witnessed her father requesting the Masses and was deeply touched knowing of her "dear King's faith and love."[94] Indeed, Papa Louis also hoped against all hope for his sweet daughter's recovery when there was absolutely no sign of hope in sight.

During Thérèse's devastating suffering, some people (particularly her uncle) were of the mindset that she shouldn't be reminded of her earnest desire to enter religious life in Carmel. But, St. Thérèse would later say, "The thought of one day becoming a Carmelite made me live."[95] She also said, "I believe the devil had received an *external* power over me but was not allowed to approach my soul nor my mind except to inspire me with great *fears* of certain things."[96]

Can we even imagine this intense turmoil and baffling struggle?

Thérèse knew without a doubt that it would take a major miracle to cure her. There was no other way out of that hellish prison. As time went on, instead of getting better, her illness escalated. Every symptom and pain heightened in intensity. One Sunday, during the novena of prayer and Masses being said for little Thérèse, her pain and other symptoms were beyond control. She suddenly called out, begging for her family to come quickly to her sick bed.

She Needed a Miracle

"Mama, Mama!" Thérèse cried out. And then she called much louder, "Mama!"[97] Thérèse's mother had already passed away, and Thérèse was calling for her sister Marie.

Her three sisters, Marie, Léonie, and Céline, all hurried to her bedside, where they knelt and prayed fervently to the Holy

Virgin, "praying with the fervor of a mother begging for the life of her child,"[98] according to Thérèse. She could hardly stand it. The Little Flower prayed with all her heart that the Mother of our Lord would take pity on her.

Saint Thérèse recalled those miraculous moments — and especially one instance in particular. "All of a sudden the Blessed Virgin appeared *beautiful* to me, so *beautiful* that never had I seen anything so attractive; her face was suffused with an ineffable benevolence and tenderness," she sweetly recalled, "but what penetrated to the very depths of my soul was the '*ravishing smile of the Blessed Virgin.*'"[99]

The miracle occurred! "At that instant," Thérèse recalled, "all my pain disappeared, and two large tears glistened on my eyelashes, and flowed down my cheeks silently, but they were tears of unmixed joy."[100]

Mary's Miraculous Holy Smile

And now, she tells us of the amazing and miraculous holy smile! Thérèse said, "Ah! I thought, the Blessed Virgin smiled at me, how happy I am, but never will I tell anyone for my *happiness would then disappear.*"[101]

She was right. And we will get to that. First, let's finish hearing about that great miracle and what transpired immediately afterwards. Thérèse could then see out of the corner of her eye that her sister Marie was lovingly looking at her, seemingly moved by what had just occurred. Thérèse could tell that Marie knew of the great healing miracle which the Virgin Mary had just performed for her — some sort of hidden grace. Thérèse attributed the "grace of the Queen of Heaven's smile" to the prayers of Marie. Thérèse kept her gaze fixed on the Blessed Virgin's statue, and Marie couldn't contain her joyful excitement.

"Thérèse is cured!"[102] Marie cried out.

However, the bliss of the miracle would quickly change. This happened after Thérèse innocently shared what had happened. Even though she did so discreetly and prudently, she recalled, "Alas! Just as I had felt, my happiness was going to disappear and change into bitterness."[103] Marie had asked Thérèse to share about the special grace from Mary. Then, she also asked permission to share it at Carmel. Thérèse agreed.

The Interrogation

At the convent, Thérèse was questioned about the special grace. She recalled, "All these questions troubled me and caused me much pain." We need to remember that Thérèse had initially desired to keep it all to herself. Thérèse tried to explain the experience, but the sisters had other ideas about what had occurred. Thérèse recalled, "Seeing that the Carmelites had imagined something else entirely (my spiritual trials beginning already with regard to my sickness), I thought I *had lied*."[104]

Poor innocent Thérèse. The path to sanctity (to which we are all called!) is a difficult one. The young saint-in-the-making deeply suffered with the aftermath for the next four years. However, it was for the benefit of her soul. She was also learning more and more about the lay of the land in the spiritual life.

Seeing with the eyes of faith, she could say, "Without a doubt, if I had kept my secret, I would also have kept my happiness …" She ardently knew the invisible spiritual gem in play and explained, "… but the Blessed Virgin permitted this torment for my soul's good, as perhaps without it I would have had some thought of vanity, whereas *humiliation* becoming my lot, I was unable to look upon myself without a feeling of *profound horror*." She concluded, "Ah! what I suffered I shall not be able to say except in heaven!"[105]

I often say that, if like spoiled children we had everything we wanted or thought we needed, we might not make it to Heaven. We need to trust God that He knows exactly what we need and when. He knows what will harm us and what will help us.

The Miraculous Statue

It's interesting to note that Thérèse writes in her autobiography that her mother also received a miracle from Our Lady when praying before the "miraculous statue" of the Blessed Virgin. The 3-foot statue of the Immaculate Conception which had been gifted to Papa was given a prominent place of honor in the Martin home. Mama Zelie had consecrated all of her nine babies to the Blessed Virgin shortly after their births. Every day the family gathered around Mary's statue to pray their daily family prayers. In addition, together, both parents prayed that their children might be consecrated to the service of her Son Jesus.

The four children who passed shortly after their births died in their baptismal innocence. The other five, Pauline, Marie, Léonie, Céline, and Thérèse, were all consecrated to God. Both religious orders they entered were of the Blessed Virgin — Our Lady of Mount Carmel and the Visitation.

Having been raised with the tender love and devotion of Mary, Thérèse placed much importance on her Mother in Heaven. After being ordered to write the story of her life, the young faithful daughter of Mary begged her Mother's help. She recalled, "Before taking up my pen, I knelt down before the statue of Mary (the one that has given so many proofs of the maternal preferences of heaven's Queen for our family), and I begged her to guide my hand that it trace no line displeasing to her."[106]

Incidentally, I was blessed to see this miraculous statue when I made a pilgrimage to Lisieux. It is located in the Basilica Shrine near the reliquary which holds the body of St. Thérèse. Millions of pilgrims journey there every year to pray and reflect at this holy site.

Thérèse's Holy Joy and Transforming Smile

As we get to know St. Thérèse, we learn that even though she was very young, she is an amazing teacher for us on our pilgrimage to Heaven. She is certainly a beautiful Pilgrim of Hope. We can strive to emulate her virtues and pray for her intercession.

Thérèse was overflowing with the supernatural gift of holy joy. She loved to serve and to show love and care to others. So, it shouldn't have been too difficult a task for her to show acts of charity to the old and infirm Sr. St. Pierre. However, the elder irritable sister was almost impossible to please. And she clearly made that known to Sr. Thérèse, who moved her will to do good and to please Jesus and His Holy Mother by always being kind and loving to the crusty nun.

Please pardon me for sounding a bit harsh with my description of Sr. St. Pierre. Sweet Thérèse herself speaks about Sister's many criticisms of her, saying, "It cost me very much to offer myself for this little service because I knew it was not easy to please Sister

St. Pierre."[107] Thérèse also knew that her elder Sister was suffering much and had a hard time handling the changes of caretakers. Still, Thérèse treated her elder Sister "with as much gentleness as possible."[108] In her autobiography, Thérèse shares that she didn't want to miss the opportunity to serve as Jesus calls us: "Whatever you do to the least of my brothers, you do to me" (Mt 25:40). Even so, Sr. St. Pierre continued to be cranky and let Thérèse know she was displeased with her care.

One day, something changed. It was when Thérèse was leaving the room and noticed Sr. St. Pierre was struggling to cut her bread. Thérèse went back in and cut it for her. But before leaving, as Thérèse explained, "I gave her my most beautiful smile."[109] It was a moment filled with love and grace. Thérèse learned later on that through her loving smile and generous assistance, she had gained the "entire good graces"[110] of Sr. St. Pierre!

I'm glad that St. Thérèse chose to include this experience in her autobiography. We can all learn volumes from her example — it's like a treatise of her little way of love. The Little Flower explained the reason she decided to mention her "little act of charity," as she called it. Firstly, she believed that she "must sing of the Lord's mercies because of it." She also believed that God allowed her to retain its vivid memory. As she recalled, "He deigned to leave its memory with me as a perfume which helps me in the practice of charity."

Do you see what I mean about her "treatise?" We learn so much from the humble and very sweet saint!

Smiles are truly transforming. I have experienced this to be true in my own life, and I'll bet you have, too. Dare I mention a time when Our Lady seemed to smile at me — lest you think I am comparing myself to St. Thérèse, a Doctor of the Church? Actually, I think I'll save that for a later chapter! I will also mention later a bit more about transforming smiles.

Of course, we can never compare our smiles to the Mother of God's smile. Yet, I believe we receive countless opportunities, even in the course of our daily, ordinary lives, to smile at someone who might need our act of kindness at that particular moment — our imparting God's mercy. It could be someone we might not particularly care to smile at. Just imagine the beautiful grace hidden beneath a tender, loving smile given towards the one who is antagonizing you.

God works the miracles when we move our will to do good.

The Holy Face of Christ

Her full religious name was "Sister Thérèse of the Child Jesus and the Holy Face"!

Saint Thérèse would come to contemplate the Holy Face of Christ and find meaning in her father's suffering and her own. She meditated upon Jesus' bruised, humiliated Sacred Face with flowing tears. She saw that Jesus abandoned Himself to the Father and had lovingly forgiven sinners. She discovered that suffering was not a contradiction of God's profound love. Instead, she could unite her sufferings with Jesus' sufferings, and the sweet Little Flower teaches us to do the same.

As our reflection comes to a close, I will add, that interestingly, just as kindred spirit St. Catherine Labouré (as mentioned in an earlier chapter) came into this world at the ringing of the *Angelus* bells on May 2, 1806, St. Thérèse distinctly heard the ringing of the *Angelus* bells shortly before she would leave this world. As the bells pealed, the Little Flower looked at the statue of the "Virgin of the Smile" for quite some time, holding tightly to her crucifix. Not too long afterwards, the humble saint closed her eyes on this earthly life and passed into eternity on September 30, 1897.

Her Last Words and Mission

At just 24 years of age, St. Thérèse spoke her last words while gazing at her crucifix: "My God, I love You!" And then, Thérèse seemed to be in ecstasy, and her face took on a healthy glow while she looked to an area above the statue of the Blessed Virgin. Her fellow sisters witnessed a smile on her lips and her beautiful glowing face as she died (which is evident in the photo her sister Céline snapped just after Thérèse breathed her last).

Towards the end of her life, during her agonizing suffering, Thérèse had written to Fr. Belliere to say, "I am not dying; I am entering into life!"[111] The unknown little saint who spent her life hidden in the cloister would soon become famous after her death. After all, she had promised to work hard in Heaven to save souls.

You know, Thérèse always wanted to be a missionary — on every continent, no less! She also desired to die a martyr's death for her faith. Yet, where did God place her to do the work? Hidden behind the cloister gate! Her great missionary work was hidden within her intercessory prayers and sacrifices for the world, enclosed by the seclusion of Carmel. Her fame and popularity (not something she desired) would quickly come about after her death.

"My mission — to make God loved — will begin after my death," she said. "I will spend my heaven doing good on earth. I will let fall a shower of roses."[112] That is why countless pilgrims pray for a sign or gift of roses from beloved St. Thérèse.

Thérèse's Writings

And her writings? Well, what had simply started off one day by her sister's decision to ask Thérèse to write about her "little way of love" so they could all enjoy reading it ended up becoming the *Story of A Soul.* When Thérèse was putting her pen to paper to fastidiously recount her precious, yet simple, love story with Jesus, she had absolutely no idea whatsoever that her *little* story would one day be considered a spiritual masterpiece, one of the most beautiful autobiographies ever written, and a permanent source of inspiration, which would end up touching countless hearts for years to come, and would wind up as a world's bestseller (with more than 500 million copies published and translated into more than 50 languages).

Saint Thérèse's feast day is October 1. The title of Our Lady of Victories has come to be known as Our Lady of the Smile or the Virgin of the Smile due to Thérèse's holy and miraculous experience. She's also called Our Lady of the Rosary, and her feast is October 7.

ACT

We have discussed a precious and very humble saint-in-the-making who one day was declared a canonized Saint and Doctor of the Church.

We see that God chose to have little Thérèse work out her salvation and pray for the salvation of others within the confines of the cloister — not where the Little Flower had first envisioned she would do her missionary work.

We have learned about her strange and intense illness and the merciful loving smile of Mother Mary, as well as so much more in our reflection above.

Thérèse also gives the wonderful example of a simple, yet sincere, smile and how it transformed her elder nun who was often irritable.

Be more ready with your smile! It's a wonderful gesture of friendliness. Smiling can even trigger happiness in ourselves and others! Perhaps it can make someone feel more hopeful and less depressed.

Thérèse spoke of vanity and humiliations and the spiritual life. Ponder it all and ask St. Thérèse to aid you along your pilgrimage through life. Ask her to bring you to Jesus and Mary.

I highly recommend that you read St. Thérèse's spiritual memoir, *Story of a Soul.* The Little Flower poured her heart out upon the pages, reflecting on God's love and mercy in her life. It will touch your heart.

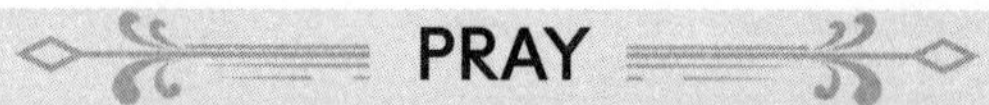

PRAY

Dear Holy Family, Jesus, Mary, and Joseph,
please bless me and pray for me.
Saint Thérèse, please pray for me.
Teach me to be a servant and trusting in my prayers.
Amen.

Dear Holy Mary, Virgin of the Smile, please smile upon me.
Mother of the Redeemer, Mother of Mercy and of hope,
thank you for being my Mother.
Gate of Heaven, strengthen my virtues of faith, hope, and love.
Seat of Wisdom, please grant to me your graces.
Mirror of Perfection, mold my heart and teach me
to believe, to hope, and to love right along with you.
Mary, my Mother, I need your help.
Please perfect my simple prayers.
Please guide my steps today and always closer
to your Son Jesus.
Star of Hope, Star of the Sea, please shine upon me
and guide me ever closer to your Son's Kingdom!
Amen.

Recite the Our Father, Hail Mary, Glory Be, Hail Holy Queen, Memorare *(pages 201-202).*

Pray the prayer to The Holy Face *(page 229).*

Or pray the prayer to Our Lady of the Smile or one of St. Thérèse's prayers *(pages 228-230).*

SAVOR

A prayer, a thought, a resolution:

11

The Hope from Poland:
Our Lady of Częstochowa

"In every stage of the march through history, the Church has benefited from the prayer and protection of the Virgin Mary."[113]

— Saint John Paul II

No matter her title, our Mother Mary always brings hope to our hearts. She assures us that her Son is the answer to all our perplexing problems and the absolute and certain door to our salvation. She forever leads us to Him. In this chapter, we will discuss Our Lady of Częstochowa, the Polish Madonna, her fascinating history, and some of the ways in which Mary touches our lives.

REFLECT

My grandmother, Alexandra Mary Uzwiak, St. Maria Faustina Kowalska, and St. John Paul II have something in common. They all loved Our Lady of Częstochowa.

Back in the day, my very prayerful Polish grandmother had a small image of Our Lady of Częstochowa displayed on the wall of her humble apartment. Alexandra was very devoted to her Polish Madonna. She prayed many a Rosary in her honor.

I always looked forward to visiting Grandma. She personified everything good and holy to me. Truth be told, I learned holiness from her — not just because she preached it to me with her loving, encouraging, and hopeful words; but mostly from observing her life of prayer, the sparkle of joy in her eyes, and her winning smile. My grandmother was a Pilgrim of Hope in my life — being with her filled my heart with hope.

If you visited my grandma, she would most likely offer you some of her homemade Polish cookies and, donned in her apron, would ask if she could cook something for you. Chances are good that she would set a cup of hot tea on the table before you and somehow masterfully slip Our Lady or her beloved Polish Pope into the conversation. As you glanced around her humble abode, in addition to vases of fresh flowers here and there and a multitude of family photos displayed everywhere, you would see a smattering of religious art all over her walls. And I mean *all over* her walls!

Among the eclectic array were pictures of Pope John Paul II. It turns out that my grandmother's birthday would become the same as the feast day of someone she loved so dearly: St. John Paul II. Of course, at the time, Grandma didn't know that her cherished Polish Pope would be canonized one day! Or did she?

After my grandmother passed on to her Eternal Reward, I became the keeper of the little, yet meaningful, Our Lady of Częstochowa icon. It's a bit worn, but nonetheless it is very special to me since it belonged to my beloved grandmother and is an image of someone to whom she was greatly devoted. The image always seemed to speak to me of a Mother's protection and love.

My Heart Felt Pummeled

So much so, that I vividly recalled the Polish Madonna when I was a young single mother of three, experiencing a very difficult situation in my life. At this time, I desperately desired, if not absolutely needed, to feel some semblance of peace in my heart. My heart felt completely pummeled. I had been abandoned by my husband and forced to make a life-changing decision that would affect not only me, but my family too. The whole idea of it deeply troubled me. My mother had already died, and I really needed a mother to swoop in.

I prayed to Our Lady of Częstochowa for help. And I decided to make a mini pilgrimage — traveling from Connecticut to a Shrine of Our Lady of Częstochowa in Doylestown, Pennsylvania to earnestly seek her help. I firmly believe that Our Lady delivered a huge dose of peace to my heart that day. It has stayed with me ever since. Mary is also known as the "Queen of Peace," after all. Her peace also brought much hope to my heart.

As I mentioned, St. John Paul II also loved Our Lady of Częstochowa. She is called the "Black Madonna" because of her dark face in the icon. I'll explain more about that soon. First, I wish to tell you something very special about St. John Paul II as a little boy.

Karol Wojtyła

The future Pontiff had a strong devotion to Our Lady of Częstochowa and claimed he would not have been a pope without her.

Karol Wojtyła grew up in a very religious family at a time when it was natural for Polish families to practice their Catholic Faith. We can say that his parents brought the Church inside their home in the truest expression of the "Domestic Church" — something we all should do! If you were to visit their small, modest apartment, you might hear the pealing of church bells from right across the street. Upon walking through the front door, one of the first things you would notice is the bowl of holy water. As you moved in a bit more, you would see the small altar in the parlor, which Karol's mother had lovingly created.

We can presume that the family's prayer life, along with the tangible holy items, had a powerful effect on the little boy who would grow up to become a priest, bishop, archbishop, cardinal, and then, amazingly, the pope! And such a beloved one at that. After which time, as we know, he was also canonized a saint in our Catholic Church.

A mother's loving and faithful example matters an awful lot.

Mercy was His Greatest Calling

Saint John Paul II would become known as the "Great Mercy Pope" because of his ties to the Divine Mercy message which was entrusted to a 20th-century Polish mystic, whom I have mentioned earlier: St. Maria Faustina Kowalska. Jesus first appeared to St. Faustina in the image of the Divine Mercy on February 22, 1931. Heaven had placed the mammoth mission of propagating the message of Divine Mercy upon her shoulders.

As a young seminarian in 1940, Karol learned of St. Faustina's revelations, and the message of Divine Mercy completely drew him in. As a priest, he often visited St. Faustina's former convent to pray and hold retreats. As the Archbishop of Krakow, he led the effort to introduce her name to the Congregation for the Causes of Saints and also strongly defended her when Rome questioned the truth of the revelations. As Pope, on November 30, 1980, he published his second encyclical, *Dives in Misericordia* ("Rich in

Mercy"). The following year, he traveled to the Shrine of Merciful Love in Collevalenza, Italy, while still recovering from gunshot wounds from an assassination attempt. There, he expressed the fact that he wholeheartedly believed that spreading the message of Divine Mercy was his greatest calling. Specifically, he said, "Right from the beginning of my ministry in St. Peter's See in Rome, I considered this message my special task. Providence has assigned it to me in the present situation of man, the Church, and the world. It could be said that precisely this situation assigned that message to me as my task before God."[114]

And so, on Divine Mercy Sunday, April 30, 2000, St. John Paul II would end up with the honor of canonizing St. Maria Faustina Kowalska as the first saint of the new millennium. He would also institute Divine Mercy Sunday (which Jesus had called for) for the entire Church as the first Sunday following Easter Sunday each year. He famously said, "Today is the happiest day of my life."

Get to Know Saint Faustina

Just a quick backdrop on humble St. Faustina (1905-1938). She was once a simple peasant farm girl who fought hard to enter religious life, became a nun, and, through God's design, became a mystic, a prophetess, and so much more. To tell you the truth, I won't be at all surprised when she is declared a Doctor of the Church. Notice I said "when." I hope it happens in my lifetime.

Saint Faustina is someone I've come close to in my years of research, writing books about her and the Divine Mercy message. I always say that she is very lovable and down-to-earth — definitely someone we should get to know. We don't have to dust off the history pages too much to get to know her, since she lived in the 20th century. She was very endearing in the way in which she conversed with Jesus and His Holy Mother, which we can see in the *Diary* that she wrote under obedience from Jesus and her spiritual director, Blessed Michael Sopoćko. Thank God for her obedience, because now we can learn from the treasure trove of her *Diary*.

Early in her religious life, Sr. Faustina spent six hours in front of the image of Our Lady of Częstochowa. She had just taken her perpetual vows and attended the pre-dawn unveiling of the image.

She would later recall in her *Diary* that it was there in front of that image where Our Lady spoke profoundly to her heart and soul. For Sr. Faustina, the hours ticked away in a flash. She recalled, "It seemed to me that I had just come … The Mother of God told me many things. I entrusted my perpetual vows to her. I felt that I was her child and that She was my Mother. She did not refuse any of my requests."[115] Earlier, when St. Faustina left her parent's home to join a convent, she followed Jesus' instructions and took a train to Warsaw, Poland. As she got off the train, not knowing where to go, she suddenly became paralyzed with fear. She immediately turned to her Mother Mary. She pleaded, "Mary, lead me, guide me."[116] And Mary did! She will guide us too. Ask her.

Can we see the similarities with the many saints who consider Mary to be their Mother?

The young mystic was so taken up with communing with the Queen of Heaven that she just about missed her train. Another nun had to go and get her from the church so she would be able to catch it. Our Lady would remain beside the young nun and greatly aid her in her mission.

I have a very tiny connection to point out. My grandmother Alexandra was born in Płock, Poland. That's the same town where Jesus first appeared to St. Faustina in the form of the Image of the Divine Mercy on February 22, 1931, in the convent of the Congregation of the Sisters of Our Lady of Mercy (which still stands).

Well, after my long rambling about two of my very favorite saints and my dear grandmother (not yet canonized!), I am finally getting to some of the history of Our Lady of Częstochowa. Perhaps I am leaving the best for last in this chapter.

Our Lady of Częstochowa History

The history of the painting of Our Lady of Częstochowa is rather incredible. The dark color was caused from the soot residue which has accumulated on the painting from years of votive lights and devotional candles burning before it.

Now, here is the really amazing part. This beautiful painting of the Madonna and the Christ Child was painted by St. Luke the Evangelist, according to legend. It gets even better! The legend tells us that St. Luke used a wooden tabletop from a table crafted by Jesus. We know that Jesus learned well from his carpenter foster father, St. Joseph. It is said that as St. Luke painted the image of Mary, the Blessed Virgin told him all the events in Jesus' life that he would later use in his Gospel.

The portrait possesses substantial history. Tradition holds that in 326 A.D., St. Helena traveled to Jerusalem on a quest to find the True Cross of Jesus. Indeed, she found it, but in the searching, she also happened to discover the painting. Saint Helena gave it to her son Constantine, who had a shrine built for it. The portrait was later displayed from the walls of Constantinople during a battle with the Saracens. The city was saved, and the portrait was credited. Next, comes Charlemagne, who became its owner. He then gifted it to Prince Leo of Ruthenia (northwest Hungary), who hung it in his palace.

In the 11th century, an invasion occurred, and the King prayed to Our Lady to protect his troops. Suddenly, an eerie darkness descended upon the enemy troops, confusing them, and they ended up attacking their own people. It is said that Our Lady had intervened, and Ruthenia was saved.

In the 14th century, Prince Ladislaus of Opola had a dream about a request that the portrait be transferred to the Mount of Light (*Jasna Gora*) in Poland.

The Painting Took Direct Hits

The beautiful portrait would take direct hits. First, in 1382, an arrow from the Tartars attacking the Prince's fortress struck the portrait and lodged in the neck of Our Lady. The fearful Prince fled with the portrait in the night and ended up in Częstochowa, where he had the portrait installed in a small church. He eventually had a Pauline monastery and church built there in order to keep the portrait safe.

The eventful history continues, and, in 1430, Our Lady's image would again be wounded. The Hussites overpowered the monastery and attempted to steal the portrait. One of the thieves thrust his sword twice into Our Lady's cheek. About to slash it again, suddenly, in great agony, he fell to the floor and died! To this day, the sword cuts and arrow wound are still clearly visible on the image.

Still later, in 1655, the forces of Sweden's King Charles X almost completely took over Poland. The monastery remained unconquered during the 40-day siege. The portrait was saved, and the invaders were driven out. Because of this seemingly miraculous intervention, Our Lady of Częstochowa became the symbol of Polish national unity. She was crowned Queen of Poland. The King of Poland placed the country under Our Lady's protection.

In 1920, the Russians invaded Poland. It is said that an image of the Blessed Virgin Mary suddenly appeared in the sky over the city of Warsaw when the enemy on the banks of the Vistula River threatened attack. The enemy troops immediately withdrew.

Peace and Hope for Pilgrims

Countless pilgrims continue to travel to Częstochowa to see the Black Madonna — seeking peace, seeking hope, and seeking answers to prayers.

One day, not too long ago, I got to travel to Poland for the first time. It was when I led a pilgrimage in the footsteps of St. John Paul II and St. Faustina, and I was so very blessed to visit the image of Our Lady of Częstochowa! In those seemingly endless, yet fleeting, moments before the image, my grandmother's Polish Madonna brought tremendous and palpable peace to my heart.

Is there someone in your life, living or deceased, who has imparted holy hope into your heart? Can you strive to be a Pilgrim of Hope to others with Mary's help?

Pray and ponder ways in which you can lend a hand to others, whether spiritually or physically. Ask Our Lady of Częstochowa to help you. Writing a friendly letter, text, or email to someone who is lonely can certainly bring a healthy dose of hope to their heart. Offering to help someone in need (a new mother, someone suffering a loss, a single mother, an elderly neighbor) can surely be the hopeful medicine they need. Befriending a widow or widower can be hopeful for both of you!

Of course, our prayers and prayerful offerings for those in need (living and deceased) are beautiful acts of mercy which can impart hope.

I'd like to mention here that St. Faustina honored her Mother Mary with many prayers. In my book *52 Weeks with Saint Faustina: A Year of Grace and Mercy* I told about St. Faustina's multitude of prayers and how the Blessed Mother, in a sense rewarded her:

> One time, as she was preparing for the Feast of the Immaculate Conception of the Mother of God, Sr. Faustina prayed even more intensely, thanking God for the great gift of Mary. She took part in the congregation's nine-day novena, but she also desired to do more. In Mary's honor, St. Faustina prayed 1,000 Hail Marys on each of the novena's nine days. On the actual feast day, Sr. Faustina saw the Blessed Mother at Mass. The Mother of God smiled at Sr. Faustina and told her that, at God's command, the Blessed Virgin Mary was to be in a special and exclusive way Sr. Faustina's mother. She added that she desired that Sr. Faustina would be, in a special way, her child. Mary then let Sr. Faustina know that she desired Sr. Faustina to especially practice three virtues: humility, purity, and love of God. She said, "As My daughter, you must especially radiate with these virtues" (*Diary*, 1412-1415). The Blessed Mother then pressed Sr. Faustina to her Heart and disappeared. Sister Faustina said her own heart became immensely attracted to these virtues, and she practiced them faithfully. It would seem that the second and third virtues mentioned by Our Lady flow forth from the first virtue of humility, which is so necessary for spiritual growth. Like Jesus, Mary very much valued the virtue of humility.[117]

While we might not be inspired or able to pray in the same way as St. Faustina, even a few extra daily prayers to our loving Holy Mother will be great!

Put on your thinking cap and list five ways that you can be a Pilgrim of Hope to others and put them into action soon.

PRAY

Dear Holy Family, Jesus, Mary, and Joseph,
please bless me and pray for me.
Dear Holy Mary, Our Lady of Częstochowa,
please bring peace to my heart.
Mother of the Redeemer, Mother of Mercy and of hope,
thank you for being my Mother.
Gate of Heaven, strengthen my virtues of faith, hope, and love.
Seat of Wisdom, please grant to me your graces.
Mirror of Perfection, mold my heart and teach me to believe,
to hope, and to love right along with you.
Mary, my Mother, I need your help.
Please perfect my simple prayers.
Please guide my steps today and always closer
to your Son Jesus.
Star of Hope, Star of the Sea, please shine upon me
and guide me ever closer to your Son's Kingdom!
Amen.

Recite the Our Father, Hail Mary, Glory Be,
Hail Holy Queen, Memorare *(pages 201-202).*

Pray a prayer to Our Lady of Częstochowa
(page 239).

SAVOR

A prayer, a thought, a resolution:

____

____

____

____

____

____

____

"The Apparition on August 21, 1879," a mosaic in Knock Basilica.

12

Hope to the Weary Heart:
Our Lady of Knock

"Man's great, true hope which holds firm in spite of all disappointments can only be God — God who has loved us and who continues to love us 'to the end,' until all 'is accomplished.'"[118]

— Pope Benedict XVI

Mary is our hope, and she lovingly delivers great hope to our hearts. She also brings warnings, as well as the means to overcome difficulties and calamities. Our Heavenly Mother soothes our weary hearts. Our Lady of Knock brought great peace and hope to the beyond exhausted, persecuted, and pummeled Irish faithful. Mary answered their prayers in the most magnificent way. Let's now delve into this great, loving apparition and the history behind it.

"I seen [sic] the Blessed Virgin, St. Joseph, and St. John the Evangelist on the gable of the church,"[119] said John Curry, more than half a century after he witnessed an apparition as a young boy. He remembered it as if it was last evening. Let's take a look at what was happening at the time when 5-year-old John experienced the Knock apparition for at least a two-hour duration.

In 1879, the Catholic Church in Ireland was going through a very dark night. It had been enduring three centuries of hideous and frightening anti-Catholic persecutions. Religious houses were suppressed, priests and bishops were in great danger of persecution, and some were put to death. Holy Mass was suppressed and outlawed. The people in "the land of saints and scholars," as Ireland has been described, were starving, sick, suffering, and poor — barely hanging on, but trying earnestly to recover from successive famines and the Great Famine.

The Irish people had lost hope. Sure, there were those faithful who had clung to their faith — hoping against all hope. Truth be told, they did not have much of anything else to hang on to. The frazzled thread was thin and was about to break. The Irish people had suffered deeply and were still suffering religiously, culturally, socially, and economically.

Trying Desperately to Survive

Let's zoom in on the map a bit. Hidden away in the west of Ireland in County Mayo, there was a humble little spot out in the middle of nowhere which would miraculously become a great pilgrimage site one day and a grand place of hope for Ireland. This fairly unknown place would enter history.

Of course, the people of that little village of about a dozen houses didn't know anything about this at the time. They were much too busy about their work, trying desperately to feed their families and simply get by — day by day. Indeed, while living in times of uncertainty, the Catholic people of Ireland were trying to emerge from the bleak times with the help of their faith as well as their faithfulness to Holy Mass, in addition to their many Rosaries — all from which they drew strength.

I have to say, Mary certainly knows how to turn hidden hamlets and unknown places into major pilgrimage sites! Think of Nazareth, Bethlehem, Lourdes, Fátima, and many other out-of-the way places.

According to Irish tradition, once upon a time, St. Patrick had traveled through that little town and predicted that it would become a very holy place one day. And so it did. We may wonder why Heaven chooses such places. We need to just look at the dire situation and the humility and faith of the people.

Mary Showed Up One Ordinary Evening

And then, it happened. One ordinary evening, enveloped in bright light, Our Blessed Mother, St. Joseph, and St. John the Evangelist appeared together at the church on the vigil of the octave of the Assumption. However, those in the apparition, although lifelike, did not utter a single word. It was a completely silent apparition — sheer stillness. Also appearing with the three aforementioned people was a white lamb on a large altar with a cross. And there were adoring angels all around the altar.

We might take a quick moment to recall that only seven years prior to this apparition, at a time when the Church seemed to be in exceptional peril, Bl. Pope Pius IX had declared St. Joseph the Patron of the Universal Church. In addition, we know how beloved St. John was and is to the Virgin Mary. We might want to crack open our Bibles and look at the Apocalypse or Book of Revelation. We see the Lamb, we see Mary, Queen of the Church, angels, the holy City of God … but wait, we are getting ahead of ourselves.

The heavenly light is what drew the 15 would-be visionaries together on August 21, 1879. "From the apparition a mysterious light seemed to emanate, sparkling at various points like diamonds, and flowing out from the figures to extend itself almost to the height and width of the gable,"[120] said one writer.

The visionaries, ranging from 5 to 75 years of age (one of them from afar), were all members of St. John the Baptist Parish, where the two-hour vision appeared on the gable of church. The littlest one, eager to see everything, had climbed up onto his cousin's shoulders. There, he wouldn't miss a thing. We will learn something quite fascinating about little John a bit later on.

A Closer Look

Now, let's get a closer look at how the apparition unfolded. It was getting to be evening, but still light, and the day's rain continued to beat down. Mary McLoughlin, the housekeeper for the parish priest, was absolutely amazed while walking by the church to see that the church's outside south wall was completely bathed in a mysterious light. Despite the rain, she could clearly see three distinct, radiant figures standing in front of the wall and assumed that Father must have installed replacements for the stone figures that had been destroyed in a storm.

The rain was picking up, and it was getting dark. Mary rushed through the rain to get to her friend Margaret Byrne's house.

After a short visit there, Mary decided to leave. Margaret's sister Mary agreed to walk home with (the first) Mary. They had to pass the church on the way. As they approached the church, they simply couldn't believe their eyes, for they saw the most amazing vision with complete clarity. Standing out from the gable and to the west of it stood the Blessed Virgin Mary, St. Joseph, and St. John the Evangelist. According to Mary Byrne:

> The Virgin stood erect, with eyes raised to Heaven, her hands elevated to the shoulders or a little higher, the palms inclined slightly toward her shoulders or bosom; she wore a large cloak of a white color, hanging in full folds and somewhat loosely around her shoulders and fastened to the neck; she wore a crown on the head — a rather large crown — and it appeared to be somewhat yellower than the dress or robes worn by Our Blessed Lady.[121]

Visionary Bridget Trench said Mary was "deep in prayer," with her eyes raised to Heaven, her hands raised to the shoulders or a little higher, the palms inclined slightly to the shoulders. "[I] went in immediately to kiss, as I thought, the feet of the Blessed Virgin; but I felt nothing in the embrace but the wall, and I wondered why I could not feel with my hands the figures which I had so plainly and so distinctly seen."[122]

Patrick Hill was on his way home that evening when, as he said in his official statement six weeks after the apparition, "Dominic Beirne came into the house and cried, 'Beautiful vision that are to be seen there!' I followed him; another man by name of Dominic Beirne (senior) and John Durcan and a small boy, John Curry, came with me."

They couldn't get there fast enough. Despite the heavy rain they rushed to see the vision, so eager were they to experience it. Patrick said:

> We ran over towards the chapel and when the gable came into view, we immediately saw the lights; a clear white light covering most of the gable, from the ground to the window and higher. It was a kind of changing bright light, going sometimes up high and again not so high. We saw figures — the Blessed Virgin, St. Joseph and St. John and an altar with a lamb on the altar, and a cross behind the lamb. I went up closer; I saw everything distinctly.[123]

The others came to quickly see it as well.

Fifteen Eyewitnesses

All in all, there were 15 eyewitnesses. Fourteen of them stood in the pouring rain to take in the mystical heavenly apparition, which seemed to pour hope right into their weary hearts. The 15th, Patrick Walsh, was about a half a mile away and had been checking on his farmland when he observed a large globe of golden light in the distance. He said, "I never saw, I thought, so brilliant a light before; it appeared high up, above and around, the gable, and it was circular in appearance."[124]

Heaven chose this humble church to have Our Lady come down from Heaven, bringing with her St. Joseph and St. John the Evangelist. Seeing the heavenly apparition prodded the group to pray the Rosary while watching the silent, yet profound, vision in amazement. Perhaps, the silent Blessed Virgin spoke to the onlookers' hearts. They "compared notes" afterwards, and, sure enough, everyone saw the exact same figures and images. Each person's heart was profoundly touched. Perhaps, in a variety of ways.

God Rewards Our Prayers

There's more to the story of Our Lady of Knock. I'll explain by stating that, as recorded in her *Diary*, our Lord Jesus revealed to St. Faustina Kowalska that He often rewards our perseverance in prayer. Specifically, He said, **"I often wait with great graces until towards the end of prayer."**[125] This profound fact was revealed to the humble mystic after she struggled in great discomfort through Holy Hours which she believed were fruitless. However, despite the feelings of uselessness, she persisted in prayer. And Jesus rewarded her!

I mention St. Faustina because I can see a similarity here with regard to the apparition at Knock. You see, there's more to the story than simply Our Lady's sudden and miraculous appearance to the faithful Catholics at the small parish church in Knock. I believe that our Lord rewarded the Catholic people of Ireland for their faith and wanted to give them a huge dose of hope after they had been through so much suffering. But, even more than that, He chose this parish specifically because of the loving sacrifice and dedication of their devout pastor, Archdeacon Cavanagh. No doubt, God rewarded his many prayers and sacrifices.

It's not a coincidence that the Our Lady of Knock's apparition occurred right after Archdeacon Cavanagh finished the 100th Mass he celebrated for those who had died in the Great Famine. This humble parish priest sacrificed all he had to help the poverty-stricken people of the Great Famine. Even as a young priest, he worked with the famine's victims and served those who died in ditches and on the sides of the road who had succumbed to the excruciating slow demise of starvation, unable to seek final absolution. Archbishop Cavanagh sold his possessions to purchase food for the starving. He used every means he could to help them practically — to ease their hunger pains and try to save their lives. For their spiritual needs, he searched them out to administer the Last Rites.

Even with doing all of this, this pastor's heart was broken, for it was impossible for him to physically reach in time all the hundreds of dying in his parish and the area. They were dying left and right.

Archdeacon Cavanagh was a true father and suffered along with his flock. He decided to offer the most precious gift ever — 100 Holy Masses to plead for God's mercy on the souls of all who had died, especially those who were not able to make their peace with God and died without the last Sacraments of our Church.

Since it was impossible to gift them with the Church's supreme act of mercy, the Archdeacon prayed that his gift of Masses would draw down God's mercy.

Heaven heard his prayers and saw his offerings. Our Lady came. Amazingly, she appeared right after the 100th Mass was celebrated. She came with the Lamb — the Lamb of the Last Rites, the Lamb of Mercy. In John 1:29, we read, "Here is the Lamb of God who takes away the sin of the world!" Yes! Jesus, the Lamb of God forgives our sins. He is the Divine Mercy. The Lamb was the figure most brilliantly illuminated in pure light. Jesus is the Sacrificial Lamb, Who won mercy for all mankind through His Passion and death on the Cross.

Our Lady was next in order of brightness of light. She is the Mother of the Church. Saint Joseph, next to Mary, is the Patron of the Universal Church. He was next in order of illumination. A priest, in the person of St. John the Evangelist, is next. He is shown as an Eastern rite priest (according to his vestments) and therefore represents the Universal Church on earth. As a priest, he is privileged to offer Holy Mass, all the while sacrificing his own life to Jesus and holy Mother Church.

What an amazing sign of consolation and great hope is found in the apparition of Our Lady of Knock. We can take a moment to ponder it all and what it meant to the people of the time and what it means even now as we read this book. The Lamb who takes away the sins of the world appeared at Knock — an amazing answer to Archdeacon Cavanagh's prayers for mercy for the victims of the famine.

Once again, I am reminded of St. Stanislaus Papczyński, who also was filled with great compassion for the souls in Purgatory. He prayed earnestly for them, often falling into ecstasy and being transported in spirit to Purgatory. He witnessed the suffering souls and did all he could to aid them with prayers, Masses, the offering of his pain and illnesses, as well as doing penance for them. He instructed his brothers to always remember this holy duty of mercy towards the dead. He added that they should commend the souls to the Blessed Virgin Mary Immaculately Conceived.

We can do the same. We can commend the Holy Souls to Mary and remember to pray for them.

Of course, we also remember St. Faustina, who, early in religious life, was led to Purgatory by her Guardian Angel to learn about the suffering souls. The young mystic had asked Jesus for whom should she pray. Our Lord let her know! Later, souls came to her in the night, and she lovingly offered prayers and penance for them.

Saint Faustina sets the example for us to do our part too.

God Was on Their Side

The Catholics of Ireland surely must have felt that God was on their side after having endured centuries of heartrending suffering in Ireland. The day following the apparition, the visionaries went to their priest and explained what had happened, for he did not see the apparition. He accepted their testimonies and wrote to the diocesan Bishop. A Church commission interviewed the witnesses. The diocesan hierarchy were skeptical at first. Yet, after several weeks of testimonies and gathering evidence, a positive report was submitted to the Archbishop, stating that the "testimony of all, taken as a whole, was trustworthy and satisfactory."[126] Townspeople and others flocked to the parish church to see the place for themselves — the first pilgrimages to Knock began in 1880.

At that time, the Archbishop stated, "It is a great blessing to the poor people of the West, in their wretchedness and misery and sufferings, that the Blessed Virgin Mary, Mother of God, has appeared among them."[127]

Two years later, Archbishop John Joseph Lynch of Toronto, Canada, visited the parish and claimed he had been healed by the Virgin of Knock.

Sacred Ground

That once unknown place out in the middle of nowhere became sacred ground when Jesus, Mary, St. Joseph, and St. John appeared. Two blind men and a little deaf girl were miraculously cured shortly after the apparition took place, and more than 600 miraculous cures and countless conversions have been reported at Knock since the apparition. The humble place of the Knock apparition is Church-approved, and the shrine now draws a million visitors a year, having become a major pilgrimage site. Knock has been visited by St. John Paul II, St. Mother Teresa of Calcutta, and Pope Francis.

The tiny village of Knock was totally transformed by the appearance of the Blessed Virgin Mary and then by the thousands of pilgrims who traveled there to commemorate the apparition and seek healing and answers to their prayers. In 1976, Our Lady, Queen of Ireland Church was constructed there to accommodate the countless pilgrims.

The Matter of John Curry

And now, there is the matter of little John Curry, the boy who sat on his older cousin's shoulders so that he could better see the vision. It turns out that in the 1930s, one of the Little Sisters of the Poor at 213 E. 70th Street in New York City was curious about something that had been prodding her. She wondered if the John Curry she knew who was residing at the Home of the Aged run by the sisters had ever heard of Knock, and if he knew of a

John Curry from Knock. After all, the John Curry she knew was from Ireland, which anyone could have guessed from his telltale, thick brogue. *He might know him!* she thought and went ahead and asked him.

"Yes," said the humble man who helped to clean the dining room and served at daily Mass. Yes, he knew of Knock. Not only that. He declared, "He is the J. Curry that serves Mass for you in the Home every morning ..."[128] Her jaw must have dropped to the floor! Can we even imagine the sister's great surprise? And the humility of John! He had never let on that he was one of the visionaries of the Knock apparition.

John had immigrated from his beloved Knock to the United States and settled in New York and worked as a laborer and an attendant at City Hospital on Welfare Island. The vision he saw as a little boy lived on in his heart. He could never forget such a holy, miraculous thing. He lived a faithful Catholic and humble life and, at 58 years of age, moved into the Home.

One day, a completely unexpected ecclesiastical summons letter arrived at the Home, requesting that John Curry appear before a tribunal of the Roman Catholic Archdiocese of New York.

John met before the tribunal, which represented the "Second Commission of Enquiry in Ireland," and three reverend judges asked him a variety of questions. John did not flinch or miss a beat, and said straight out," Yes, sir, I am the very John Curry ... I seen [sic] the Blessed Virgin, St. Joseph, and St. John the Evangelist on the gable of the church." He explained every detail to them, adding, "What I gave you here was out of my head and not out of any book."[129]

I don't know about you, but John's forthright, true words give me goose bumps!

John Curry died in 1943 at the age of 68. The Little Sisters of the Poor had John buried in a communal cemetery plot they owned in Farmingdale, on Long Island. However, in God's Providence, in 2015, Cardinal Timothy Dolan of New York would make a pilgrimage to the Knock Shrine where he learned that the youngest visionary was buried in an obscure unmarked grave on Long Island in New York. Cardinal Dolan knew he had to change that. Upon his instructions, John Curry's body was reinterred in the small cemetery of the Basilica of St. Patrick's Old Cathedral in lower Manhattan.

A seemingly insignificant and humble Irish immigrant, without notable worldly accomplishments to speak of, who died stone broke and was buried in an obscure grave without so much as a headstone, would eventually be acknowledged after his death and honored with a permanent headstone. The chiseled statement upon blue-black granite announced, "Witness to the apparition at Knock."

Imagine that!

ACT

Once again, we see how Mary brings great hope to weary hearts. She allays their fears. We learn of humble, faith-filled parishioners, standing in the pouring rain to take in all that Our Lady of Knock has brought them. Finally, after seemingly endless years of suffering — hope fills their hearts.

Take time to ponder it all. Close your eyes and put yourself in the scene of the apparition and pray to Mother Mary. Ask her for everything you need to get to Heaven and bring others with you! Pray to emulate her virtues — especially humility.

While you are at it, give your misery to Jesus. Give Him all of your sufferings and sorrows. When you offer all to Jesus, you will become much lighter, less burdened, and will possess an abundance of hope in your heart!

Consider praying more regularly for the Holy Souls in Purgatory and the dying. If possible, have Masses said for the Holy Souls.

PRAY

Dear Holy Family, Jesus, Mary, and Joseph,
please bless me and pray for me.
Dear Holy Mary, Our Lady of Knock,
please bring hope and healing.
Mother of the Redeemer, Mother of Mercy and of hope,
thank you for being my Mother.
Gate of Heaven, strengthen my virtues of faith, hope, and love.
Seat of Wisdom, please grant to me your graces.
Mirror of Perfection, mold my heart and teach me to believe,
to hope, and to love right along with you.
Mary, my Mother, I need your help.
Please perfect my simple prayers.
Please guide my steps today and always closer to your Son Jesus.
Star of Hope, Star of the Sea, please shine upon me
and guide me ever closer to your Son's Kingdom!
Amen.

Recite the Our Father, Hail Mary, Glory Be,
Hail Holy Queen, Memorare *(pages 201-202).*

Pray the prayers to Our Lady of Knock
(pages 231-232).

SAVOR

A prayer, a thought, a resolution:

13

Hope from Champion: "I Am the Queen of Heaven"

"I Am the Queen of Heaven who prays for the conversion of sinners."[130]

— Our Lady of Champion

The Queen of Heaven stoops low to the earth to comfort and teach her children. She continuously prays for the conversion of sinners and, at times, chooses helpers to carry out her work. Let's learn about Our Lady of Champion and how she equipped a partially blind young woman to lovingly teach and preach the Faith with tender dedication. Let's see how Our Lady brought the faithful through a devastating and terrifying attack of killer fire. I will take the liberty of beginning our chapter with a personal story.

During the writing of this book, I met a woman who already knew me. This happens at times when I am out and about. I bump into one of my "fans" — one of my followers. It's someone who has read my books and might have seen some of my shows on television. For instance, one time when I was leading a pilgrimage to Lourdes, France, a married couple from Ireland was also visiting the area and approached me in a little restaurant. The woman excitedly declared, "Donna-Marie! We watch you on the telly every day!" It sure brought a smile to my face and opened up a beautiful conversation.

I marvel how our Lord and His Holy Mother bring people together all over the world. Add to that, no matter how often this happens, I am always taken aback for a moment — totally taken by surprise because I feel amazed that people know me even as I try to keep a "low profile." I wish I could put a smiley emoji here!

The woman I mentioned first, whom I said already *knew* me, exclaimed, "You *are* Donna-Marie Cooper O'Boyle. Right?" I smiled and nodded.

Just moments before her question, I had sat down next to her in a waiting area at a hair salon. I hadn't expected anything other than a hair trim that morning. But I always pray that God will use me to help others, especially every day in my Morning Offering prayer to God. And suddenly, here was this woman, seemingly very delighted to see me in person. I don't believe in coincidences, by the way. I couldn't wait to see what our Lord and Our Lady had in mind.

"I have read your books!" she said. "I have seen your interviews and shows on EWTN television. Your story is powerful!"

This woman (and I'll call her Marie) used to live in another state and had recently moved to a town not too far from my own. She said that ever since she moved to Connecticut, she had wondered if she would ever cross paths with me.

"It's very nice to meet you!" I said as I smiled and extended my hand. She quickly proceeded to tell me that, first of all, she couldn't believe that I was actually there. And then she mentioned a quote from St. Teresa of Calcutta (whom I still call Mother Teresa) which I had shared during at least one of the television interviews she had seen.

"Mary, Mother of Jesus, be Mother to me now," Marie quoted to me.

"Yes, that's it," I replied. Could I ever forget Mother Teresa's special prayer? Impossible! The petite Saint of the Gutters had instructed me to pray those earnest words as I was trying to preserve the life of my unborn baby and my own life while on complete bed rest with a heart condition and a massive pool of blood in my uterus.

Did you notice that Mother Teresa's prayer is not asking Mary to be "a Mother" to us. She is asking her to be "Mother to us!" Do you see the difference? She acknowledges that Mary is MOTHER! Not just any mother. She is THE Mother!

After hearing me talk about this on a television show, Marie had written this quote on a slip of paper and posted it on her refrigerator. It has continuously given her hope in tough times.

That morning, our serendipitous encounter affected the salon's stylists too. That's because the woman told her stylist how she *knew* me, but only just now met me in person, and the rest of the wonderful back story. I had to tell my stylist a bit too, because I wanted to quickly explain why at one point (with her permission), I suddenly decided to leave my seat for a moment. It was so that I could bring a blessed Miraculous Medal over to Marie. I told my stylist that the woman knew me through my books and television shows and now was very pleased to meet me in person. My stylist then told me that she would like to read my books someday and that she was Catholic! I had not known that until all this had unfolded.

Mary is Our True Mother

"Mary, Mother of Jesus, be Mother to me now." Yes, Mary desires to be our Mother. We should call upon her at any time. But what does this all have to do with a young, devout Belgian farm woman named Adele Brise and Our Lady of Champion?

Well, we need to switch gears and step back to the year 1859 to understand. And we will also see why Champion, Wisconsin, would become the first and only approved Marian apparition site in the United States where, we are told, Our Lady appeared and "gave words of solace and comfort and a bold and challenging mission for the young immigrant woman."[131]

Mother Mary and Adele Brise

Adele, who was born on January 30, 1831, grew up to be a very cheerful and religious young lady, despite a childhood accident that left her blind in one eye. On the day of her First Holy Communion, she promised the Blessed Virgin Mary that she would devote her life to becoming a religious teaching sister in Belgium.

Would this come to fruition?

Her holy desire might as well have gone up in smoke. Adele's parents decided to move the family to America, along with other Belgian settlers. It would seem that it had become impossible for her to achieve her inspiration now. However, Adele's confessor reassured her that she should not be concerned — if our Lord wanted this of her, it would happen in America. What Adele did not know at the time was that her confessor was spot on. Even better yet, her desired vocation would manifest in a most miraculous way! Something Adele would never have dreamed of!

Nonetheless, it was a tough life in a rugged and scary new land. The winters at their new settlement in Wisconsin were extremely harsh, and some settlers died due to the piercing and raw sub-zero conditions. Adele and her family made their new life by living with other immigrants in the largest Belgian settlement of that time. Adele helped her parents by bundling up to ward off the freezing temperatures every day and carrying the family grain on foot to the grist mill.

Mary Appears

One day, while walking on a trail in the area of Robinsonville (now Champion), Wisconsin, Adele was surprised to see a bright light, which took on the form of a lady dressed in dazzling white. The Lady was silent as she was a bit elevated and between a maple tree and a hemlock tree. Shortly after, she slowly vanished and left a pure, brilliant white cloud behind her.

Adele wondered deeply what this encounter could be. *What did it mean?* She quickly shared it with her parents upon reaching home. Her parents believed that she had seen something mystical and important. They surmised that it must be a Holy Soul from Purgatory in need of prayer.

A few days later, on Sunday, October 9, 1859, Adele, her sister, and a friend made their 10-mile journey to Mass. Once again, Adele saw the mysterious Lady. She was between the trees. Yet Adele's companions didn't notice anything. However, she knew what she needed to do. Nothing could stand in the way. Holy Mass prepared her heart. Right after Mass, Adele didn't hesitate in mentioning her two encounters to the priest. He listened carefully and gave her clear instructions. He told Adele to ask the Lady, "In God's name, who are you and what do you want of me?"[132]

On the way back home from Mass, Adele saw the heavenly light for the third time and the mysterious Lady within it. The Lady was surrounded by pure white light and dressed in brilliant white with a yellow sash around her waist. Her long golden wavy hair fell naturally over her shoulders. A crown of stars adorned her head. Her resplendent dress fell in graceful folds to touch her feet.

Adele did as she had been told by the parish priest and might have been very surprised to immediately receive her answer from the heavenly visitor.

"I Am the Queen of Heaven"

The Lady said, "I am the Queen of Heaven who prays for the conversion of sinners, and I wish you to do the same. You received Holy Communion this morning and that is well. But you must do more. Make a general Confession and offer Communion for the conversion of sinners. If they do not convert and do penance, my Son will be obliged to punish them."[133]

Adele's companions could not see or hear the Lady. However, they asked what was happening. Adele told them to kneel down because the visitor said she was from Heaven. The Blessed Mother seemed pleased to see them kneeling. She gazed upon them kindly, saying, "Blessed are they that believe without seeing." Then, the Blessed Mother looked at Adele and asked, "What are you doing here in idleness while your companions are working in the vineyard of my Son?"[134]

In other words, there was work that needed to be done. Adele felt inept and sincerely did not know what else she should be doing and, importantly, how she might be able to accomplish it. She asked the Lady, "But how shall I teach them who know so little myself?"[135] She could neither read nor write!

Our Lady was crystal-clear in her answer: "Teach them their catechism, how to sign themselves with the sign of the Cross, and how to approach the sacraments; that is what I wish you to do. Go and fear nothing, I will help you."[136]

Our Lady's requests were for simple teachings, yet they are so necessary in laying the foundation of Faith for children. We notice that the Queen of Heaven also allayed Adele's fears, assuring her of her holy help.

The radiant Blessed Virgin Mary then lifted her holy hands in what seemed like a blessing. She then slowly vanished from Adele's sight. Adele lay prostrate on the ground. We can only dare to imagine what must have been going through her mind and heart. She was given heavenly instructions — a call to action — a mission from the Mother of God!

The young lady would take every bit of it seriously. She did as Our Lady instructed. Nothing deterred her — inclement weather, exhaustion, ridicule, or anything else for that matter. She was on a mission for our Lord and Our Lady.

Writing these words now, knowing the great measures that Adele took to teach the children in the Wild West, makes me feel like a wimp compared to courageous and faithful Adele. At times (and let's not forget that she was blind in one eye!), she would travel as far as 50 miles to reach children so that she could teach them the catechism. How blessed were they to have her as their teacher! Just imagine how their hearts must have been touched by such love and holy dedication. Adele surely must have inspired them to go on and teach others as well. When Heaven gives a task to us, and we strive to do it well for the glory of God, our little and bigger efforts affect countless souls.

Adele's father built a small family chapel after the apparitions on the site. After a few years of teaching alone, Adele recruited her women friends to help in her teaching mission. Adele and the women were sisters in the mission and lived as Third Order Franciscans. God was very generous in providing for every need. In 1861, many came forward to support the teaching efforts and built a school, convent, and larger chapel. The words "*Notre Dame De Bon Secours, Priez Pour Nous*" were inscribed on a sign placed above the chapel's door: "Our Lady of Good Help, Pray for Us."

The Queen of Heaven's Teachers Persevere on God's Providence

Indeed, Adele prayed to the Mother of God for help in the mission of teaching. And now, with other sisters to feed, as well as herself, they met in the chapel to beg Mary's assistance since they lacked provisions for their next meal. Without fail, shortly thereafter, through God's great Providence, with Mary's intercession, a supply of meat, a bag of flour, and many other provisions were brought to their door.

Though it was arduous work, Adele was happy to the core of her innermost being to be doing what she had been asked by Our Lady. She successfully enlisted help for the mission, and within a few short years after the apparitions, the buildings were up and in use. And much evangelization work was being accomplished.[137]

The Great Peshtigo Fire

Though nothing could have prepared Adele for the tornado of fire which was unleashed on the area and devastated it on October 8, 1871. It had been almost 12 years since Our Lady had appeared and suddenly everything there — everything they had worked so hard to build in order to serve the children — was about to be destroyed. The attacking evil monster was the "Great Peshtigo Fire," which to this day is considered the worst fire in U.S. history. It killed as many as 2,400 people and burned 1.2 million acres because of dry land and high winds. Some say it roared like a tornado of fire, and it was headed straight for the Shrine!

Adele and the sisters did not leave the chapel. They decided to stay put, and they prayed and prayed earnestly with all of the others who had come to join together to pray for the protection of the Shrine and the people there. They courageously and trustingly lifted Mary's statue high and begged her help. They prayed the Rosary and belted out hymns to Jesus and Mary with great gusto. When the winds threatened suffocation, they turned their heads in another direction away from the smoke and continued their fervent prayers. They dug their heels in. They refused to stop praying.

Heavenly Rain

A steady rain came in the early morning, and the fire was extinguished.

Father Peter Pernin, a local priest, described how the Shrine grounds looked after the horrendous fiery assault. He said, "After hours of horror and suspense, the heavens sent relief in the form of a downpour. The fervent prayers to the Mother of God were heard." He continued, "The convent, school, and chapel on the holy land consecrated to the Virgin Mary shone like an emerald isle in a sea of ashes."

He said, "Tongues of fire had reached the chapel fence, and threatened destruction to all within its confines; the fire had not entered the Chapel grounds."[138]

It was truly a miracle. The charred scars on the outside of the Shrine's fence serve as mementos of the miracle.

Teaching and catechizing the children went on long after the catastrophic fire. Adele and her sisters were not going to give up.

They knew they were on a holy mission bestowed by the Mother of God. Their holy, steadfast, and loving presence had a lasting effect on the townspeople and those in surrounding communities.

Because Adele Brice never learned to read or write, she shared about all of her experiences with the Blessed Virgin Mary verbally. And so, the written history of the apparitions has been developed from her oral history and sources close to her, as well as historical documents and third-hand accounts which were discovered in the Shrine's archives. We may see a few slight variations in the recorded history since this is how it was compiled.

National Shrine

Adele died on July 5, 1896. She is buried in the cemetery located near the Apparition Chapel on the grounds of what is now called the National Shrine of Our Lady of Champion. The sisterly comrades who had helped Adele in the teaching mission disbanded after their beloved visionary trailblazer died in 1896.

Shortly after, in 1902, Bishop Messmer asked the Sisters of St. Francis of Bay Settlement to assume responsibility for the work of Adele Brice. The sisters agreed, and one of the founding sisters, Pauline La Plante, made note in her diary of the special day she arrived on the scene. She wrote, "I left my loved mission to come to the Chapel on October 28, 1902. Sweet will of God be forever praised. I found two Sisters, twenty children and forty-two cents."[139] Through love, much perseverance, and loads of great hope, for more than 50 years the sisters continued the work to instruct the children and the many orphans.

The years rolled along, and the sisters turned the facilities into a home and school for crippled children in 1933. Later, in 1953, they took on the formation of young women who wanted to enter their religious community. In 1971, a house of prayer and retreat center was established by the sisters. Ninety years of ministry by the sisters transformed the minds and hearts of countless people. The sisters' kindness was rewarded by Heaven because their heroic efforts deeply affected the sisters' lives too, as they witnessed the great faith of the people who sought the intercession of the Mother of God.

Sisters Eugene DeGrand, Mary Jean Gauthier, and Jeanne Jarvis, representing the Community of Sisters of St. Francis of the

Holy Cross (formerly known as the Sisters of St. Francis of Bay Settlement), were present on December 8, 2010, when Bishop David L. Ricken of Green Bay celebrated Mass at the Shrine of Our Lady of Champion and declared the Marian apparitions to Adele Brice "worthy of belief."

Just six years after the 2010 decree of authenticity was proclaimed, the United States Conference of Catholic Bishops designated the site in Champion as a National Shrine. It had been formerly called Our Lady of Good Help, and, on April 20, 2023, the name was changed to the "National Shrine of Our Lady of Champion."

Thousands of pilgrims visit the National Shrine of Our Lady of Champion to seek help and healing. The Shrine holds many events and prayer services, staying true to Mary's request to Adele to foster the teaching of children and adults. It is holy place in which to encounter Jesus in the Sacraments of the Holy Eucharist, Reconciliation, and Anointing of the Sick. The official website states, "These events, along with their pilgrimages, retreats, and spiritual experiences, make Champion Shrine a home for all seeking a deeper relationship with Jesus through His Mother."[140]

Mother Mary Works Everything For the Glory of God

Mother Mary is always calling to us! Let's be attentive to her calls to our hearts. And, you know, I want to share a bit more about the woman I mentioned at the beginning of this chapter. Well, Marie got in touch with me by email after that "chance" encounter and after I wrote the beginning of this chapter. She wanted to show me a photo of the blessed Miraculous Medal I had given her that day and also explain something that she had not yet shared. Marie told me that, shortly after her mother died, she moved to where she is living now.

She explained what happened after she arrived at her new home: "I reached out to my local Catholic Church and did not receive the support I needed at the time." This caused Marie to leave the Catholic Church and seek out another denomination where she has been attending ever since.

"As a lifelong cradle Catholic, this was a difficult choice for me," she explained. "So when I met you at the salon, I thought this might be a prodding from the Lord to return to the Catholic Church."

You, dear Reader, can probably imagine how my heart felt upon reading this in her email. Marie added, "There are no accidents, and bumping into you appeared to be an invitation from our Lord. Especially, since I am so very familiar with your books." My sentiments precisely. There are no coincidences. God always has a Divine Plan. After all, He is our Divine Physician.

She also told me that she had read my book about the Miraculous Medal and was very touched by it. She is still unpacking boxes after her move, and she told me that after meeting me, she hoped to find that book. That day, she went home and opened the first box, and there it was, right on the top. Marie is excited and feels she is being led home to our Catholic Church.

I am firmly convinced that Mother Mary made a way for this encounter and everything associated with it to unfold in Marie's life. Interestingly, I believe Mother Mary also inspired me to gift that blessed Miraculous Medal to Marie that day. I'm sure that Mary is calling Marie to come back to the Church of her Baptism. By the way, Marie and I have plans to get together.

ACT

There's much to think about when meditating upon this reflection. Adele was faithful and wanted what God wanted for her. Through all kinds of difficulties and circumstances, she worked very hard to carry out her mission from the Blessed Mother to catechize children. She sets a beautiful example for us all.

Take time to consider the possibility of teaching the Faith to children. It could be in your own family or faith formation programs at your parish. In addition, consider making a General Confession like Adele did, following Mary's advice, or offer your Holy Communion for the conversion of sinners.

Something else to consider: Strive to be attentive. Surely, there are plenty of times when we walk right past an opportunity to do some good.

With regard to my story about Marie, you just never know how much a *chance* encounter and Mary's blessed sacramental can completely turn things around and cause great transformations! It's so important to be welcoming. We don't want to inadvertently turn someone away for the Church or from God because we don't show care or concern. Our encounters with Mary through prayer and our encounters with those we meet and those we know can certainly bring a great abundance of hope to hearts!

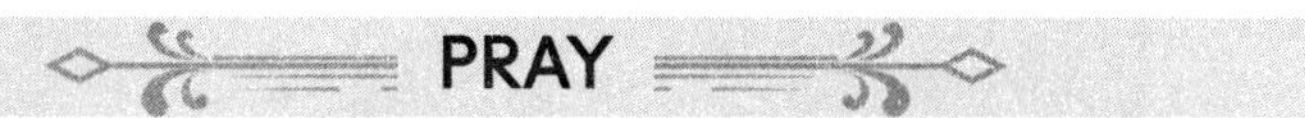

Dear Holy Family, Jesus, Mary, and Joseph,
please bless me and pray for me.
Dear Holy Mary, Our Lady of Champion,
please douse the "fires" which seek to attack me.
Help me to be a vibrant example and teacher of the Faith.
Mother of the Redeemer, Mother of Mercy and of hope,
thank you for being my Mother.
Gate of Heaven, strengthen my virtues of faith, hope, and love.
Seat of Wisdom, please grant me your graces.
Mirror of Perfection, mold my heart and teach me to believe,
to hope, and to love right along with you.
Mary, my Mother, I need your help. Please perfect my simple
prayers. Please guide my steps today and
always closer to your Son Jesus.
Star of Hope, Star of the Sea, please shine upon me
and guide me ever closer to your Son's Kingdom!
Amen.

Recite the Our Father, Hail Mary, Glory Be,
Hail Holy Queen, Memorare *(pages 201-202).*

Pray the prayer to Our Lady of Champion (page 237).

SAVOR

A prayer, a thought, a resolution:

Saint Mother Teresa of Calcutta.

Venerable Servant of God Cardinal Nguyễn Văn Thuận.

14

Hope, Suffering, and Joy:
Learning to Walk with Mary

"Keep the JOY of loving Jesus ever burning in your heart and share this joy with others."[141]

— Mother Teresa

Life can seem like a crazy adventure! Throughout the many stages of life, one day to the next, we can sometimes feel kept on our toes as another, sometimes precarious adventure suddenly unfolds. Or perhaps we are waiting for the proverbial other shoe to drop. Just how does joy tie into our lives? From time to time, we might find it difficult to recognize joy in our lives. Our pilgrimage through life can be arduous. Yet, truth be told, joy should reside in our hearts. It should hold a prominent place! But how can we discover a pure and holy joy despite the challenges we face? Let's allow Our Lady, Mother Teresa, and a saint-in-the-making to enlighten us.

Joy is a beautiful gift which is meant to be shared. Loving our Lord Jesus can cause us to be joyful. Mother Teresa often ended each letter she wrote me with a powerful and encouraging instruction. I've used one of her teachings in today's quotation: "Keep the JOY of loving Jesus ever burning in your heart and share this joy with others." This petite nun firmly believed that to love Jesus was to be joyful.

Joy should be woven into our spiritual journeys. It seems very appropriate as we near the end of our book, reflecting upon our Mother Mary as a beautiful Pilgrim of Hope for us, that we should also discuss the gift of joy and how it ties in as an essential part of our journey.

Mother Teresa said, "Our prayer each day should be, 'Let the joy of the Lord be my strength.' Cheerfulness and joy were Our Lady's strength. This made her a willing handmaid of God."

Mother explained, "Only joy could have given her the strength to go in haste over the hills of Judea to her cousin Elizabeth, there to do the work of a handmaid. If we are to be true handmaids of the Lord, then we, too, each day, must go cheerfully in haste over the hills of difficulties."[142]

This is, as we know, exactly what the young Mary did after giving her wondrous Fiat to the Lord, declaring herself His handmaid, after the Angel Gabriel had greeted her with the amazing message that she would become the Mother of God. We discussed the beautiful times of the Annunciation and the Visitation earlier in this book.

What is Joy?

It's important to note that we won't always *feel* joyful, especially if we are going through a trying time. There's nothing wrong with you if you can't feel the joy all the time. So, you can take that pressure off your shoulders right now. However, let's be clear: Joy is not the same as happiness, which we can sometimes muster up by ourselves (by having a special dessert, enjoying a hobby, watching a great movie, spending time with a friend or loved one, etc.). Joy is much deeper and more meaningful.

That is because joy is actually a fruit of the Holy Spirit, stemming from the gifts of the Holy Spirit. Joy can certainly reside in our hearts through pain or sorrow — a holy and hopeful joy — possible by knowing of the promise of something better — an Eternal Life which follows what we experience here on planet Earth. In addition, joy can fill our hearts by knowing that our tough times and sorrows can actually bring about good when we lovingly offer them to Jesus and ask Him to unite them to His Passion and redeem them for His glory and for the good of souls.

The Holy Spirit's fruit of joy was very important to the feisty Saint of the Gutters. So important was joy to Mother Teresa, that she even made sure that it was included in the Missionaries of Charity Constitution, which stipulates, "A spirit of joy should permeate the daily life of the novitiate, and the novices should be encouraged to regard the communication of this joy as a necessary part of their apostolate" (No. 203).

Let's allow that to sink in. It's not only a very important, even essential, instruction for Mother Teresa's sisters — but for us too!

Because joy is such an important fruit of the Holy Spirit, and because the poor and unfortunate need to be cared for with great love, Mother Teresa made sure that her sisters possessed the beautiful gift of joy so they wouldn't inadvertently pass along any sadness or grumpiness to those for whom they cared. The poor surely didn't need a bombardment of "baggage" from a sister who was lacking that special fruit of the Holy Spirit.

Agony and Joy Intertwined

Whenever I had the privilege of looking into Mother's shining eyes, I beheld radiating joy. I wouldn't learn until after her death that while her utterly selfless life was radiating such pure, holy joy, she was, at the same time, suffering in great pain due to a 50-year-long dark night in her spiritual life. Jesus' joy shining through her was not stifled in the least because of Mother Teresa's innermost agony in feeling completely abandoned by God. No. The steady resplendent joy radiated out of her like sun beams!

I must add here that even though Mother Teresa felt this way, her heart knew otherwise. She was not going to give up on God. Jesus was allowing her to feel the great pains of abandonment that He Himself felt as He hung from the Cross, thirsting for souls and dying for our salvation. We might think now about the fact that Jesus often allows those He loves so dearly to experience and endure some of what He Himself went through.

I am also thinking of St. Faustina now. She was also allowed to taste Jesus' Passion. Though St. Faustina deeply suffered in the spiritual life (experiencing two dark nights of suffering), she joyfully offered it all to Jesus. In time, she became completely united with Him mystically.

One time on a Good Friday, she heard Jesus calling from the Cross to her about His thirst for the salvation of souls. The young mystic offered herself to Jesus on the Cross. I'll let her tell you. She recorded in her *Diary*:

> At three o'clock, I saw the Lord Jesus, crucified, who looked at me and said, **I thirst.** Then I saw two rays

> issue from His side, just as they appear in the image. I then felt in my soul the desire to save souls and to empty myself for the sake of poor sinners. I offered myself, together with the dying Jesus, to the Eternal Father, for the salvation of the whole world.[143]

Whenever I spent time with Mother Teresa or her Missionaries of Charity Sisters, I experienced profound joy. It was strikingly palpable. There was no question about it — to see them in action was to be touched by the inexhaustible joy in their hearts. But they did not amass this special gift for themselves. No. They joyfully gave it away in their loving service to others — most times, the very unfortunate and difficult cases — cleaning wounds, feeding the hungry, pulling maggots out of people left for dead in the gutters, and so much more.

Mother was also acutely aware of the starvation in the Western world, the feelings of loneliness, abandonment, and of being unloved. Receiving Jesus in the Holy Eucharist gave them the absolute and necessary strength, courage, and joy to walk forward in faith every single day — to serve Jesus in others.

Thank God for the great gift of the Eucharist — the miracle of Jesus! — Who loves us so much that He humbles Himself to remain with us in the form of Bread, so we can be nourished and healed by His love for us.

Mother Teresa, so close to the Blessed Mother, explained how Mary thanked God in her Magnificat. She said:

> The Magnificat is Our Lady's prayer of thanks. She can help us to love Jesus best; she is the one who can show us the shortest way to Jesus. Mary was the one whose intercession led Jesus to work the first miracle. "They have no wine," she said to Jesus. "Do whatever he tells you," she said to the servants. We take the part of the servants. Let us go to her with great love and trust.[144]

Walk with Mary

Mother Teresa lovingly pushes us forth to walk with Mary — to go forward with our Mother Mary with great love and trust. In overseeing her religious congregation and in serving the poorest of the poor all over the world, Mother Teresa relied upon the Blessed Mother each day. She prayed fervently and trustingly to Mary to help transform her heart and soul.

Mother Teresa even negotiated a cease fire with Mother Mary! I detailed this in my book *Small Things with Great Love: A 9-Day Novena to Mother Teresa, Saint of the Gutters.* It occurred in 1982 during the war in Lebanon. One hundred disabled and ill children were left abandoned in an orphanage in Beirut because it had been bombed. Bombs and war didn't scare her. The abandonment of the children was a holy call to action for the humble Saint of the Gutters. Like I mentioned, she actually arranged for a cease fire with the Mother of God so that she could rescue the children! It would happen on the eve of Mary's feast day — the Assumption. Mother Teresa scooped up all the children and brought them to a Christian suburb of Beirut. We can just imagine the many hugs and smiles of the children after being in Mother's loving care!

In knowing Mother, I have learned Mother's way of sending up an emergency flare to Mary. When in urgent need, Mother and her sisters prayed a special novena. It consisted of 10 *Memorare* prayers in a row — nine of them for the novena and the 10th in thanksgiving, no matter the outcome. I have prayed this way often. You can too. It works!

We can also pray Mother Teresa's prayer to Mary:

> Mary, I depend on you totally as a child on its mother, that in return you may possess me, protect me, and transform me into Jesus. May the light of your faith dispel the darkness of my mind; may your profound humility take the place of my pride; may your contemplation replace the distractions of my wandering imagination; and may your virtues take the place of my sins. Lead me deeper into the mystery of the cross that you may share your experience of Jesus's thirst with me.[145]

Mother Teresa would often mention that joy was, in fact, a holy net of love with which to catch souls. She was right! The fruit of joy is utterly contagious! Like a holy magnet, it attracts us — beckoning us to cling to it. And Mother Teresa and her sisters' virtuous, joyful witness fills our hearts with great hope.

Cardinal Francis-Xavier Nguyễn Văn Thuận

I'd like to introduce you to someone who will stir your heart. Have you heard of Cardinal Nguyễn Văn Thuận? I want to tell you about him. I feel it's important to include him in this book, which is all about holy hope. He is someone whom I deeply admire and who profoundly inspires me.

Cardinal Văn Thuận was born in Vietnam in 1928. His family members were faithful Catholics who had endured a seemingly unacceptable amount of suffering. He was taken as a prisoner when Saigon fell to the North Vietnamese Army. That was on August 15, 1975, the Feast of the Assumption. Loving the Blessed Virgin Mary as he did, the timing of his arrest was significant to him. Mother Mary would become Cardinal Văn Thuận's constant companion while he endured prison life and tried to make sense of it.

Cardinal Văn Thuận suffered deeply in captivity for 13 years, nine of which were in solitary confinement. However, let's back up just a bit in order to understand more. Before this unfair imprisonment, in 1945, when Cardinal Văn Thuận was in the seminary, his Uncle Khoi and his son were executed by the Communists. Later, in 1963, his Uncle Diem and Uncle Can were both assassinated by the Viet Cong. These losses and how they occurred were almost too much for him to take. But his mother's holy example helped Cardinal Văn Thuận to eventually forgive the killers.

Another significant piece to the spiritual puzzle, which was under Cardinal Văn Thuận's belt before he was suddenly imprisoned, was the amazing pilgrimage he had decided to take in 1957, while studying in Rome. He visited the Lourdes Shrine. While taking it all in, there in that sacred place where Mary appeared to St. Bernadette, he deeply reflected upon the words of the Blessed Virgin Mary to St. Bernadette: "I do not promise you joys and consolations on this earth, but rather trials and sufferings."

Cardinal Văn Thuận took these words to his own heart, embracing them and believing Mary was telling this to him as well. He must have been given a special grace to recognize this. At that time, he sincerely told Mother Mary, "For your Son's Name and yours, Mary, I accept trials and sufferings."[146]

Cardinal Văn Thuận was called to a deeper life of faith and suffering and was granted graces to understand this suffering. In addition, he cooperated with these graces. He could have turned a deaf ear to them, become bitter over his situation, or decide to completely ignore the calling; but because of his faithfulness and cooperation with God's grace, those of us who learn his story have been given an amazing witness to hope to inspire our lives.

After he had been imprisoned for quite some time, Cardinal Văn Thuận felt rather useless since he felt he could no longer help his flock. He said, "My heart is torn to pieces for having been taken away from my people."[147] After all, this was his vocation. He felt utterly useless.

Though he didn't like to mention the stark, negative realities of his grueling imprisonment, later on he openly shared, "The harsh years in prison pass very slowly. While suffering humiliation and abandonment, my only support and hope was the love of Mary, Our Blessed Mother."[148] Later on, Cardinal Văn Thuận would write what he called the "Ten Rules of Life." One rule was, "I will have one very special love: The Blessed Virgin Mary."

Embracing the Cross

At times, Cardinal Văn Thuận could barely recite a prayer (though they were welling up from his heart). Sometimes, he could hardly catch his breath in the small dark and dingy room in which he was placed when in solitary confinement. He often got down on his knees to put his nose to the little narrow crack at the bottom of the door in order to get some air. Through it all, as he prayerfully looked to the Cross of Christ, Cardinal Văn Thuận began to recognize his captivity as a unique opportunity for grace and an incomparable opportunity to offer his suffering to God for souls.

By outward appearances, Jesus also looked useless as He was dying on the Cross for our salvation. In time, with God's grace and Mary's help, Cardinal Văn Thuận recognized his seemingly endless days — one after the other — as a road of hope — a road *to* hope. He was not useless after all. He also remembered wonderful Marian saints, whose inspiration fueled him to go on with great faith as they kept company with him, all the while a reminder of Mother Mary's love and protection.

The faithful servants of Mother Mary — St. Louis de Montfort, St. John Bosco, and St. Maximilian Kolbe — were his companions on the road of hope, for they inspired him and gave him an unwavering trust in the love of Mary, the Queen of Apostles and Martyrs.

By God's grace and Cardinal Văn Thuận's cooperation with grace, he did amazing things on very dark days and nights. He made a firm decision to live in the present moment and totally trust God as to whether he would ever get released. Whether he did or not, he wasn't ever going to give up on hope and whatever it was that God wanted him to do. He also felt his people needed him. He was inspired to stay in touch with his people as St. Paul did from his prison cell. He would imitate St. Paul.

For instance, he devised a way to scribble inspiring reflections on scraps of paper and smuggle them out to his people through the help of a little boy and his mother. These notes would later be collected in his book, *The Road of Hope*. Eventually, he even taught one of the guards to sing Latin hymns! And, later on, sympathetic guards smuggled in a small piece of wood and some wire so that Cardinal Văn Thuận could fashion a cross. This was completely against the rules and extremely risky business to do. However, God made a way.

As amazing as all of the above is, perhaps more importantly was how Cardinal Văn Thuận managed to celebrate Holy Mass during his solitary confinement.

Mass in Secret

Having a tiny piece of bread, just three drops of wine, and one drop of water put into the palm of his hand, Cardinal Văn Thuận pronounced the words of Consecration, and by God's grace, Jesus burst into the dark prison cell. He was able to secretly consecrate bread and wine (no matter how minuscule) into the Body and Blood, Soul, and Divinity of Jesus Christ, truly present in the Eucharist. To me, this is utterly inspiring.

Cardinal Văn Thuận was as brilliant as he was resourceful. He asked for "medicine" to help his ailing stomach, and his family immediately knew that he meant altar wine, which they put in a small bottle marked as "medicine." They also smuggled in bits of unconsecrated hosts in a flashlight. When he used the two of these, Holy Mass came alive in his depressing cell. Celebrating Mass and receiving our Lord in the Eucharist sustained the humble Cardinal through the darkest of times. After a while, he was able to secretly give Holy Communion to other prisoners and, in time, to villagers too.

Day after day, Cardinal Văn Thuận's irresistible Christian love and amazing Eucharistic joy won over prisoners and guards alike. Because of this, he was often moved to other prison camps or placed in solitary confinement, and his guards were rotated. That didn't stop God from working through this saint-in-the-making.

Certainly Mary continued to help him help others and spread holy hope. Villagers became his allies, and the Communist network of village spies completely fell apart! Cardinal Văn Thuận was being used by God in many areas! His Christian love brought much hope during hopeless circumstances, including helping a suicidal man decide not to end his life.

During his long prison spell, Cardinal Văn Thuận totally resigned himself to God's holy will, knowing that He alone knew what was best for his life. He wholeheartedly trusted God with every single thing. Cardinal Văn Thuận was told he would never be released. Still, he trusted God and relied on Mary's help and was satisfied with whatever God wanted for him.

Mary Arranged His Miracle

One day, he prayed to his Mother in Heaven, "Mary, my Mother, if you know that I cannot be of any more use to the Church, grant me the grace to die here in prison and consummate my sacrifice. If you know that I can still be of use to the Church, grant me the grace of freedom on one of your feast days."[149] You might recall now that he was arrested on one of Mary's feast days.

On November 21, 1988, the Cardinal was fixing his meal when he heard a telephone ring. He had a strong feeling something was going on regarding him. He was taken to the Minister of

Police, and, surprisingly, the minister asked him if he had anything to request.

"I would like to be freed." He responded as naturally as if he was asking for a cup of coffee.

The official was taken aback and asked him, "When do you want to be freed?"

"Today," was Cardinal Văn Thuận's simple response. [150]

The Minister of Police seemed extremely surprised to hear such a forthright, yet honest, answer. Seeing the look of amazement on his face, Cardinal Văn Thuận calmly responded, "You see, Mr. Minister, I have been in prison for three pontificates: Paul VI, John Paul I, John Paul II. I have been here during the offices of four Secretary Generals of the Communist Party: Brezhnev, Andropov, Chernenko and Gorbachev."[151]

With that, his request was immediately and miraculously granted! On the Feast of the Presentation of Mary, and Cardinal Văn Thuận's parents' 63rd wedding anniversary, no less!

God's Will: A Road to Hope

After his release, Cardinal Văn Thuận worked tirelessly on behalf of marginalized and oppressed people. He visited Vietnamese communities, spoke of his experiences, and encouraged them in their faith journey. Most of all, his witness was abounding in hope.

Saint John Paul II appointed him to the Pontifical Council for Justice and Peace. Cardinal Văn Thuận later became its president. He taught that obstacles in life are a path to holiness. He wrote several best-selling religious books, including *The Road of Hope*, which was distributed worldwide. In this book, he stated, "God uses trials and sufferings to teach us to better understand and be more patient with the sufferings of others."[152]

The year 2001 was when he was made a cardinal, a Prince of the Church. He had been diagnosed with cancer by then and later died peacefully on September 16, 2002, a true Pilgrim of Hope.

On May 4, 2017, Pope Francis declared Cardinal Francis-Xavier Nguyễn Văn Thuận to be a Venerable Servant of God. Thus, the cause for his beatification has opened and is being investigated as I type these words.

I'll leave you with an inspiring prayer which Cardinal Văn Thuận wrote while in his prison cell:

> I sing of Your mercy in the darkness, in my weakness, in my annihilation. I accept my cross, and I plant it, with my own two hands, in my heart. If You were to permit me to choose, I would change nothing, because You are with me! I am no longer afraid, I have understood. I am following You in Your Passion and in Your Resurrection.[153]

ACT

Take time to ponder your life. Are you a joyful person? Ask yourself if you have room to grow in this area. If possible, sometime soon, be present with our Lord Jesus in the Blessed Sacrament in a time of Adoration. Certainly, endeavor to be present with our Lord wherever you are. Quiet your mind, close your eyes, and prayerfully reflect upon a few experiences and encounters in your life.

Was there a time when someone's pure joy touched your heart in a special way? Was there a time when your joyful spirit helped someone or when you could have chosen to act in a joyful manner, but instead acted in a negative way? Ponder these things in a sort of examination of conscience. Take your time with it. Make a resolution to change for the better.

Ask Jesus to heal your heart of past wounds. These wounds can cause suffering, sometimes even unbeknownst to you. These same wounds can stand in the way of spiritual growth. Take time to ponder times in your life when you have been hurt by others. Pray for the graces to forgive the offenders. This does not mean that you condone the sin. With God's grace and your cooperation, you can indeed forgive and ask for forgiveness. The floodgates of peace will inundate your heart.

Pray to the Holy Spirit and ask for the fruit of joy to reside in your heart. Strive to become a joyful giver. Offer your sufferings to Jesus and ask Him to redeem them for the sanctification of your soul and others.

Give of yourself, not grudgingly, but with joy, aided by the Blessed Mother, St. Mother Teresa of Calcutta, and Venerable

Servant of God Cardinal Văn Thuận. You can then become a beautiful and effective missionary of hope to our world today.

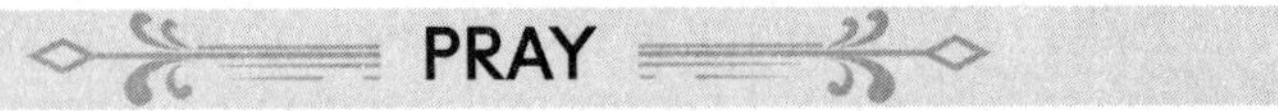

PRAY

Dear Jesus, please heal me.
Dear Holy Spirit, please come to my aid.
Help me to possess the fruit of joy in my heart.
Pray the "Come Holy Spirit" prayer (page 216).

Dear Holy Family, Jesus, Mary, and Joseph,
please bless me and pray for me. Saint Teresa of Calcutta
and Venerable Cardinal Văn Thuận, please pray for me.
Dear Holy Mary, Mother of the Redeemer, Mother of Mercy
and of hope, thank you for being my Mother.
Gate of Heaven, strengthen my virtues of faith, hope, and love.
Seat of Wisdom, please grant to me your graces.
Mirror of Perfection, mold my heart and teach me to believe,
to hope, and to love right along with you.
Mary, my Mother, I need your help.
Please perfect my simple prayers.
Please guide my steps today and always
closer to your Son Jesus.
Star of Hope, Star of the Sea, please shine upon me
and guide me ever closer to your Son's Kingdom!
Amen.

Recite the Our Father, Hail Mary, Glory Be,
Hail Holy Queen, Memorare *(pages 201-202).*

Pray "Mother Teresa's Prayer to Mary"
and Cardinal Van Thuan's prayer to Mary
(pages 224-225).

SAVOR

A prayer, a thought, a resolution:

15

Hope and Penance:
Our Lady of Fátima's Message

"My Immaculate Heart will never abandon you."

— Our Lady of Fátima

Our Lady continues to call to our hearts. She has so much to teach us. As our true Mother, she loves us and wants us in Heaven one day. Mary also asks that we give of ourselves to help save other souls. Our pilgrimage through life is not about just making it to Heaven one day (by the skin of our teeth!), but it is about lovingly praying and sacrificing for others to help them get there too. Let's see what Our Lady of Fátima has to tell us and what we can learn from three young, innocent, and faithful children.

REFLECT

I felt a tear trickle from the corner of my eye. I was in church waiting for Mass to begin on May 13, the feast of Our Lady of Fátima. I felt inspired that morning — which happens to be *this* morning! Yes, that's right. I am writing this chapter on the feast of Our Lady of Fátima! Well, it had happened that I felt inspired to grab a copy of my children's book, *Our Lady's Message to Three Shepherd Children and the World*, before leaving my house for Mass. I planned to gift it to the little girls who sit in the pew in front of me at church. I wanted them to know the story of Our Lady and the faithful shepherd children.

After I handed my book to the little 4-year-old (who looks just like St. Jacinta, by the way), she excitedly thanked me and then so quietly whispered in an angelic voice, "Could you stay a little longer after Mass?" Her question seemed very familiar. I told her I would try. I knew I had to get back home to write this book! She seemed satisfied with my answer, turned around, and leaned against her mother. She held a prayer card of St. Jacinta, which she studiously gazed upon.

Seconds later, Mass was about to begin, and that is when the unexpected tear came to my eye. I had suddenly realized that the little girl's invitation for me to stay seemed to come straight from Mother Mary, who beckons us to stay with her Son and pray. My heart felt profoundly touched. I knew then what Mary had asked me. She had asked me this very thing in the past.

With regard to the apparitions of Fátima, or any apparition, we see that Heaven works through humble souls. We have observed this throughout history and within every Marian apparition. Most especially, we see that the greatest example of humility was manifested through Jesus Christ Himself. His Holy Mother is next in order of the greatest expression and example of humility. Mary is honored by God for her most pure humility. Though Mary is the Mother of God and the Queen of Heaven and earth, she always comported herself and acted in deep humility during her life on earth. She consistently sought to be of service to others.

The Mother of God chose the lowly tasks and has always operated through humility in order to praise, honor, and glorify her Son's unequaled humility. Mary's thoughts, words, and actions and her entire being continually seek to glorify God.

If we could only strive to be more like Mary!

A Little Hamlet Called Aljustrel

Let's now step back to the year 1917, to a little hamlet called Aljustrel in Portugal so that we can reflect upon Our Lady of Fátima and why she visited planet Earth at that time in the first place. It was a time of upheaval and tensions between governments. World War I was raging, and Pope Benedict XV had pleaded for world peace. In May 1917, the pontiff appealed to the Blessed Mother to intercede for peace. Our Lady didn't waste time. She began to appear to the three young Fátima visionaries about a week later.

Through Our Lady of Fátima, the supernatural events in the lives of a trio of peasant farm children-turned-visionaries would impact and change the world. Brother and sister, 8 and 6 years old, Francisco and Jacinta Marto, along with their older cousin, Lucia dos Santos, 9, were chosen by Heaven to receive the great sobering, yet hopeful, messages from Our Lady of Fátima.

The events actually started in 1916, with visits from the Angel of Peace of Portugal, who prepared the shepherd children for Our Lady's visits the following year.

The Angel's Visits

Beginning in the spring of 1916, these supernatural events occurred during ordinary days when these faithful Catholic children were tending their family's flocks of sheep. Each of the three angelic visits was profoundly enlightening. On the first visit, the radiant Angel, as white as snow, told them, "Do not be afraid. I am the Angel of Peace. Pray with me."[154] The children were absolutely astounded, but also at complete peace.

And so, throughout these visits in 1916, the Angel taught the shepherd children to pray, to adore our Lord, and to offer intercessory prayers and about the need to sacrifice for sinners. One time, the Angel of Peace told them, "Pray! Pray very much! The Hearts of Jesus and Mary have designs of mercy on you. Offer prayers and sacrifices constantly to the Most High."[155]

The simple yet faith-filled children were very impacted by the angelic visits. The Angel of Peace told them, "Pray thus. The hearts of Jesus and Mary are attentive to the voice of your supplications."[156]

They did not yet fully understand the necessity of these angelic instructions of preparation or why they had been chosen. They didn't know what lay ahead with Our Lady. Still, the Angel's words enraptured their hearts. They would not forget them. Jesus and Mary were "attentive to the voice" of their supplications. They took it all deeply into their hearts.

Pretty incredible!

Our Lady of Fátima Appears to the Shepherd Children

Our Lady of Fátima's appearance to them the following year in 1917 would come as a complete surprise. Again, it happened out in the pastures as the young ones watched over their flocks.

On May 13, 1917, the three little shepherds were grazing their sheep at the Cova da Iria (or Cove of Irene, meaning "peace"). As the sheep were nibbling away at the grass, suddenly the entire sky lit up with a flash, appearing like lightning. The shepherd children jumped into action to begin to get their flocks safely home because of what they thought was an emerging serious storm.

Another flash! Then, suddenly, there she was! A beautiful Lady all in white, hovering above an old holm oak tree.

Lucia said she was more radiant than the sun and that she radiated a beautiful crystal light. The heavenly visitor put the children's minds at ease. Similar to the Angel of Peace, Our Lady (they would later find out her identity) said, "Do not be afraid. I will do you no harm."[157]

Our Lady's Invitation

Our Lady asked them to come back to the Cova at the same hour on the 13th day of the month for the next six months. She then posed a question: "Are you willing to offer yourselves to God and bear all the sufferings He wills to send you as an act of reparation for the conversion of sinners?" The children said they were up to the task and would devote the remainder of their lives to saving souls.

Through a series of six visits, between May 13 and October 13, 1917, the Mother of God appeared to the three shepherd children. Our Lady would appear twice more to Lucia later on after her younger cousins had gone to Heaven. In July's apparition, Mary promised that on October 13 she would tell them who she was and would perform a miracle for all to see and believe. It was the Miracle of the Sun, a miracle which Our Lady of Fátima performed to prove that her visits were authentic.

There's an awful lot contained in the apparitions of Our Lady of Fátima. I will only mention highlights of her messages (otherwise I would be writing another book here in this chapter!).

In June, Our Lady told the three shepherds that Francisco and Jacinta would go to Heaven soon, but Lucia would need to remain on earth a while longer so she could fulfill Jesus' desire to spread devotion to her Immaculate Heart throughout the world. She also revealed her Immaculate Heart in need of reparation. Our Lady reassured Lucia that she would never forsake her, and that Lucia could take refuge in her Immaculate Heart.

Lucia would have much work to do. It's a good thing Lucia could depend upon Mary's promise and take refuge in her

Immaculate Heart because Lucia would end up staying in this world a very long time after her cousins went to Heaven. Lucia lived to just short of her 98th birthday!

Our Lady Reveals Secrets

In July, Our Lady revealed three parts of a secret. The first and second parts were a vision of hell and prophesies. Seeing hell in all its gory detail was beyond frightening for the children. Yet, Mary did not hesitate to show them the existence of hell and the consequence for sin.

This terrible vision made a lasting impression on the children. Knowing of this sad reality, the faithful children would learn about making sacrifices for sinners, which they did lovingly because they wanted to help save their souls. They devoted the remainder of their lives to prayer and penance.

Our Lady spoke much to them. She impressed upon them the way in which sinners will be saved from the eternal fires of hell. "You have seen hell where the souls of poor sinners go. To save them, God wishes to establish in the world devotion to my Immaculate Heart."

Later, Sr. Lucia would state, "Thus we see that devotion to the Immaculate Heart of Mary must be established in the world by means of a true consecration, through conversion and self-giving."[158]

"Penance, Penance, Penance!"

The third part of the secret, about an Angel with a flaming sword calling for "Penance, Penance, Penance!" is very intense and has much history behind it. It is connected to St. John Paul II. As he was recovering in 1981 from bullet wounds from a would-be assassin, he recognized with complete clarity that he was the "Bishop dressed in white" who was mentioned. He would later claim that Fátima was the greatest apparition of the 20th century and, possibly, of all time.

Our Lady of Fátima gave important instructions to avoid another war: "To prevent this, I shall come to ask for the consecration of Russia to my Immaculate Heart and the Communion of Reparation on the First Saturdays." She also said, "In the end, my Immaculate Heart will triumph."[159] We can hang on to these precious, comforting words.

Our Lady gave these final words at the July apparition: "When you pray the Rosary, say after each mystery: 'O my Jesus, forgive us our sins, save us from the fires of hell. Lead all souls to heaven, especially those in most need of thy mercy'" (the Decade Prayer).

In August, Our Lady said, "Pray, pray very much, and make sacrifices for sinners; for many souls go to hell, because there are none to sacrifice themselves and pray for them." Her words again made a deep impression on the children, who redoubled their prayer efforts.

In September's apparition, Our Lady said, "Continue to pray the Rosary in order to obtain the end of the war. In October Our Lord will come, as well as Our Lady of Sorrows and Our Lady of Mount Carmel. St. Joseph will appear with the Child Jesus to bless the world. God is pleased with your sacrifices."

Our Lady Performed the Great Miracle of the Sun

In October, as I mentioned, the Great Miracle of the Sun occurred, when the sun danced and did crazy miraculous things, such as spinning out of control and hurling itself towards the earth, capturing the attention of 70,000 eyewitnesses. The young visionaries received other visions simultaneously.

Our Lady also gave very specific instructions while revealing her name. "I want to tell you that a chapel is to be built here in my honor," she said. "I am the Lady of the Rosary. Continue always to pray the Rosary every day. The war is going to end, and the soldiers will soon return to their homes."[160]

Mary's requested chapel was built, and it is now the Sanctuary of Our Lady of Fátima, which attracts 4 to 6 million visitors a year. It's important to note that Mary always asks for a chapel for her Son Jesus. He will be there in the Blessed Sacrament, available to the faithful pilgrims!

I was blessed to lead a pilgrimage to Fátima during the centennial year (2017) and was deeply moved to visit the place where Our Lady appeared to the shepherd children and also very moved to venerate the visionaries' burial places.

Mary's Immaculate Heart

Sister Lucia would later recall in her memoirs that "God began the work of our redemption in the Heart of Mary, given that it was through her 'fiat' that the redemption began to come about."[161] Let's permit these profound words to sink into our hearts.

Regarding Our Lady's request for the world to be consecrated to her Immaculate Heart, yes, the world was consecrated as Our Lady requested. According to the World Apostolate of Fátima USA, "Pope Pius XII consecrated the whole world to Mary's Immaculate Heart in 1942 and carried out a similar consecration of Russia in 1952, but neither of these fulfilled Mary's request at Fátima. This collegial consecration, in union with a 'moral totality' of the world's bishops, was finally carried out by St. John Paul II on March 25, 1984."[162]

The youngest visionaries, Francisco and Jacinta, are now canonized saints because of their lives of heroic virtues. It's important to recognize that people don't get canonized because they have seen the Blessed Mother, Jesus, or any other holy apparition. It's because of their lives of heroic virtue.

Francisco and Jacinta's feast day is February 20. Sister Lucia, who lived to almost 98 years, labored her entire life to spreading the Immaculate Heart of Mary devotion and the messages of Our Lady of Fátima. Lucia's cause for canonization is well under way. Since she lived a long life, it will take some time for all the information of her life to be studied and scrutinized before she can be declared a saint. I have no doubt it will happen eventually.

Our Response to Our Lady of Fátima

Pope Benedict XVI gave us a way to respond to the message of Our Lady of Fátima. He said, "To be an 'apostle' of Our Lady: LEARN the message of Fátima, LIVE the message of Fátima, and SPREAD the message of Fátima."[163]

My friend, Fr. Andrew Apostoli, CFR, of happy memory wrote, "We see how dangerous the world situation is in terms of potential violence: war, even nuclear war; terrorism; the loss of respect for human life from conception to natural death. At the same time, how many people have abandoned any faith in God."

Now, about eight years after Fr. Andrew's statement, we see that the world is still going in the wrong direction.

He added, "Our Lady said to three shepherd children, Lucia, Francisco, and Jacinta: 'Many souls are lost from God because there is no one to pray and offer sacrifices for their conversion.' We must all respond to Our Lady's request if there is to be world peace."[164]

Yes, indeed, Our Lady calls to us to pray for the salvation of souls. She asks us to "stay a little longer" to visit with her and prayerfully make reparation for sins committed. Our Lady's words, "my Immaculate Heart will triumph," bring great hope to our hearts. We can all embrace Our Lady of Fátima's call to prayer, penance, and conversion to bring about peace in the world.

Special Favors from Mary

I'd like to share a couple of personal experiences if I may. I hinted at an experience earlier in the book. One time I was visiting a parish in Louisiana to give several talks on Our Lady of Fátima. I flew in from Connecticut the day prior and had a terrible experience after dinner that evening. I had an allergic reaction to shellfish which had slipped into my dinner by mistake at a restaurant. The situation caused much suffering, which meant no sleep at all. However, I prayed fervently through the night.

So, when it came time to be at the parish church bright and early in the morning, I managed to make it there. I sat in the front pew by myself, praying, waiting to begin, wondering how I'd do it all, and looking lovingly upon a large statue of Our Lady of Fátima before me. The church was full behind me and the pastor suddenly came over to me on the side of my pew and bent down to quietly and quickly welcome me before he would introduce me to everyone before I would begin.

Fully aware that I would be giving five talks that day, and because I was feeling greatly depleted and under a very dark heavy cloud, I quickly seized the opportunity to whisper a plea in his ear.

"Please pray for me, I didn't get any sleep last night."

His answer was immediate: "It's the devil!"

"I know!" I said in a loud whisper. "That's why I need your prayers!"

Just then, he put his strong hand firmly down on my right shoulder. Poof! The darkness lifted immediately! Just then, Our Lady of Fátima smiled at me from her statue! I'll never forget it. In addition, I believe that Mary granted abundant powerful graces all day long to sustain me.

I dare share just one more special favor from Mother Mary. It was when the COVID-19 worldwide pandemic had begun in our country and my husband and I came down with the dreaded illness shortly after it hit. It was a scary time because little was known about curing it and people seemed to be dying left and right. My husband was especially doing poorly. I had to be on the phone with the doctor that late afternoon. It was a very dark cloudy day. I guess it kind of matched our predicament. Feverish myself, I took the phone to our bedroom so as not to disturb my feverish husband, who was resting on the couch. The bedroom was dark.

The doctor confirmed our positive COVID diagnoses over the phone. However, amid the terrifying uncertainty of it all, I could suddenly feel as if hope jumped right into my heart. It was a huge dose of holy hope which filled my heart with profound peace!

I'll try to explain. As we were talking, the sun, which had not shown its face all day, suddenly, without warning, burst through like a torpedo from behind the thick wall of clouds, to explode its surprising and brilliant rays through my bedroom window to reveal a beautiful detailed image of Our Lady of Fátima on the wall!

You see, when the sun pierced through the window, it displayed on to the wall, a distinct crisp shadow of my tall statue of Our Lady of Fátima. It looked exactly as if it had been painted there. The detail was extraordinary. Mother Mary seemed to come alive for a couple of minutes. I wholeheartedly felt her telling me that it would be okay. *Everything* would be okay. She would be with us. There would be suffering, but we should not be afraid. She would be with us, and she would get us through.

We should not fear.

I found myself praying constantly throughout my illness (which lingered a very long time) a prayer that Our Lady of Fátima taught the shepherd children: "O Jesus, it is for love of You, for the conversion of sinners and in reparation for the sins committed against the Immaculate Heart of Mary."

You certainly don't need to believe my stories above. I share them candidly as one friend to another. You probably know by now that I've been known to wear my heart on my sleeve. Even so, I hardly ever share such personal spiritual experiences publicly. Most of it, I feel is best kept between my Lord and me. However, I was very much reminded of these happenings as I wrote this book for you. My sincere desire is that reading them will bring hope to your heart. Our beautiful Heavenly Mother loves us very much.

Let's take time to learn, live, and spread the message of Our Lady of Fátima.

Let's stay close to Mary, who always leads us to her Son Jesus! Turn your gaze to Mary. Pray to her often. Be attentive to her calls to your heart. Let's stay longer with her.

ACT

Consider doing the Five First Saturdays devotion if you haven't already. Don't stop at five. Try to continue it — endlessly. Make Mother Mary happy!

If you have not already made a consecration to Jesus through Mary, now is a good time. It's a beautiful and loving act and a way of life, turning to our true Mother, who was gifted to us by her Son Jesus Christ as He was hanging from the Cross for our salvation. You can use a 33-day preparation to do so,[165] or some other way. Consecrations can be made more than once, and it is a good idea to renew your consecration daily with even a simple short prayer. You'll see consecration prayers and information on the Five First Saturdays Devotion in the Appendix of this book.

There's much more to learn about Our Lady of Fátima, her apparitions, and her messages. I encourage you to do your own research, being sure to use Church-approved sources. I recommend sources from the World Apostolate of Fátima, USA. Most importantly, take time to turn to Mother Mary, to stay awhile with her, and ask her for guidance, help and protection.

In addition, I encourage you to take time to meditate on the pure faith of the three shepherd children, who dedicated their lives to saving souls. Pray to be more childlike in your faith, as well as more loving and generous with your prayers and sacrifices for others. Wholeheartedly, trust Jesus with your life.

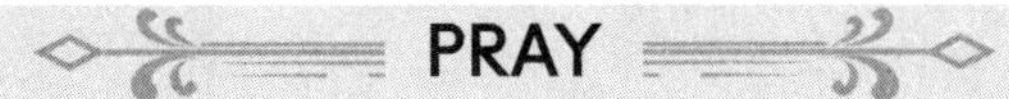

PRAY

Dear Holy Family, Jesus, Mary, and Joseph,
please bless me and pray for me.
Dear St. Jacinta, St. Francisco, and Servant of God Sr. Lucia,
please pray for me.
Dear Holy Mary, Our Lady of Fátima, Mother of the Redeemer,
Mother of Mercy and of hope, thank you for being my Mother.
Gate of Heaven, strengthen my virtues of faith, hope, and love.
Seat of Wisdom, please grant me your graces.
Mirror of Perfection, mold my heart and teach me to believe,
to hope, and to love right along with you.
Mary, my Mother, I need your help.
Please perfect my simple prayers. Please guide my steps today
and always closer to your Son Jesus.
Star of Hope, Star of the Sea, please shine upon me
and guide me ever closer to your Son's Kingdom!
Amen.

O my Jesus, forgive us our sins, save us from the fires of hell. Lead all souls to Heaven, especially those in most need of thy mercy.

Recite the Our Father, Hail Mary, Glory Be,
Hail Holy Queen, Memorare *(pages 201-202).*

Pray any of the Fátima prayers (pages 225-227).

SAVOR

A prayer, a thought, a resolution:

____

____

____

____

____

____

____

I took this photo of St. Finbarr's Church on the island of Gougane Barra in County Cork, Ireland.

AFTERWORD:
My Pilgrimage of Hope

Christian hope endures even during the darkest of times. Holy hope can come out of tragedy.

I began my own "Pilgrimage of Hope" a bit early. You see, my brother Gene passed away suddenly and unexpectedly. I was not allowed the chance to say goodbye.

What can I say about Gene, a beloved brother to seven siblings and a husband and father of three children? He was a beautiful, caring soul in love with God and his neighbor. He lived in Europe most of his life, spoke eight languages fluently, was a university professor of theology and an author. He played the violin like a maestro in many concert halls and even in the Swiss Alps. He skied all over Europe, loved golf, and, for a time, worked for the Von Trapp family in Stowe, Vermont.

We were very close — he, being the second child, and me, the seventh out of eight. Despite the age difference and the ocean between us, we shared the same deep Catholic Faith and understood one another. Not only that, Gene had always been a steady rock for me — a wonderful and saintly big brother.

During the writing of this book, I set out on a voyage to Ireland to attend his funeral and be present as my dear brother's body was put to rest. My pilgrimage with Mary, our life, our sweetness, and our hope, was not without a few jarring splinters from the Cross. However, I won't belabor you with those details — the very ones which pierced my already aching heart, an unexpected hurtful blow beforehand, with more to follow upon reaching the Emerald Isle.

As it would turn out, by God's amazing Providence, I would find myself on a pilgrimage to the Knock Shrine before arriving at my brother's funeral. I truly believe that Mother Mary kept me company throughout the pilgrimage. In fact, Mary has been taking me on a pilgrimage throughout my life.

Mother Mary in a Myriad Details

My mother named me after Mother Mary, hence my first name: "Donna-Marie" (Lady Mary). She suggested I take Anne for my Confirmation name in honor of Mary's mother. I was baptized at a St. Mary's Church. I made all my Sacraments, including Matrimony, at another St. Mary's Church. Mary seemed to be following me all over!

Looking back, I realize that Mary took me by the hand to lead me to the Our Lady of Częstochowa Shrine in Pennsylvania, where she gifted me with profound peace. My Mother Mary brought me to Fátima, Portugal, and Poland, where she helped me encounter dear St. Jacinta, St. Francisco, and Venerable Sr. Lucia — as well as St. Faustina in a more profound way, as a sister on my Pilgrimage of Hope towards Heaven. Mary was with me when I venerated her holy image of the Black Madonna in the Chapel of the Virgin Mary in the Pauline monastery of Jasna Gora in Częstochowa, Poland. Mary certainly brought me closer to St. John Paul II (whom I had seen a few times during his audiences and trips) while in Poland. She brought me to the Knock Shrine and to the Lourdes Grotto in France.

As the years of my life rolled along, in so many places and within an extraordinary myriad of details, Mary showed me she was there. At times, I didn't fully notice it or even understand. In other instances, my heart was pierced in the sure knowledge that Mary was lovingly interceding for me, protecting me, and drawing me closer to her beloved Son. One time in particular, a mysterious Rosary showed up unexpectedly at a time when I was in captivity (which I tell about in my memoir, *The Kiss of Jesus*). This caused a thunderous ray of hope to penetrate my heart.

Another time in my life, Mother Mary was with me when I received the troubling news (twice!) that my 16-week-old unborn baby had died. I experienced tremendous sorrow. I wrote "twice" regarding receiving the shocking news, because I didn't believe it when I was told the first time. The following day, after a night of painful hemorrhaging, a second ultrasound was necessary to confirm this reality for me. I had to be absolutely sure because surgery was needed. In my case, urgently needed. However, if my baby was alive, I wouldn't go through with the surgery. My very caring Christian doctor shed a few tears as he confirmed the sad decisive news. I was immediately wheeled into emergency surgery since I was losing far too much blood.

No doubt, Mother Mary was still with me when I was feeling pretty bewildered upon coming out of the anesthesia after surgery and saw two intravenous lines (one in each arm), rather than the one I had started off with prior to my surgery. Blood plasma was dripping slowly into one of my arms, and the nurse came in the room to check on me. She said I wouldn't be going home for a while. *Huh?* I was perplexed. She told me I had lost way too much blood. I was supposed to go home to my family right after the procedure. Be that as it may, I almost died on the operating table due to a severe hemorrhage that occurred as soon as I went under the anesthesia. My blood pressure had plummeted to just about nothing. My doctor later told me that if I had been any place other than that operating table, there would have been absolutely no hope of saving my life. Even so, the medical team had to hasten with great measures, including intubation in order to save my life. *Wow.* I could hardly comprehend it.

I talked my doctor (practically twisted his arm) into allowing me to go home after my blood transfusion was complete. I didn't want my small children to worry. As long as I promised to stay in bed for a couple of weeks, he would let me go. So, there I was, at home in bed, the day after the surgery trying to take in all that he had explained to me over the phone. It wasn't until then that I learned that I had been rescued from the brink of death.

Reflecting on my sorrowful experience in losing my beloved unborn baby, I realized that Mother Mary was surely with me. She certainly consoled me in my deep sorrow, and I believe she even made sure I didn't die. There was work to be done, after all. In the meanwhile, there would be plenty of time to pray many prayers of thanksgiving to Mama Mary while I recuperated.

In God's Divine Providence, I would come to know saints in my life who all had a special devotion to Mary. As I mentioned earlier, one would be Mother Teresa, who would become a special mother, teacher, and spiritual guide to me. Father John Hardon, SJ, another saintly friend, was very close to the Mother of God, especially after she performed that Miraculous Medal miracle to his great surprise and right under his very skeptical nose! Incidentally, Fr. Hardon had a succinct catchphrase: "There's work to be done!" He would say so often. And you knew he was talking about you! And Fr. Andrew Apostoli, CFR, who dearly loved Mary and was a world leading Fátima expert, would give me the most amazing blessings. In person or over the phone, Fr. Andrew would invoke Mother Mary to place her protective mantle over me. I felt it! Every time! It was always a powerful blessing.

I might add here, dear Reader, that you shouldn't hesitate to ask for blessings and prayers from a holy priest.

Mother Mary Escorted Me Back to Knock

Now, this unexpected Marian pilgrimage would unfold in my life. Without any planning on my part, Mother Mary escorted me to the Knock Shrine on my journey to my brother's funeral. Since I would be in Ireland, it made complete sense for me to go back to Knock to pray for graces while there.

In addition, amazingly, with absolutely no advance planning, I arrived in Ireland along with some of my family right on my brother's birthday. It hadn't dawned on me until a couple of days before boarding the flight that I would be setting foot on that *little bit of Heaven* (as Ireland is often called) on such a special occasion, in light of the fact that the entire purpose of the trip was for Gene.

After checking into our hotel, though quite exhausted, I decided to take a little walk because the church with the huge steeple down the street was calling my name. I wanted to give thanks to Jesus in person for a safe trip. Jesus, Who was there waiting in the tabernacle. I also wanted to light a candle for my brother Gene on his birthday. I knew that doing so would bring a certain peace to my heart. I also knew I needed to make the effort to get there since it would have been much easier to lie down and take a nap.

A very tall and exceedingly old statue of Mary greeted me outside the church. I paused to say hello. Once inside, I observed a plaque with an inscription explaining that the church was built in 1858 and had been destroyed by storms twice and rebuilt. After lighting two candles — one for Gene and one for the family — I knelt before a statue of Mary who was holding Baby Jesus, and I began the Rosary. My husband Dave joined me. It was a very moving Rosary, with many quiet tears shed as I knelt on weary knees. These were grateful tears and grieving tears. Though I was beyond exhausted, I was so very grateful to God to be there in a Catholic Church to pray in thanksgiving for getting there safely and for dear Gene's soul. It was the most perfect way to start this Irish Marian Pilgrimage of Hope.

Just then, one of my daughters (named after Mother Mary!) quietly walked into the church as we were praying. She lit a candle and knelt down before the statue of Mother Mary. My heart was singing. The theme of Mary leading me through life was so fresh on my heart. Another part of it was unfolding before my eyes at that moment. This adult daughter was the one who had resided in my womb amid much uncertainty about our survival, when dear Mother Teresa gave me the words, "Mary, Mother of Jesus, be Mother to me now." Mother Mary surely saw us both through that precarious pregnancy when I was on complete bedrest.

Certainly, on this unexpected early Pilgrimage of Hope, Mary would reveal special things to me, bring me to grateful tears, and impart peace and hope to my heart all along the way. I'll share snippets of some of the experiences.

Gene's Voyage

Just a few years before his passing on to Eternal Life, I sent a special photo to Gene. I had come across it in a worn cardboard box of old photos, and I just knew that my brother would want to have it. It was an old photograph of Gene standing with our mother and father and two of our brothers, Tim and Gary. They were on board the *Queen Elizabeth I* before it was to set sail to bring Gene to Louvain, Belgium, to continue his studies in theology. My parents and two of my brothers were there to send him off on his *bon voyage*.

Gene absolutely loved receiving the photo from me. That time on the ship seemed like a lifetime ago. He told me in a message, "Brilliant, Donna! This photo is now in my photo album, and I can send it to our children. Thanks a million!"

After Gene's passing, regarding the striking photograph, his son Brian remarked to me, "It was the voyage that made our lives possible." You see, Gene met his beloved wife in Europe.

Wow! My nephew's statement pierced my heart. It was absolutely true and amazing to think about all these years later — about God's Providence, our decisions, and how life turns out.

Knock, Once Again

The second day in Ireland was a Sunday. Our Sunday Mass would be celebrated at the Knock Shrine. Imagine that! I was still extremely tired due to not having gotten much sleep (at all!), but very grateful to travel to Knock. What a blessing!

The rain was lashing down, though. *Too bad.* I had hoped for a good weather day while in Knock. Yet, the weather brought to mind the rainy evening when Our Lady of Knock appeared in front of the church gable to the 15 eyewitnesses on August 21, 1879. (Incidentally, when I wrote the earlier chapter on Knock for this book, I had no idea that I would pilgrimage there once again and so soon after penning that chapter.)

My husband and I walked through the gates and into the grounds of the Shrine. I immediately spotted the figures of the Lamb, the Cross, Mary, St. Joseph, St. John, and the angels — all as white as snow. I drew near them in the stunning Apparition Chapel and found a place to kneel and pray, first, in thanksgiving for being there, and then for all the needs I had, especially for the repose of my brother's soul. Being there just about took my breath away.

The sun suddenly came out in all its glory as the clouds moved out of sight. It was as if holy angels had pushed them away to allow the sun's vibrant rays to shower down on Mary's pilgrims. The sky was a glorious heavenly blue in that holy place. We checked out the bookstore, and I was delighted to see that they carried my books. Then, we were off to the Basilica ahead of Mass to have a time of prayer.

We were blessed to be there in time for a beautiful Anointing of the Sick service available to the faithful. Both Dave and I took part. We would end up receiving three Sacraments that day: the Anointing, Holy Communion at Mass, and Confession afterwards. The Mass was followed up by a very beautiful time of Adoration and a Eucharistic procession around the inside of the Basilica. The Blessed Sacrament in the Monstrance was absolutely huge.

I was moved to tears as Jesus, hidden in the Blessed Sacrament, came around the church, stopping at various places to give Benediction to the faithful. We both wiped away the tears from our faces. I felt deeply blessed by the Lord. I even imagined Jesus there just as He was when He walked the earth. There He was, walking around the church and blessing everyone — healing everyone's wounds, especially their wounded hearts — pouring out His unfathomable Divine Mercy and love. I took it all in. It was truly an amazing experience.

Confession followed. Though we had made a point to receive the Sacrament of Penance before embarking on the trip, we didn't want to miss out on the opportunity for additional grace.

After a while, it would be time to leave the Shrine and get back to the place we were staying. I said my goodbyes to Jesus and Mary, sorry to leave, but knowing there was more we needed to do. We had to move on. Before doing so, I filled some bottles with Knock Holy Water.

The next day, as we traversed wildly around the tightest corners on the skinniest roads I had ever seen, nearly missing high scratchy hedges and jagged stone walls which tightly gripped the routes, I stopped short in awe. No, I did not stop the car. I was not the driver, after all. It was my mind stopping short. Completely. My heart and my soul were in a sort of sudden holy jubilation, realizing something of profound significance. That is, that the Holy Family of Nazareth appeared in Knock on the night the devout Archdeacon Cavanaugh had finished his 100 Masses for the dead. It really hit me in that moment. Yes, indeed, it was the Holy Family. The Lamb, Mary, and St. Joseph (in the company of St. John the Evangelist). Moreover, you might recall, I began this book with placing the Holy Family right there at the very beginning to guide you on this Pilgrimage of Hope.

Saint Brigid

I knew of St. Brigid before this pilgrimage and have an image of one of her iconic woven crosses in my home. She is one of the three beloved Patron Saints of Ireland, alongside Sts. Patrick and Columba. Saint Brigid was inspired by St. Patrick's teachings and became a Christian like her mother. She had a sure heart for the poor. In time she built several monasteries and founded a school of art.

The story of her unique cross goes that she was at the bedside of an elderly pagan chieftain who was on his deathbed. She had been called by his servants to calm him. She spoke to him with great love and began picking up some rushes (commonly found in homes to keep the floors warm) from the floor of his room. Saint Brigid wove the rushes into the shape of a cross to tell the man about the life of Jesus. She explained the Cross of Christ and His loving Paschal mystery, which caused the old pagan to be overcome with emotion. He suddenly thrust his hand over his heart and was converted by grace and baptized right before he died.

My daughters became interested in St. Brigid and I bought them replicas of her cross while in Ireland. They even made their own crosses from rushes they found in fields. We continually saw versions of the beautiful Cross of St. Brigid all over Ireland. I loved seeing them displayed in shop and restaurant windows. Not for sale, but as a display of Faith.

Saint Brigid's life and holiness caused conversions. She is beloved all over the world, not simply in Ireland. She has been venerated for centuries in the Eastern Orthodox Church too!

I began to pray for her intercession every day we were in Ireland (I've included some of the prayers on page 240). After all, she was so devoted to the Mother of God that she is known as "Mary of the Gael" by the Irish.

Gougane Barra

I was just 13 years old when I traveled to Ireland the first time. I have emotive memories from that visit of seeing little humble makeshift Marian Shrines — from rustic to elaborate at the ends of almost every street or in people's yards. These affectionate commemorations to Mary spoke volumes to my heart, and no doubt, to passersby. At that time, I traveled there with my mother and older sister for Gene's wedding. He and his bride were married by their dear priest friend in St. Finbarr's, a most stunning little stone church on a small island in Gougane Barra. The nearly hidden sacred place is surrounded by mountains. The sheer beauty of the surroundings almost takes your breath away.

As a way to honor my brother Gene, I made a point to visit the church again, all these years later. What a sight! Truly a peaceful place. The church holds a lot of history. It dates back to the sixth century. According to Cardinal Timothy Manning, "The surrounding mountains were his [St. Finbarr's] cloister and the lake was for him the mirror of God's grandeur; stone cells commemorate his hermitage. From here he journeyed the river-way of the Lee to become the first bishop and founder of the church and city of Cork."[166] I took my time while there, in awe at being in that sacred place once again, after more than 50 years. It truly is mind-boggling how the years fly by.

I prayed inside the church and explored outside. I found a small heart-shaped rock outside the church, put it into my pocket, and brought it back home with me to America. I also snapped some lovely photos of the outside of the church, which captured the vivid reflection of the church on the water. It was difficult for me to leave that holy place, but it was only a part of the special journey. I had to move along.

My Brother's Funeral

We finally arrived in the little town where my brother had his cottage and where I would, in a few days, say goodbye to Gene. We got situated in our place. At my first chance, my husband and I set out to find the little village church which I had visited more than 30 years ago, during my last visit to Ireland. After arriving, I quickly got out of the car and hurriedly walked to the gate, leaving Dave many steps behind me. I couldn't wait to get inside to the church grounds.

I felt as if Mary greeted me. An extremely tall, vivid blue statue of Mary was standing just outside the church gracing the lawn. Her back was against the green Irish hills and the pastures walled with stone, which were dotted with farm animals in the distance. What a sight. I could barely take it in. That vision of Mary against the lush Irish farmlands spoke volumes to my grateful heart. I paused there to greet and thank her. I prayed the Rosary, asking help from Mary for our time in the village and for the funeral.

The day arrived for my brother's funeral Mass and for his body to be put to rest. I had asked Mother Mary to give me strength and help me through Gene's funeral. I was asked to be one of the readers at Mass. Thankfully, I was able to deliver the reading without tears.

Earlier, I had gently prepared with my grandsons before the funeral. I wanted them to know that his burial was not the end. There is the great blessing, gift, and reward of Eternal Life. I had told them, even when we know this to be true, many times, we still cry after we lose our loved one or when we say farewell to our loved one at a funeral. We miss them even as we trust God.

At the end of the funeral Mass, when it was time for the family to process out of the church following my brother Gene, my oldest grandson (just 9 years old), without warning, came quietly running to my side. Without a fuss, he simply slipped right in front of my husband and took his place beside me. My heart was lifted and profoundly touched. What a sweet child he was, sensing I would want him close to me and that his little heart could comfort mine. We processed down the aisle with my arm around his shoulder. There were some quiet tears. I tried to hold them back as much as I could. And then, "How Great Thou Art" resounded from somewhere in the heart of the church. It was as if the Heavens opened wide. Unexpectedly, my heart let out a sudden deep and audible yet ephemeral cry, coming from the depths of my being. I was surprised by that emotion. That little cry of anguish escaped from my heart. But I deeply knew — my big brother Gene was going to be put to rest. Oh my goodness. Thank God for the gift of faith, hope, and love and Eternal Life!

What would we do without our faith and the sublime gift of hope? What exalted gifts!

I was told later that "How Great Thou Art" was one of my brother's very favorite hymns. Mine too. I'll never be the same whenever I hear it again.

Our Lady of Knock, St. Finbarr, St. Patrick, and St. Brigid, please pray for us.

A Special Spiritual Journey

I have thought of you and prayed for you as I wrote this book. I pray that this book is a great source of hope for you. It was a blessing for me to write this book in the month of May, which is Mary's month!

Writing this book was also a special spiritual journey for me as I meditated upon our wonderful, loving Mother Mary and all of the other Pilgrims of Hope we met along the way. In addition, I have shared many very personal experiences from my own life which I did not plan to share before setting out to write this book. Yet, I felt compelled to do so — actually going back and adding to what I had already written. Perhaps, my sharing will make this book even a bit more *bona fide.*

Surely, you must have noticed my mention of traversing the winding, crazy, narrow roads in rural Ireland. Well, as we near the ending of this Pilgrimage of Hope with Mary, I would like to share that I think life is like a winding, and at times precarious and unpredictable, narrow road. Our pilgrimage towards Heaven is not without many unexpected twists and turns, blinding and turbulent weather, and major malfunctions in our mode of transportation.

So, what do we need to stay safely on the right route? A map? Yes! A spiritual road map to life! What is it exactly? Well, I think that our essential spiritual road map in life is comprised of the two greatest Commandments. Simply put, to love God with all our heart, soul, and mind, and our neighbor as ourself (see Mt 22:34–40). If we can only get those two things right, well, we would be on our way to Heaven, to Paradise! Correct? Sounds fairly simple when we think of it this way. Our ticket to Heaven is following these Commandments!

That said, I'm afraid we might get stuck on the second one — the loving our neighbor part. That is precisely because among the good-natured characters, God often puts the persnickety and difficult personalities into our lives too. He wants us to love them with His love, to pray for them, to guide them to Heaven. It's not always easy to do so through the contradictions and, perhaps, pain and suffering too. Trust me. I am not saying that we need to invite everyone to our home for dinner! Yet, we do need to take notice of these people in our lives, and rather than get put out and annoyed, we need to pray for them and set a good example, reaching out to them when appropriate.

As a quick note of hope here, St. Faustina told Jesus towards the end of her life that she could finally love others with His Divine love. It's a process. Day by day, we get better at it with God's grace. But we have to keep it going — not give in to discouragement and the tricks of the devil, who tries to instill fear into our hearts. Mother Mary will protect us, but we need to stay close to her and ask her for help.

Jesus told St. Faustina that He demands works of mercy. He used the word "demand." It's not a suggestion or mere recommendation. It is required. Specifically, Jesus told His Secretary of Mercy:

> **I demand from you deeds of mercy, which are to arise out of love for Me. You are to show mercy to your neighbors always and everywhere. You must not shrink from this or try to excuse or absolve yourself from it.**
>
> **I am giving you three ways of exercising mercy toward your neighbor: the first – by deed, the second – by word, the third – by prayer. In these three degrees is contained the fullness of mercy, and it is an unquestionable proof of love for me. By this means a soul glorifies and pays reverence to My mercy.**[167]

These deeds of mercy, performed with our loving care — whether by deed, word, or prayer — will help our own souls and the souls of the people we are serving. Precisely within the intricate details of these human encounters is where the rubber meets the road. In other words, it is in our very responses to the contradictions and annoyances of life, along with the joyful moments too, (let's not forget about the joy!) where we indeed come face-to-face with the choices to move our will to do good, or kick it to the curb (or under the bus!), completely neglecting the need (a.k.a. the opportunity!) which God has provided for us to ascend the ladder of perfection. That said, perhaps we are hoping for an elevator like St. Thérèse! Nonetheless, Mother Mary provides the graces we need to move our wills to choose the good. Whether a ladder, an elevator, or bumpy, scary road, we must ask her to help us persevere all the way to Heaven.

In addition, we must remember that faith without works is dead (see James 2:14–17). We must love our neighbor and help him or her get to Heaven — all along the winding path — this holy pilgrimage through life.

So, my dear Reader, to traverse the mysterious road of life, we must take serious note of Jesus' instructions. At times, it means that we need to take our eyes off our devices and cellphones to interact with the very people whom God has placed into our lives. After all, it is within the nitty gritty details of our daily life where we indeed work out our salvation. And this, dear Reader, is how we can strive to prayerfully follow the two greatest Commandments. Thanks be to God for the most eminent gift of Mother Mary, who will guide us every step of the way.

I want to share something that I feel will be beneficial for your spiritual journey, which Mother Teresa shared with me. Mother's letters were filled with beautiful spiritual direction. She always encouraged me to pray the Rosary and to stay close to Mama Mary, who will always lead me closer to Jesus. I quoted from one of her letters in the Preface, and I'll add here another amazing nugget of wisdom from that same letter because I really think it will be helpful. She wrote, "Christ calls us to be one with Him in love through unconditional surrender to His plan for us. Let us allow Jesus to use us without consulting us by taking what He gives and giving what He takes."[168] Her powerful words will greatly aid us, and Mother Mary will grant the graces for us to surrender our lives to God's holy will. Let's ask her.

You know, there's so much we can learn from Mother Mary, who always leads us to her Son Jesus. In this volume, I have provided a mere sampling of her wonders, marvels, miracles, mysteries, and great love — all leading to a great big dose of hope for our hearts. However, I must mention that we must do our part too — not simply accept the great gift of hope, but also pray deeply and lead good and holy lives. By doing so, we can be a great light of hope for others who are struggling.

I encourage you to do your own research on Mary's titles and Church-approved apparitions. You might very well discover fascinating facts which will stir your heart to a greater mission of prayer. Most of all, I hope and pray that you remain close to Mary's Immaculate Heart. She will most definitely lead you closer to her Son Jesus' Sacred Heart. Take her into your life, your home, and your family.

Before I go on, discussing the road ahead in our lives, I am excited to share something incredible with you.

Remember Marie? I mentioned her earlier in the book. She had "serendipitously" met me in a hair salon. Well, just before this book was to go out to be printed, on a beautiful Marian feast day, at my encouragement, Marie met with a Catholic priest. He was very welcoming and made her feel very comfortable in sharing what was on her heart — all that was troubling her. Afterwards, he invited her to go to Confession, which she happily embraced. This beautiful Sacrament ushered her back into the Catholic Church! I am not surprised. Simply, I am deeply grateful! To the point of tears. May God be praised!

Thank you, Mother Mary, for your grace and unspeakable intercession — working it all out! I have no doubt that Mary interceded and offered great hope to Marie, as well as granted graces to her through her Miraculous Medal — the medal she designed herself!

The Road Ahead

If we had our druthers, would we choose an unpredictable road? What about taking the straight route — nice and straight — all the way to Heaven? After all, I have always heard that the shortest distance between two points is a straight line.

Here's the thing. While that might seem to make sense, and possibly be less scary, would we get to Heaven?

Life doesn't unfold in such a neat and tidy way. We might be called to take the "scenic" route! I did! So far, anyway. God knows exactly what we need and what is absolutely best for each of us. And He also brings much good out of the bad stuff that happens in our lives.

Remember too, even though the road ahead might appear to be pretty scary at times, or downright unpredictable, still, we can absolutely count on the sure HOPE in Jesus' promises to us. We can!

I have earlier referred to our path ahead as mysterious. And it is to some extent. Nonetheless, it is not entirely mysterious because we are indeed assured that Jesus has prepared a place for us! He tells us, "Do not let your hearts be troubled." There is no need to fear the mysterious road. Jesus assures us that He will come for us (see John 14:1–3). Our Mother Mary told us that she will crush the head of the serpent and that her Immaculate Heart will triumph! Hope, hope, hope! Immense hope for our hearts!

Mary always brings hope. She also delivers warnings for our safety and our salvation, and as a means to overcome difficulties and calamities. She assures us that her Son is the answer to all of our perplexing problems and for our very salvation.

We must remember, though, that Mary was not all smiles when she appeared in her apparitions. Most times, she was very serious or sad. Yes, she truly brings great hope, even within her warnings for us. Let us be attentive and step up to the plate to become whom we are called to be! Let us ask Mary to help us.

Please also remember, dear Reader, Mary is not our last resort — like a "Hail Mary pass"! One time, someone commented to me (after I suggested prayer as a solution to a problem) that prayer is a last resort — something to use when all else fails. When nothing else works, we can pray. She believed that.

But, no, my dear Reader, prayer is *not* a last resort. I'm confident that you already know this. Mary is *not* our last resort. Mary is our hope NOW! We need her now!

As St. John Paul II, a great witness to hope, reminded us over and over again, "Be not afraid." He also said, "No difficulty, no fear is so great that it can completely suffocate the hope that springs eternal in the hearts of the young. … Do not let that hope die! Stake your lives on it!"[169]

And as Pope Francis suggested, "Let us lift up our hearts to Christ and become *singers of hope*."[170]

One last thing. I would like to share with you is something that is very personal to me, which came from my dear spiritual mother, Mother Teresa. It was when she allayed my fears and sent me directly to Mother Mary. She said:

> Do not be afraid. Just put yourself in the Hands of our Blessed Mother and let her take care of you. When you are afraid or sad or troubled just tell her so. Pray often: "Mary, Mother of Jesus, make me alright"; Mary, Mother of Jesus, be Mother to me now. … She has done wonders for others and she will do so for you too. Just trust and pray.[171]

Do not be afraid! Jesus has told us endlessly throughout the Scriptures to be not afraid. The saints have reminded us. Over and over again. I'm telling you right now. Be not afraid! This is coming from your friend who was pretty much afraid of her own shadow as a young girl and as a young woman growing up in this wild world. Mary protects us from the tricks of the devil, who incessantly endeavors to plague our hearts with fear and discouragement.

Ask Mary for help. Give your fears to Mary, and she will allay them. Not only that, she'll show you how to face your fears with grace.

Mary is our HOPE! Stay close to her. Take her hand. Walk with her. She shows us the way!

> God is the foundation of hope: not any god, but the God who has a human face and who has loved us to the end, each one of us and humanity in its entirety. His Kingdom is not an imaginary hereafter, situated in a future that will never arrive; his Kingdom is present wherever he is loved and wherever his love reaches us. His love alone gives us the possibility of soberly persevering day by day, without ceasing to be spurred on by hope, in a world which by its very nature is imperfect. His love is at the same time our guarantee of the existence of what we only vaguely sense and which nevertheless, in our deepest self, we await: a life that is "truly" life.[172]

— Pope Benedict XVI

ONLINE RESOURCES

OUR LADY OF THE MIRACULOUS MEDAL:
www.chapellenotredamedelamedaillemiraculeuse.com
USA: www.miraculousmedal.org

OUR LADY OF GUADALUPE: www.virgendeguadalupe.org.mx
USA: www.guadalupeshrine.org

OUR LADY OF LOURDES: www.lourdes-france.org
USA: www.nsgrotto.org

OUR LADY OF KIBEHO: www.kibeho-cana.org
USA: www.immaculee.com

OUR LADY OF CZĘSTOCHOWA: https://en.jasnagora.pl
USA: www.czestochowa.us

OUR LADY OF KNOCK: www.knockshrine.ie

OUR LADY OF CHAMPION: www.championshrine.org

OUR LADY OF FATIMA: www.fatima.pt/en
USA: www.bluearmyshrine.com

SAINT MOTHER TERESA: www.motherteresa.org
www.missionariesofcharity.org

CARDINAL NGUYỄN VĂN THUẬN: www.nguyenvanthuan.com

SAINT THÉRÈSE OF LISIEUX: www.littleflower.org

SAINT FAUSTINA AND DIVINE MERCY:
www.TheDivineMercy.org

MICHAEL O'NEILL'S "THE MIRACLE HUNTER":
www.miraclehunter.com

MARIAN APPARITION TALKS BY FR. CHRIS ALAR, MIC:
www.DivineMercyPlus.org/tags/explaining-faith

NEW VATICAN DOCUMENT ON APPARITIONS, "Norms for Proceeding in the Discernment of Alleged Supernatural Phenomena," Dicastery for the Doctrine of the Faith, May 17, 2024: www.vatican.va/roman_curia/congregations/cfaith/documents/rc_ddf_doc_20240517_norme-fenomeni-soprannaturali_en.html

APPENDIX OF PRAYERS

"Rejoice in hope, be patient in suffering,
persevere in prayer."

— Romans 12:12

Hail Holy Queen

Hail, Holy Queen, Mother of Mercy, our life, our sweetness, and our hope, to thee do we cry, poor banished children of Eve; to thee do we send up our sighs, mourning and weeping in this valley of tears; turn, then, most gracious Advocate, thine eyes of mercy towards us, and after this, our exile, show unto us the blessed fruit of thy womb, Jesus. O clement, O loving, O sweet Virgin Mary! Pray for us, O holy Mother of God, that we may be made worthy of the promises of Christ.

The Hail, Holy Queen (*Salve Regina*) has been a most beloved prayer and hymn of devotion to Mary for the past 900 years. The prayer expresses our faith in the Mother of God who imparts her love and mercy to us. It is the traditional concluding prayer to the Liturgy of Hours, the end of the Rosary, as well as a traditional hymn to be sung at the end of the day.

Tradition holds that on his voyage in 1492 to the New World, Christopher Columbus called his men together every evening to sing the *Salve Regina,* seeking and believing in the Blessed Mother's protection. An old tradition tells us that St. Bernard of Clairvaux (1090-1153) composed this prayer. The saint's deep devotion to Mary is seen within his writings, but some historical scholars say that the prayer was actually written by a German monk, Blessed Herman the Lame (1013-1054), also known as Herman Contractus (the Latin form). The current form of this prayer is said to have come from the 12th century Abbey of Cluny. Over the centuries, countless saints have embraced and promoted it.

Whatever the precise origin may be, this beautiful prayer and hymn is customarily recited in the evening before bed and is observed from the conclusion of the Eastertide season until Advent begins. It is a most wondrous prayer in honor of Mary, our Hope, to be prayed at any time.

Memorare

Remember, O most compassionate Virgin Mary, that never was it known that anyone who fled to your protection, implored your assistance, or sought your intercession, was left unaided. Inspired with this confidence, we fly unto you, O Virgin of Virgins, our Mother; to you we come; before you we kneel, sinful and sorrowful. O Mother of the Word Incarnate, despise not our petitions, but, in your clemency, hear and answer them. Amen.

Consecration to the Immaculate Heart of Mary

Most Holy Virgin Mary, tender Mother of men, to fulfill the desires of the Sacred Heart of Jesus and the request of the Vicar of Your Son on earth, we consecrate ourselves and our families to your Sorrowful and Immaculate Heart, O Queen of the Most Holy Rosary, and we recommend to You, all the people of our country and all the world.

Please accept our consecration, dearest Mother, and use us as You wish to accomplish Your designs in the world.

O Sorrowful and Immaculate Heart of Mary, Queen of the Most Holy Rosary, and Queen of the World, rule over us, together with the Sacred Heart of Jesus Christ, Our King. Save us from the spreading flood of modern paganism; kindle in our hearts and homes the love of purity, the practice of a virtuous life, an ardent zeal for souls, and a desire to pray the Rosary more faithfully.

We come with confidence to You, O Throne of Grace and Mother of Fair Love. Inflame us with the same Divine Fire which has inflamed Your own Sorrowful and Immaculate Heart. Make our hearts and homes Your shrine, and through us, make the Heart of Jesus, together with your rule, triumph in every heart and home. Amen.

Saint Louis de Montfort's Consecration to Mary Prayer

I, _______________ , a faithless sinner, renew and ratify today in thy hands the vows of my Baptism; I renounce forever Satan, his pomps and works; and I give myself entirely to Jesus Christ, the Incarnate Wisdom, to carry my cross after Him all the days of my life, and to be more faithful to Him than I have ever been before.

In the presence of all the heavenly court I choose thee this day for my Mother and Mistress. I deliver and consecrate to thee, as thy slave, my body and soul, my goods, both interior and exterior, and even the value of all my good actions, past, present and future; leaving to thee the entire and full right of disposing of me, and all that belongs to me, without exception, according to thy good pleasure, for the greater glory of God in time and in eternity. Amen.

Solemn Act of Consecration

by St. Maximilian Kolbe

O Immaculate Queen of heaven and earth, Refuge of sinners and our most loving Mother, God has willed to entrust the entire order of mercy to You. I, an unworthy sinner, cast myself at Your feet, humbly imploring You to take me, with all that I am and have, wholly to Yourself as Your possession and property. Please make of me, of all my powers of soul and body, of my whole life, death, and eternity, whatever pleases You. If it pleases You, use all that I am and have without reserve, wholly to accomplish what has been said of You: "She will crush your head," and "You alone have destroyed all heresies in the whole world." Let me be a fit instrument in Your immaculate and most merciful hands for introducing and increasing Your glory to the maximum in all the many strayed and indifferent souls, and thus help extend as far as possible the blessed Kingdom of the Most Sacred Heart of Jesus. For, wherever You enter, You obtain the grace of conversion and sanctification, since it is through Your hands that all graces come to us from the Most Sacred Heart of Jesus.

V. Allow me to praise You, O most holy Virgin.
R. *Give me strength against Your enemies.*

Ave Maris Stella

Hail, bright star of ocean,
God's own Mother blest,
Ever sinless Virgin,
Gate of heavenly rest.

Taking that sweet *Ave*
Which from Gabriel came,
Peace confirms within us,
Changing Eva's name.
Break the captives' fetters,
Light on blindness pour,
All our ills expelling,
Every bliss implore.

Show thyself a Mother;
May the Word Divine,
Born for us thy Infant,
Hear our prayers through thine.

Virgin all excelling,
Mildest of the mild,
Freed from guilt, preserve us,
Pure and undefiled.

Keep our life all spotless,
Make our way secure,
Till we find in Jesus,
Joy forevermore.

Through the highest heaven
To the Almighty Three,
Father, Son and Spirit,
One same glory be. Amen.

The Holy Rosary

1. Make the Sign of the Cross and say the "Apostles' Creed."
2. Say the "Our Father."
3. Say three "Hail Marys."
4. Say the "Glory be to the Father."
5. Announce the First Mystery; then say the "Our Father."
6. Say 10 "Hail Marys" while meditating on the Mystery.
7. Say the "Glory be to the Father." After each decade, say the following prayer requested by the Blessed Virgin Mary at Fátima:
   "O my Jesus, forgive us our sins, save us from the fires of hell. Lead all souls to Heaven, especially those in most need of Thy mercy."
8. Announce the Second Mystery: then say the "Our Father." Repeat 6 and 7 and continue with the Third, Fourth, and Fifth Mysteries in the same manner.
9. Say the "Hail, Holy Queen" on the medal after the five decades are completed.

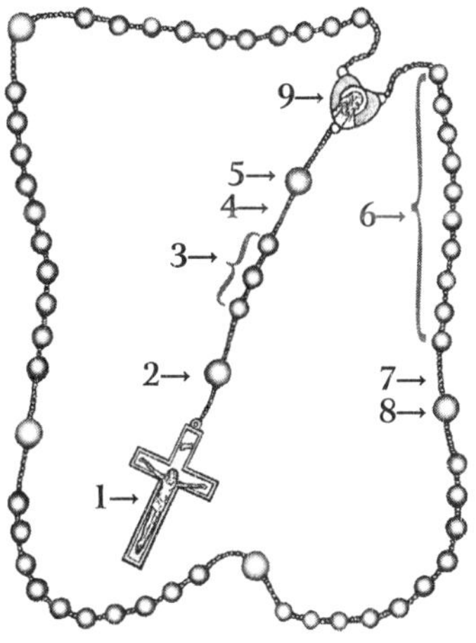

As a general rule, depending on the season, the Joyful Mysteries are said on Monday and Saturday; the Sorrowful Mysteries on Tuesday and Friday; the Glorious Mysteries on Wednesday and Sunday; and the Luminous Mysteries on Thursday.

Prayers of the Rosary

The Sign of the Cross: In the name of the Father, and of the Son, and of the Holy Spirit. Amen.

The Apostles' Creed: I believe in God, the Father almighty, Creator of heaven and earth, and in Jesus Christ, his only Son, our Lord, who was conceived by the Holy Spirit, born of the Virgin

Mary, suffered under Pontius Pilate, was crucified, died, and was buried; he descended into hell; on the third day he rose again from the dead; he ascended into heaven, and is seated at the right hand of God the Father almighty; from there he will come to judge the living and the dead. I believe in the Holy Spirit, the holy catholic Church, the communion of saints, the forgiveness of sins, the resurrection of the body, and life everlasting. Amen.*

The Our Father: Our Father, who art in heaven; hallowed be thy name; thy kingdom come, thy will be done on earth as it is in heaven. Give us this day our daily bread, and forgive us our trespasses, as we forgive those who trespass against us; and lead us not into temptation, but deliver us from evil. Amen.

The Hail Mary: Hail Mary, full of grace. The Lord is with thee. Blessed art thou among women, and blessed is the fruit of thy womb, Jesus. Holy Mary, Mother of God, pray for us sinners, now and at the hour of our death. Amen.

Glory be to the Father: Glory be to the Father, and to the Son, and to the Holy Spirit, as it was in the beginning, is now, and ever shall be, world without end. Amen.

Hail, Holy Queen.

*The wording of the Apostles' Creed conforms with the *Roman Missal.*

Mysteries of the Rosary

JOYFUL MYSTERIES

1. THE ANNUNCIATION

And when the angel had come to her, he said, "Hail, full of grace, the Lord is with you" (Lk 1:28).

FRUIT OF THE MYSTERY: HUMILITY.

2. THE VISITATION

Elizabeth, filled with the holy Spirit, cried out in a loud voice and said, "Most blessed are you among women, and blessed is the fruit of your womb" (Lk 1:41–42).

FRUIT OF THE MYSTERY: LOVE OF NEIGHBOR.

3. THE BIRTH OF JESUS

She gave birth to her firstborn Son. She wrapped Him in swaddling clothes and laid Him in a manger, because there was no room for them in the inn (Lk 2:7).

FRUIT OF THE MYSTERY: POVERTY IN SPIRIT.

4. THE PRESENTATION

When the days were completed for their purification according to the law of Moses, they took Him up to Jerusalem to present Him to the Lord, just as it is written in the law of the Lord, "Every male that opens the womb shall be consecrated to the Lord" (Lk 2:22–23).

FRUIT OF THE MYSTERY: OBEDIENCE.

5. THE CHILD JESUS IN THE TEMPLE

After three days they found Him in the temple, sitting in the midst of the teachers, listening to them and asking them questions (Lk 2:46).

FRUIT OF THE MYSTERY: JOY IN FINDING JESUS.

LUMINOUS MYSTERIES

1. BAPTISM OF JESUS

After Jesus was baptized, … the heavens were opened [for Him], and He saw the Spirit of God descending like a dove [and] coming upon Him. And a voice came from the heavens, saying, "This is My beloved Son, with whom I am well pleased" (Mt 3:16–17).

FRUIT OF THE MYSTERY: OPENNESS TO THE HOLY SPIRIT.

2. WEDDING AT CANA

His mother said to the servers, "Do whatever He tells you." … Jesus told them, "Fill the jars with water." So they filled them to the brim (Jn 2:5–7).

FRUIT OF THE MYSTERY: TO JESUS THROUGH MARY.

3. PROCLAIMING THE KINGDOM

"As you go, make this proclamation: 'The kingdom of heaven is at hand. 'Cure the sick, raise the dead, cleanse lepers, drive out demons. Without cost you have received; without cost you are to give" (Mt 10:7–8).

FRUIT OF THE MYSTERY: REPENTANCE AND TRUST IN GOD.

4. TRANSFIGURATION

While He was praying, His face changed in appearance and His clothing became dazzling white. Then from the cloud came a voice that said, "This is My chosen Son; listen to Him" (Lk 9:29, 35).

FRUIT OF THE MYSTERY: DESIRE FOR HOLINESS.

5. INSTITUTION OF THE EUCHARIST

Then He took the bread, said the blessing, broke it, and gave it to them, saying, "This is My body, which will be given for you ..." And likewise the cup after they had eaten, saying, "This cup is the new covenant in My blood" (Lk 22:19–20).

FRUIT OF THE MYSTERY: ADORATION.

SORROWFUL MYSTERIES

1. THE AGONY IN THE GARDEN

He was in such agony and He prayed so fervently that His sweat became like drops of blood falling on the ground. When He rose from prayer and returned to His disciples, He found them sleeping from grief (Lk 22:44–45).

FRUIT OF THE MYSTERY: SORROW FOR SIN.

2. SCOURGING AT THE PILLAR

Then Pilate took Jesus and had Him scourged (Jn 19:1).

FRUIT OF THE MYSTERY: PURITY.

3. CROWNING WITH THORNS

They stripped off His clothes and threw a scarlet military cloak about Him. Weaving a crown out of thorns, they placed it on His head, and a reed in His right hand (Mt 27:28–29).

FRUIT OF THE MYSTERY: COURAGE.

4. CARRYING OF THE CROSS

And carrying the cross Himself, He went out to what is called the Place of the Skull, in Hebrew, Golgotha (Jn 19:17)

FRUIT OF THE MYSTERY: PATIENCE.

5. THE CRUCIFIXION

Jesus cried out in a loud voice, “Father, into Your hands I commend My spirit”; and when He had said this He breathed His last (Lk 23:46).

FRUIT OF THE MYSTERY: PERSEVERANCE.

GLORIOUS MYSTERIES

1. THE RESURRECTION

"Do not be amazed! You seek Jesus of Nazareth, the crucified. He has been raised; He is not here. Behold the place where they laid Him" (Mk 16:6).

FRUIT OF THE MYSTERY: FAITH.

2. THE ASCENSION

So then the Lord Jesus, after He spoke to them, was taken up into heaven and took His seat at the right hand of God (Mk 16:19).

FRUIT OF THE MYSTERY: HOPE.

3. DESCENT OF THE HOLY SPIRIT

And they were all filled with the Holy Spirit and began to speak in different tongues, as the Spirit enabled them to proclaim (Acts 2:4).

FRUIT OF THE MYSTERY: LOVE OF GOD.

4. THE ASSUMPTION OF MARY

"You are the glory of Jerusalem! ... You are the great boast of our nation! ... You have done good things for Israel, and God is pleased with them. May the Almighty Lord bless you forever!" (Jud 15:9–10).

FRUIT OF THE MYSTERY: GRACE OF A HAPPY DEATH.

5. THE CORONATION OF MARY

A great sign appeared in the sky, a woman clothed with the sun, with the moon under her feet, and on her head a crown of twelve stars (Rev 12:1).

FRUIT OF THE MYSTERY: TRUST IN MARY'S INTERCESSION.

The Divine Mercy Chaplet

The Chaplet of Divine Mercy is recited using ordinary Rosary beads of five decades. At the National Shrine of The Divine Mercy in Stockbridge, Massachusetts, the Chaplet is preceded by two opening prayers from the *Diary of Saint Maria Faustina Kowalska* and followed by a closing prayer.

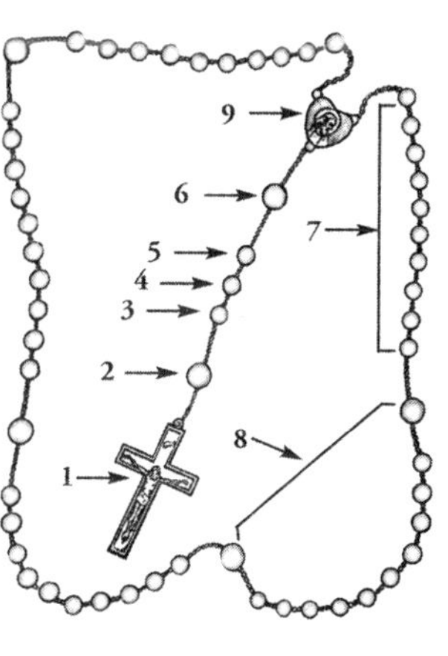

1. Make the Sign of the Cross.
2. Say the optional Opening Prayer.
3. Say the "Our Father."
4. Say the "Hail Mary."
5. Say the Apostles 'Creed.
6. Say the "Eternal Father."
7. Say 10 "For the sake of His sorrowful Passion" on the "Hail Mary" beads.
8. Repeat for four more decades, saying "Eternal Father" on the "Our Father" bead and then 10 "For the Sake of His sorrowful Passion" on the following "Hail Mary" beads.
9. At the conclusion of the five decades, on the medallion say the "Holy God," the concluding doxology, three times.
10. Say the optional Closing Prayer.

Prayers of the Chaplet of Divine Mercy

Opening Prayers (optional): You expired, Jesus, but the source of life gushed forth for souls, and the ocean of mercy opened up for the whole world. O Fount of Life, unfathomable Divine Mercy, envelop the whole world and empty Yourself out upon us (*Diary*, 1319). Or, O Blood and Water, which gushed forth from the Heart of Jesus as a fount of mercy for us, I trust in You! (three times) (*Diary*, 84).

Eternal Father, I offer You the Body and Blood, Soul and Divinity of Your dearly beloved Son, Our Lord Jesus Christ, in atonement for our sins and those of the whole world (*Diary*, 476).

For the sake of His sorrowful Passion, have mercy on us and on the whole world (*Diary*, 476).

Holy God, Holy Mighty One, Holy Immortal One, have mercy on us and on the whole world (*Diary*, 476).

Closing Prayer (optional): Eternal God, in whom mercy is endless, and the treasury of compassion inexhaustible, look kindly upon us, and increase Your mercy in us, that in difficult moments we might not despair, nor become despondent, but with great confidence, submit ourselves to Your holy will, which is Love and Mercy Itself. Amen (*Diary*, 950).

The Chaplet of Divine Mercy as a Novena

In addition to the Novena to Divine Mercy (see *Diary*, 1209–1229), which our Lord gave to St. Maria Faustina for her own personal use, He revealed to her a powerful prayer that He wanted everyone to say — the Chaplet of Divine Mercy. Saint Faustina prayed the Chaplet almost constantly, especially for the dying, and the Lord urged her to encourage others to say it too, promising extraordinary graces to those who would recite this special prayer.

The Chaplet can be said anytime, but the Lord specifically asked that it be recited as a novena, especially on the nine days before the Feast of Divine Mercy. And He promised, "By this Novena [of Chaplets] I will grant every possible grace to souls" (*Diary*, 796).

We can pray this Novena of Chaplets for our own personal intentions, or we can offer it together with the Novena to Divine Mercy for the daily intentions dictated by our Lord to St. Faustina.

A Prayer For Divine Mercy

O Greatly Merciful God, Infinite Goodness, today all mankind calls out from the abyss of its misery to Your mercy — to Your compassion, O God; and it is with its mighty voice of misery that it cries out: Gracious God, do not reject the prayer of this earth's exiles! O Lord, Goodness beyond our understanding, Who are acquainted with our misery through and through and know that by our own power we cannot ascend to You, we implore You, anticipate us with Your grace and keep on increasing Your mercy in us, that we may faithfully do Your holy will all through our life and at death's hour.

Let the omnipotence of Your mercy shield us from the darts of our salvation's enemies, that we may with confidence, as Your children, await Your final coming — that day known to You alone. And we expect to obtain everything promised us by Jesus in spite of all our wretchedness. For Jesus is our Hope: through His merciful Heart as through an open gate we pass through to heaven (*Diary*, 1570). Amen.

Star of Hope

by Pope Benedict XVI[173]

Teach us, Mary, to believe, to hope, to love with you; show us the way that leads to peace, the way to the Kingdom of Jesus. You, Star of Hope, who wait for us anxiously in the everlasting light of the eternal Homeland, shine upon us and guide us through daily events, now and at the hour of our death. Amen!

Saint Faustina's Consecration to the Blessed Mother[174]

O Mary, my Mother and my Lady, I offer you my soul, my body, my life and my death, all that will follow it. I place everything in your hands. O my Mother, cover my soul with your virginal mantle and grant me the grace of purity of heart, soul and body. Defend me with your power against all enemies, and especially against those who hide their malice behind the mask of virtue. O lovely lily! You are for me a mirror, O my Mother!

Christifideles Laici Prayer,

Pope John Paul II[175]

O Most Blessed Virgin Mary,
Mother of Christ and Mother of the Church,
With joy and wonder we seek to make our own your Magnificat,
joining you in your hymn of thankfulness and love.

With you we give thanks to God,
"whose mercy is from generation to generation,"
for the exalted vocation
and the many forms of mission
entrusted to the lay faithful.
God has called each of them by name
to live his own communion of love and holiness
and to be one in the great family of God's children.
He has sent them forth
to shine with the light of Christ
and to communicate the fire of the Spirit
in every part of society
through their life inspired by the gospel.

O Virgin of the Magnificat,
fill their hearts
with a gratitude and enthusiasm
for this vocation and mission.
With humility and magnanimity
you were the "handmaid of the Lord";
give us your unreserved willingness for service to God
and the salvation of the world.

Open our hearts to the great anticipation
of the Kingdom of God
and of the proclamation of the Gospel
to the whole of creation.
Your mother's heart
is ever mindful of the many dangers
and evils which threaten
to overpower men and women in our time.

At the same time your heart also takes notice
of the many initiatives undertaken for good,
the great yearning for values,
and the progress achieved in bringing forth
the abundant fruits of salvation.
O Virgin full of courage,
may your spiritual strength
and trust in God inspire us,
so that we might know how to overcome all the obstacles
that we encounter in accomplishing our mission.
Teach us to treat the affairs of the world
with a real sense of Christian responsibility
and a joyful hope
of the coming of God's Kingdom,
and of a "new heaven and a new earth."

You who were gathered in prayer
with the Apostles in the Cenacle,
awaiting the coming of the Spirit at Pentecost,
implore his renewed outpouring
on all the faithful, men and women alike,
so that they might more fully respond
to their vocation and mission,
as branches engrafted to the true vine,
called to bear much fruit for the life of the world.
O Virgin Mother, guide and sustain us
so that we might always live
as true sons and daughters of the Church of your Son.
Enable us to do our part in helping to establish on earth
the civilization of truth and love,
as God wills it, for his glory.
Amen.

Come, Holy Spirit

Come, Holy Spirit, Creator blest,
and in our souls take up Thy rest;
come with Thy grace and heavenly aid
to fill the hearts which Thou hast made.

O Comforter, to Thee we cry,
O heavenly gift of God Most High,
O fount of life and fire of love,
and sweet anointing from above.

Thou in Thy sevenfold gifts are known;
Thou, finger of God's hand we own;
Thou, promise of the Father, Thou
Who dost the tongue with power imbue.

Kindle our sense from above,
and make our hearts o'erflow with love;
with patience firm and virtue high
the weakness of our flesh supply.

Far from us drive the foe we dread,
and grant us Thy peace instead;
so shall we not, with Thee for guide,
turn from the path of life aside.

Oh, may Thy grace on us bestow
the Father and the Son to know;
and Thee, through endless times confessed,
of both the eternal Spirit blest.

Now to the Father and the Son,
Who rose from death, be glory given,
with Thou, O Holy Comforter,
henceforth by all in earth and heaven. Amen.

Prayer to the Holy Spirit

Come, Holy Spirit, fill the hearts of your faithful
and kindle in them the fire of your love.
Send forth your Spirit and they shall be created,
and you shall renew the face of the earth.
Let us pray.
O God, who have taught the hearts of the faithful
by the light of the Holy Spirit,
grant that in the same Spirit we may be truly wise
and ever rejoice in his consolation.
Through Christ our Lord. Amen.

Litany of the Holy Spirit

Lord, have mercy on us, *Lord, have mercy on us.*
Lord, have mercy on us.

God the Father of Heaven, *have mercy on us.*
God the Son, Redeemer of the world, *have mercy on us.*
God the Holy Spirit, *have mercy on us.*
Holy Trinity, One God, *have mercy on us.*
Divine Essence, one true God, *have mercy on us.*

Spirit of truth and wisdom, *have mercy on us.*
Spirit of holiness and justice, *have mercy on us.*
Spirit of understanding and counsel, *have mercy on us.*
Spirit of love and joy, *have mercy on us.*
Spirit of peace and patience, *have mercy on us.*
Spirit of longanimity and meekness, *have mercy on us.*
Spirit of benignity and goodness, *have mercy on us.*

Love substantial of the Father and the Son, *have mercy on us.*
Love and life of saintly souls, *have mercy on us.*
Fire ever burning, *have mercy on us.*
Living water to quench the thirst of hearts, *have mercy on us.*
From all evil, *deliver us, O Holy Spirit.*

From all impurity of soul and body, *deliver us, O Holy Spirit.*
From all gluttony and sensuality, *deliver us, O Holy Spirit.*

From all attachments to the things of the earth,
deliver us, O Holy Spirit.
From all hypocrisy and pretense, *deliver us, O Holy Spirit.*
From all imperfections and deliberate faults,
deliver us, O Holy Spirit.
From our own will, *deliver us, O Holy Spirit.*
From slander, *deliver us, O Holy Spirit.*
From deceiving our neighbors, *deliver us, O Holy Spirit.*
From our passions and disorderly appetites,
deliver us, O Holy Spirit.
From our inattentiveness to Thy holy inspirations,
deliver us, O Holy Spirit.
From despising little things, *deliver us, O Holy Spirit.*
From debauchery and malice, *deliver us, O Holy Spirit.*
From love of comfort and luxury, *deliver us, O Holy Spirit.*
From wishing to seek or desire anything other than Thee,
deliver us, O Holy Spirit.
From everything that displeases Thee, *deliver us, O Holy Spirit.*

Most loving Father, *forgive us.*
Divine Word, *have pity on us.*
Holy and divine Spirit, *leave us not until we are in possession of the Divine Essence, Heaven of heavens.*

Lamb of God, Who takes away the sins of the world,
send us the divine Consoler.
Lamb of God, Who takes away the sins of the world,
fill us with the gifts of Thy Spirit.
Lamb of God, Who takes away the sins of the world,
make the fruits of the Holy Spirit increase within us.

V. Come, O Holy Spirit, fill the hearts of Thy faithful,
R. *And enkindle in them the fire of Thy love.*

V. Send forth Thy Spirit and they shall be created,
R. *And Thou shalt renew the face of the earth.*

Let Us Pray:
God, Who by the light of the Holy Spirit
instructed the hearts of the faithful,
grant us by the same Spirit to be truly wise
and ever to rejoice in His consolation.
Through Jesus Christ Our Lord, Amen.

Litany of Loreto

Lord have mercy.
Christ have mercy.
Lord have mercy.
Christ hear us.
Christ graciously hear us.
God, the Father of heaven,
have mercy on us.
God the Son, Redeemer of the world,
God the Holy Spirit,
Holy Trinity, one God,
Holy Mary,
pray for us.
Holy Mother of God,
pray for us.
Holy Virgin of virgins,
pray for us.
Mother of Christ,
pray for us.
Mother of the Church,
pray for us.
Mother of Mercy,
pray for us.
Mother of divine grace,
pray for us.
Mother of Hope,
pray for us.
Mother most pure,
pray for us.

Mother most chaste,
pray for us.
Mother inviolate,
pray for us.
Mother undefiled,
pray for us.
Mother most amiable,
pray for us.
Mother admirable,
pray for us.
Mother of good counsel,
pray for us.
Mother of our Creator,
pray for us.
Mother of our Savior,
pray for us.
Virgin most prudent,
pray for us.
Virgin most venerable,
pray for us.
Virgin most renowned,
pray for us.
Virgin most powerful,
pray for us.
Virgin most merciful,
pray for us.
Virgin most faithful,
pray for us.
Mirror of justice,
pray for us.
Seat of wisdom,
pray for us.
Cause of our joy,
pray for us.
Spiritual vessel,
pray for us.
Vessel of honor,
pray for us.

Singular vessel of devotion,
pray for us.
Mystical rose,
pray for us.
Tower of David,
pray for us.
Tower if ivory,
pray for us.
House of gold,
pray for us.
Ark of the covenant,
pray for us.
Gate of heaven,
pray for us.
Morning star,
pray for us.
Health of the sick,
pray for us.
Refuge of sinners,
pray for us.
Solace of Migrants,
pray for us.
Comfort of the afflicted,
pray for us.
Help of Christians,
pray for us.
Queen of angels,
pray for us.
Queen of patriarchs,
pray for us.
Queen of prophets,
pray for us.
Queen of apostles,
pray for us.
Queen of martyrs,
pray for us.
Queen of confessors,
pray for us.

Queen of virgins,
pray for us.
Queen of all saints,
pray for us.
Queen conceived without original sin,
pray for us.
Queen assumed into heaven,
pray for us.
Queen of the most holy Rosary,
pray for us.
Queen of families,
pray for us.
Queen of peace,
pray for us.

Lamb of God, who takes away the sins of the world,
spare us, O Lord.
Lamb of God, who takes away the sins of the world,
graciously hear us, O Lord.
Lamb of God, who takes away the sins of the world,
have mercy on us.
Pray for us, O holy Mother of God.
That we may be made worthy of the promises of Christ.

Let Us Pray.
Grant, we beseech thee,
O Lord God,
that we, your servants,
may enjoy perpetual health of mind and body;
and by the glorious intercession of the Blessed Mary, ever Virgin,
may be delivered from present sorrow,
and obtain eternal joy.
Through Christ our Lord.
Amen.

Star of the Sea

by St. John Paul II[176]

O Mary,
bright dawn of the new world,
Mother of the living,
to you do we entrust the cause of life.

Look down, O Mother,
upon the vast numbers
of babies not allowed to be born,
of the poor whose lives are made difficult,
of men and women
who are victims of brutal violence,
of the elderly and the sick killed
by indifference or out of misguided mercy.

Grant that all who believe in your Son
may proclaim the Gospel of life
with honesty and love
to the people of our time.
Obtain for them the grace
to accept that Gospel
as a gift ever new,
the joy of celebrating it with gratitude
throughout their lives,
and the courage to bear witness to it
resolutely, in order to build,
together with all people of good will,
the civilization of truth and love,
to the praise and glory of God,
the Creator and lover of life.

Mary, my Mother

Written in prison on a scrap of paper by Cardinal Francis Xavier Nguyễn Văn Thuận in 1987

Mary, Mother of Jesus. My mother.
I want to call you our Mother
to feel close to Jesus
And all my brothers and sisters.

Come live in me, Mary,
with Jesus, your beloved Son,
in silence and in waiting, in prayer and in offering,
in communion with the Holy Trinity,
And the Church,
in the fervor of your *Magnificat*,
that message of complete renewal;
in union with Joseph, your most holy spouse;
in your humble and loving work
to accomplish Jesus' will;
in your love for Jesus, for Joseph,
for the Church, and for all humanity;
in your unshakable faith
in the midst of so many trials
Endured for the Kingdom;
in your ceaselessly active hope,
to build a new world of righteousness and peace,
Of happiness and true tenderness;
in the perfection of your virtues
in the Holy Spirit,
So as to become a witness of the Good News,
an apostle of the Gospel.

Continue, O Mother,
To pray, to love and to sacrifice in me;
continue to carry out the Father's will,
Continue to be the Mother of humanity;
Continue to live Jesus' Passion
and Resurrection in me.

O Mother, I consecrate myself entirely to you,
Now and forever.
In living your spirit and that of Joseph,
I shall live the Spirit of Jesus.
I love you, O our Mother,
With Jesus, Joseph, the angels, the saints,
And all people.

I will share your labors and cares,
and your struggle
for the Kingdom of the Lord Jesus. Amen.

Mother Teresa's Prayer to Mary

Mary, I depend on you totally as a child on its mother, that in return you may possess me, protect me, and transform me into Jesus. May the light of your faith dispel the darkness of my mind; may your profound humility take the place of my pride; may your contemplation replace the distractions of my wandering imagination; and may your virtues take the place of my sins. Lead me deeper into the mystery of the cross that you may share your experience of Jesus's thirst with me.

Prayer to Our Lady of Fátima

by Pope St. John Paul II[177]

Mother of all individuals and peoples, you know all their sufferings and hopes. In your motherly heart you feel all the struggles between good and evil, between light and darkness, that convulse the world: accept the plea which we make in the Holy Spirit directly to your heart, and embrace with the love of the Mother and Handmaid of the Lord those who most await this embrace, and also those whose act of entrustment you too await in a particular way. Take under your motherly protection the whole human family, which with affectionate love we entrust to you, O Mother. May there dawn for everyone the time of peace and freedom, the time of truth, of justice, and of hope.

Our Lady of Fátima's First Saturday Devotion

The Blessed Virgin Mary appeared to Sr. Lucia when she was a Dorothean nun and requested the Communion of Reparation. Sister Lucia's spiritual director asked her to write it down and to write it in the third person. This is what she wrote:

> On Dec. 10, 1925, the most holy Virgin appeared to her, and by her side, elevated on a luminous cloud, was [the Christ] Child. The most holy Virgin rested her hand on [Sr. Lucia's] shoulder, and as she did so, she showed her a heart encircled in thorns, which she was holding in her other hand. At the same time, the [Christ] Child said: "Have compassion on the Heart of your most holy Mother, covered with thorns, with which ungrateful men pierce it at every moment, and there is no one to make an act of reparation to remove them."
>
> Then the most holy Virgin said: "Look, my daughter, at my Heart, surrounded with thorns with which ungrateful men pierce me at every moment by their blasphemies and ingratitude. You at least try to console me and say that I promise to assist at the hour of death, with the graces necessary for salvation, all those who, on the first Saturday of five consecutive months, shall confess [their sins], receive Holy Communion, recite five decades of the Rosary, and keep me company for fifteen minutes while meditating on the fifteen mysteries of the Rosary, with the intention of making reparation to me."[178]

Mary gave Sr. Lucia and the world a great plan to use to make reparation; it is referred to as Communion of Reparation, or the Five First Saturdays devotion. This devotion is to be done on the first Saturday of five consecutive months, and it is to be done with the intention of making reparation to Our Lady for the sins of ingratitude and blasphemy committed against her. Our Lady explained that there are four main parts to carrying out this devotion:

1. Go to Confession on that Saturday or during the week before or after it.
2. Receive Holy Communion on the day if possible. With good reason it can be done on the Sunday.
3. Recite five decades of the Rosary.
4. Keep Our Lady company for 15 minutes by meditating on the mysteries of the Rosary. This is in addition to praying the Rosary.

The Fátima Prayer

O My Jesus, forgive us our sins, save us from the fires of hell,
lead all souls to Heaven, especially those
in most need of Thy mercy. Amen.

(Our Lady of Fátima told the shepherd children that we should add this prayer to the end of each decade of the Rosary.)

The Pardon Prayer

My God, I believe, I adore, I hope, and I love Thee.
I beg pardon for all those that do not believe, do not adore,
do not hope, and do not love Thee. Amen

The Angel of Peace Prayer

O most Holy Trinity, Father, Son, and Holy Spirit, I adore Thee profoundly.

I offer Thee the most Precious Body, Blood, Soul, and Divinity of Jesus Christ present in all the tabernacles of the world, in reparation for the outrages, sacrileges, and indifferences by which He is offended. Amen.

(The Angel of Peace taught this to the Fátima children as well as the one below.)

The Eucharistic Prayer

Most Holy Trinity, I adore Thee!
My God, my God, I love Thee in the Most Blessed Sacrament.
Amen.

(During this apparition, a Eucharistic host and chalice were suspended in the air, and the Angel of Peace led the children in kneeling before it, adoring Jesus, and praying this prayer.)

The Sacrifice Prayer

Oh Jesus, it is for the love of Thee in reparation for the offenses committed against the Immaculate Heart of Mary and for the conversion of poor sinners. Amen.

(Mary gave the children this prayer, as well as the Decade Prayer, on June 13, 1917. It is meant to be prayed when offering a suffering to God.)

Prayer to Our Lady of the Smile

O Mary, Mother of Jesus,
and our gentle Mother too,
with a visible and radiant smile
you consoled and cured
your beloved child, St. Thérèse of the Child Jesus.
We ask you now to smile on us,
amid the troubles of our lives.
May your gentle smile bring light and healing
to the darkness and disease of our body, mind, and spirit.
Instill us with hope and deepen our faith
so that we enjoy forever
your maternal and enrapturing smile in heaven.
Amen.

Saint Thérèse's Prayer to The Holy Face of Jesus

O Jesus, who, in Thy cruel Passion didst become the "reproach of men and the Man of Sorrows," I worship Thy divine Face. Once it shone with the beauty and sweetness of the Divinity; but now, for my sake, it is become as "the face of a leper." Yet, in that disfigured Countenance, I recognize Thy infinite love, and I am consumed with the desire of making Thee loved by all mankind. The tears that flowed so abundantly from Thy Eyes are to me as precious pearls that I delight to gather, that with their worth I may ransom the souls of poor sinners. O Jesus, whose Face is the sole beauty that ravishes my heart, I may not see here below the sweetness of Thy glance, nor feel the ineffable tenderness of Thy kiss; I bow to Thy Will — but I pray Thee to imprint in me Thy divine likeness, and I implore Thee so to inflame me with Thy love, that it may quickly consume me, and that I may soon reach the vision of Thy glorious Face in heaven. Amen.

Saint Thérèse's Canticle to The Holy Face

Jesus! Thy dear and holy Face
Is the bright star that guides my way;
Thy gentle glance, so full of grace,
Is my true heaven on earth, today.
My love finds out the holy charm
Of Thy dear eyes with tear-drops wet;
Through mine own tears I smile at Thee,
And in Thy griefs my pains forget.
Oh! I would gladly live unknown,
Thus to console Thy aching heart.
Thy veiled beauty, it is shown
To those who live from earth apart.
Fain would I fly to Thee alone!
Thy Face it is my fatherland;
It is the sunshine of my days;
My realm of love, my sunlit land,
Where through the hours I sing Thy praise;
It is the lily of the vale,

Whose mystic perfume, freely given,
Brings comfort, when I faint and fail,
And makes me taste the peace of heaven.
Thy face, in its unearthly grace,
Is like the divinest myrrh to me,
That on my heart I gladly place;
It is my lyre of melody;
My rest — my comfort — is Thy Face.
My only wealth, Lord! is thy Face;
Naught ask I more than this from Thee;
Hidden in the secret of Thy Face,
The more I shall resemble Thee!
Leave on me the divine impress
Of Thy sweet, patient Face of love,
And soon I shall become a saint,
And draw men's hearts to Thee above.
So, in the secret of Thy Face,
Oh! hide me, hide me, Jesus blest!
There let me find its hidden grace,
Its holy fires, and, in heaven's rest,
Its rapturous kiss, in Thy embrace!

Saint Thérèse's Holy Face Prayer For Sinners

Eternal Father, since Thou hast given me for my inheritance the Adorable Face of Thy Divine Son, I offer that Face to Thee, and I beg Thee, in exchange for this coin of infinite value, to forget the ingratitude of souls dedicated to Thee and to pardon all poor sinners.

Prayer to Our Lady of Kibeho

Blessed Virgin Mary, Mother of the Word,
Mother of all those who believe in Him,
and who welcome Him into their life,
we are here before you to contemplate You.
We believe that you are among us,
like a mother in the midst of her children,
even though we do not see You with our bodily eyes.
We bless You, The Sure Way that leads us to Jesus the Savior,

for all the favors which You endlessly pour out upon us,
especially, that, in your meekness, You were gracious
enough to appear miraculously in Kibeho, just when our
world needed it most.
Grant us always the light and the strength necessary to
accept, with all seriousness, Your call to us to be converted,
to repent, and to live according to your Son's Gospel.
Teach us how to pray with sincerity, and how to love one
another as He loved us, so that, just as You have requested,
we may always be beautiful flowers diffusing their pleasant
fragrance everywhere and upon everyone.
Holy Mary, Our Lady of Sorrows,
teach us to understand the value of the cross in our lives,
so that whatever is still lacking to the sufferings of Christ
we may fill up in our own bodies for His mystical Body,
which is the Church.
And when our pilgrimage on this earth comes to an end,
may we live eternally with You in the kingdom of Heaven.

Imprimatur: Gikongoro, Rwanda, the 25th of March, 2006
Augustin Misago, Bishop of Gikongoro

Prayer to Our Lady of Knock

Our Lady of Knock, Queen of Ireland, you gave hope to your people in a time of distress and comforted them in sorrow. You have inspired countless pilgrims to pray with confidence to your divine Son, remembering His promise, "Ask and you shall receive, seek and you shall find." Help me to remember that we are all pilgrims on the road to Heaven. Fill me with love and concern for my brothers and sisters in Christ, especially those who live with me. Comfort me when I am sick, lonely, or depressed. Teach me how to take part ever more reverently in the Holy Mass. Give me a greater love of Jesus in the Blessed Sacrament. Pray for me now and at the hour of my death. Amen.

Novena to Our Lady of Knock

In the name of the Father, and of the Son, and of the Holy Spirit. Amen.

Give praise to the Father Almighty, to His Son, Jesus Christ the Lord, to the Spirit who lives in our hearts, both now and forever. Amen. Our Lady of Knock, Queen of Ireland, you gave hope to your people in a time of distress and comforted them in sorrow. You have inspired countless pilgrims to pray with confidence to your divine Son, remembering His promise, "Ask and you shall receive, seek and you shall find."

Help me to remember that we are all pilgrims on the road to heaven. Fill me with love and concern for my brothers and sisters in Christ, especially those who live with me. Comfort me when I am sick, lonely, or depressed. Teach me how to take part ever more reverently in the Holy Mass. Give me a greater love of Jesus in the Blessed Sacrament. Pray for me now, and at the hour of my death. Amen.

Lamb of God, you take away the sins of the world,
have mercy on us.
Lamb of God, you take away the sins of the world,
have mercy on us.
Lamb of God, you take away the sins of the world,
grant us peace.

ST. JOSEPH, chosen by God to be the Husband of Mary, the Protector of the Holy Family, the Guardian of the Church, *protect all families in their work and recreation and guard us on our journey through life.*

(Repeat – Lamb of God, etc.)

ST. JOHN, Beloved Disciple of the Lord, faithful priest, teacher of the Word of God, *help us to hunger for the Word, to be loyal to the Mass, and to love one another.*

(Repeat – Lamb of God, etc.)

Our Lady of Knock, *pray for us.*
Refuge of Sinners, *pray for us.*

Queen Assumed into Heaven, *pray for us.*
Queen of the Rosary, *pray for us.*
Mother of Nazareth, *pray for us.*
Queen of Virgins, *pray for us.*
Help of Christians, *pray for us.*
Health of the Sick, *pray for us.*
Queen of Peace, *pray for us.*
Our Lady, Queen and Mother, *pray for us.*
Our Lady, Mother of the Church, *pray for us.*
(Here mention your own special intentions.)

With the Angels and Saints, let us pray: Give praise to the Father Almighty, to His Son, Jesus Christ the Lord, to the Spirit who lives in our hearts, both now and forever. Amen.

Instruction: The Rosary or Mass and Holy Communion is recommended each day.

Novena Prayer to Our Lady of the Miraculous Medal

O Immaculate Virgin Mary, Mother of Our Lord Jesus and our Mother, penetrated with the most lively confidence in your all-powerful and never-failing intercession, manifested so often through the Miraculous Medal, we, your loving and trustful children, implore you to obtain for us the graces and favors we ask during this Novena, if they be beneficial to our immortal souls, and the souls for whom we pray. (Here privately form your petitions.)

You know, O Mary, how often our souls have been the sanctuaries of your Son who hates iniquity. Obtain for us, then, a deep hatred of sin and that purity of heart which will attach us to God alone, so that our every thought, word, and deed may tend to His greater glory. Obtain for us also a spirit of prayer and self-denial, that we may recover by penance what we have lost by sin and at length attain to that blessed abode where you are the Queen of angels and of men. Amen.

An Act of Consecration to Our Lady of the Miraculous Medal

O Virgin Mother of God, Mary Immaculate, we dedicate and consecrate ourselves to you under the title of Our Lady of the Miraculous Medal. May this Medal be for each one of us a sure sign of your affection for us and a constant reminder of our duties toward you. Ever while wearing it, may we be blessed by your loving protection and preserved in the grace of your Son. O most powerful Virgin, Mother of our Savior, keep us close to you every moment of our lives. Obtain for us, your children, the grace of a happy death; so that, in union with you, we may enjoy the bliss of heaven forever. Amen.

Repeat 3 times:

Priest: O Mary, conceived without sin,

People: *pray for us who have recourse to you.*

Prayer to Our Mother of Mercy

Mary, Mother of God, I turn to you in all my pressing needs and difficulties as to a most sure refuge. I implore the help of your protection and choose you as my advocate. I entrust my cause to you who are the Mother of Mercy, and I wish to offer you day by day my most reverent love. But that my devotion may be pleasing to you, help me to maintain my soul and body in the spotlessness of your purity, help me to try as best I can to walk in your footsteps, humbly seeking to be like you.

Even if I have committed all possible sins, let me never lose confidence in you, for I know I shall always find your Heart filled with mercy. The Son of God has His justice, but you, the Mother, have only your mercy. You desire more to do good to me than I can desire to receive favors from you, for your Heart is all love and mercy.

Mary, My Mother, how shall I stand before my Judge at the day of judgment? How shall I answer for the wasted days and years which God has given me to serve Him alone? I look to you, Mother of Mercy. You are all-merciful that you may obtain for me pardon and mercy. You are kind and loving for you have a mother's heart, full of pity for the erring. You are a Mother of Mercy to the sinner and the fallen; have pity on me!

Saint John Paul II's Prayer to the Immaculate Heart of Mary

O Immaculate Heart! Help us to conquer the menace of evil, which so easily takes root in the hearts of the people of today, and whose immeasurable effects already weigh down upon our modern world and seem to block the paths towards the future!

From famine and war, deliver us.
From nuclear war, from incalculable self-destruction,
from every kind of war, deliver us.
From sins against the life of man from its very beginning,
deliver us.
From hatred and from the demeaning of the dignity of the
children of God, deliver us.
From every kind of injustice in the life of society,
both national and international, deliver us.
From readiness to trample on the commandments of God,
deliver us.
From sins against the Holy Spirit, deliver us, deliver us.

Accept, O Mother of Christ, this cry laden with the sufferings of all individual human beings, laden with the sufferings of whole societies.

Let there be revealed once more in the history of the world the infinite power of merciful Love. May it put a stop to evil. May it transform consciences. May your Immaculate Heart reveal for all the light of hope! Amen.

Prayer to Our Lady of Guadalupe

by St. John Paul II[179]

O Immaculate Virgin, Mother of the true God and Mother of the Church, who from this place reveal your clemency and your pity to all those who ask for your protection, hear the prayer that we address to you with filial trust, and present it to your Son Jesus, our sole Redeemer.

Mother of Mercy, Teacher of hidden and silent sacrifice, to you, who come to meet us sinners, we dedicate on this day all our being and all our love. We also dedicate to you our life, our work, our joys, our infirmities, and our sorrows. Grant peace, justice, and prosperity to our peoples; for we entrust to your care all that we have and all that we are, our Lady and Mother. We wish to be entirely yours and to walk with you along the way of complete faithfulness to Jesus Christ in His Church; hold us always with your loving hand.

Virgin of Guadalupe, Mother of the Americas, we pray to you for all the Bishops, that they may lead the faithful along paths of intense Christian life, of love and humble service of God and souls. Contemplate this immense harvest, and intercede with the Lord that He may instill a hunger for holiness in the whole people of God, and grant abundant vocations of priests and religious, strong in the faith and zealous dispensers of God's mysteries.

Grant to our homes the grace of loving and respecting life in its beginnings, with the same love with which you conceived in your womb the life of the Son of God. Blessed Virgin Mary, protect our families, so that they may always be united, and bless the upbringing of our children.

Our hope, look upon us with compassion, teach us to go continually to Jesus and, if we fall, help us to rise again, to return to Him, by means of the confession of our faults and sins in the Sacrament of Penance, which gives peace to the soul.

We beg you to grant us a great love for all the holy Sacraments, which are, as it were, the signs that your Son left us on earth.

Thus, Most Holy Mother, with the peace of God in our conscience, with our hearts free from evil and hatred, we will be able to bring to all true joy and true peace, which come to us from your Son, our Lord Jesus Christ, who with God the Father and the Holy Spirit, lives and reigns for ever and ever. Amen.

Novena Prayer to Our Lady of Lourdes

Be blessed, O most pure Virgin, for having vouchsafed to manifest your shining life, sweetness, and beauty in the Grotto of Lourdes, saying to the child, St. Bernadette: "I am the Immaculate Conception." A thousand times we congratulate you upon your Immaculate Conception. And now, O ever Immaculate Virgin, Mother of mercy, Health of the sick, Refuge of sinners, Comforter of the afflicted, you know our wants, our troubles, our sufferings: deign to cast upon us a look of mercy.

By appearing in the Grotto of Lourdes, you were pleased to make it a privileged sanctuary, whence you dispense your favors, and already many have obtained the cure of their infirmities, both spiritual and physical. We come, therefore, with the most unbounded confidence to implore your maternal intercession. Obtain for us, O loving Mother, the granting of our request. (State your request.)

Through gratitude for your favors, we will endeavor to imitate your virtues, that we may one day share your glory.

Our Lady of Lourdes, Mother of Christ, you had influence with your Divine Son while upon earth. You have the same influence now in Heaven. Pray for us; obtain for us from your Divine Son our special requests if it be the Divine Will. Amen.

Our Lady of Lourdes, *pray for us.*

Saint Bernadette, *pray for us.*

Prayer to Our Lady of Champion

by Bishop David L. Ricken[180]

O Dear Lady of Champion, you revealed yourself as the Queen of Heaven to your servant Adele. You gave her a mission to pray for the conversion of sinners, to bring the Good News of Jesus Christ to others, and to prepare the children for the reception of the sacraments.

I trust that as you called Adele to holiness, you are calling me, in my station in life, to live a holy life, devoted to Jesus Christ with the help of your maternal love.

I bring before you now my worries and anxieties. I abandon my attachments to them and place them at your feet. I ask you to hear the deepest longings of my heart as I pray most earnestly for: ____________________ (your intention).

Dear Lady, you told Adele, and you say to all of us, "Do not be afraid; I will help you." Help me now as I place this intention with complete confidence and trust.

Recite the Our Father, Hail Mary, Glory Be.

Our Lady of Champion, pray for us.

Saint Louis Marie de Montfort's Prayer to Mary

Hail Mary, beloved Daughter of the Eternal Father! Hail Mary, admirable Mother of the Son! Hail Mary, faithful Spouse of the Holy Ghost! Hail Mary, my dear Mother, my loving Mistress, my powerful sovereign! Hail my joy, my glory, my heart, and my soul! Thou art all mine by mercy, and I am all thine by justice. But I am not yet sufficiently thine. I now give myself wholly to thee without keeping anything back for myself or others. If thou still seest in me anything which does not belong to thee, I beseech thee to take it and to make thyself the absolute Mistress of all that is mine. Destroy in me all that may be displeasing to God; root it up and bring it to naught; place and cultivate in me everything that is pleasing to thee.

May the light of thy faith dispel the darkness of my mind; may thy profound humility take the place of my pride; may thy sublime contemplation check the distractions of my wandering imagination; may thy continuous sight of God fill my memory with His presence; may the burning love of thy heart inflame the lukewarmness of mine; may thy virtues take the place of my sins; may thy merits be my only adornment in the sight of God and make up for all that is wanting in me.

Finally, dearly beloved Mother, grant, if it be possible, that I may have no other spirit but thine, to know Jesus and His divine will; that I may have no other soul but thine, to praise and glorify the Lord; that I may have no other heart but thine, to love God with a love as pure and ardent as thine.

I do not ask thee for visions, revelations, sensible devotion, or spiritual pleasures. It is thy privilege to see God clearly; it is thy privilege to enjoy heavenly bliss; it is thy privilege to triumph gloriously in Heaven at the right hand of thy Son and to hold absolute sway over angels, men, and demons; it is thy privilege to dispose of all the gifts of God just as thou willest.

Such is, O heavenly Mary, the "best part," which the Lord has given thee and which shall never be taken away from thee — and this thought fills my heart with joy. As for my part here below, I wish for no other than that which was thine: to believe sincerely without spiritual pleasures; to suffer joyfully without human consolation; to die continually to myself without respite; and to work zealously and unselfishly for thee until death as the humblest of thy servants.

The only grace I beg thee to obtain for me is that every day and every moment of my life I may say, "Amen; so be it" — to all that thou didst do while on earth; "Amen; so be it" — to all that thou art now doing in Heaven; "Amen; so be it" — to all that thou art doing in my soul, so that thou alone mayest fully glorify Jesus in me for time and eternity. Amen.

Prayer to Our Lady of Częstochowa

by Pope St. John Paul II[181]

Faithful Daughter of the Eternal Father, Temple of the Love that embraces heaven and earth, I entrust to you the service of the Church in the world, a world which so needs love.

Mother of God, Mother of the only-begotten Son who gave us as the principle of life, the new commandment of love, help us to become builders of a united world, in which peace triumphs over war, and the civilization of death is replaced by love for life …

May humanity stand firmly with God, to whom belongs the whole world.

Mother of Unity and Peace, strengthen the bond of communion within the Church of your Son, enliven ecumenical efforts so that all Christians, by the power of the Holy Spirit, may become one family of sisters and brothers of Jesus Christ, the one Savior of the world yesterday, today, and forever (cf. Heb. 13:8). …

O clement, O loving, O sweet Virgin Mary, accept our trust, strengthen it in our hearts, and present it before the face of the one God in the Holy Trinity. Amen.

Saint Brigid's Blessing of the House

May Brigid bless the house wherein we dwell.
Bless every fireside, every wall and door.
Bless every heart that beats beneath its roof.
Bless every hand that toils to bring its joy.
Bless every foot that walks portals through.
May Brigid bless the house that shelters us. Amen.

Prayer to St. Brigid

(Often prayed for those with anxiety)

Saint Brigid, you were a woman of peace. You brought harmony where there was conflict. You brought light to the darkness. You brought hope to the downcast. May the mantle of your peace cover those who are troubled and anxious, and may peace be firmly rooted in our hearts and in our world. Inspire us to act justly and to reverence all God has made. Brigid, you were a voice for the wounded and the weary. Strengthen what is weak within us. Calm us into a quietness that heals and listens. May we grow each day into greater wholeness in mind, body, and spirit. Amen.

Prayer to St. Brigid for Protection

Saint Brigid, Mary of the Gael,
may your protection never fail.
Spread your mantle over me,
where 'ere I am, where 'ere I be.
Cover me with God's joy and peace,
let my faith and hope never cease.
Shine your light where there is darkness,
strengthen me in any weakness.
Heal all within that may be ill,
give me the desire each day to do God's will,
'till I rest, my journey o'er,
with God and you forever more.
St. Brigid, patron of Kildare and Leighlin,
pray for us. Amen.

ACKNOWLEDGEMENTS

I am deeply grateful to my parents, Eugene Joseph and Alexandra Mary Cooper, for bringing me into the world and raising me in a large Catholic family. How amazing it is that my mother came into this world weighing only a pound and a half! She almost didn't survive. Because of God's loving grace and mercy, through thick and thin, she grew to become a loving mother of eight children and a grandmother of many.

Thank you to my grandmother, Alexandra Mary Uzwiak, for always setting a beautiful, prayerful example. And my beautiful godmother, Aunt Bertha. To my brothers and sisters — Alice Jean, Gene, Gary, Barbara, Tim, Michael, and David — thank you for being a wonderful part of my life.

My heartfelt, loving gratitude goes to my husband, Dave, and my beloved children — Justin, Chaldea, Jessica, Joseph, and Mary-Catherine — for their continued love and support, and to my precious grandsons, Shepherd and Leo. I love you all dearly!

I am grateful to my friend, Servant of God Fr. John Hardon, SJ, who spiritually directed and encouraged me, and is no doubt continuing to do so from Heaven! Also, an exuberant thank you to dear Mother Teresa for playing a huge role in shaping me spiritually, which I know she continues to do even now. Thank you to Fr. Andrew Apostoli, CFR, a dear friend and spiritual director, now helping me from Heaven!

I owe very special thanks to Marian Press for asking me to write this book for the Jubilee Year of Hope in 2025 and beyond. To Fr. Chris Alar, MIC, Dr. Joe McAleer, Chris Sparks, Robert A. Stackpole, STD, and the wonderful team at Marian Press, all of whom have helped get this book out to you, I thank you!

Finally, I am extremely thankful for my readership, viewership, and listenership, and to all those I meet in my travels. I pray for you every day. Thank you for being part of my fascinating journey through life! Please pray for me, too.

Stay close to Jesus and Mary! May God bless you in great abundance! *Totus Tuus!*

ABOUT THE AUTHOR

Known the world over, Donna-Marie Cooper O'Boyle is a wife, mother, and grandmother whose love for children and teaching the Faith spurred her on to be a catechist for over 30 years. She is an award-winning and best-selling author of more than 35 books on faith, family, and the saints and angels; some have been translated into foreign languages, as well as in Braille. Her memoir is *The Kiss of Jesus: How Mother Teresa and the Saints Helped Me to Discover the Beauty of the Cross.*

She is the EWTN television host of "Everyday Blessings for Catholic Moms," "Catholic Mom's Cafe," and "Feeding Your Family's Soul," which she created to teach, encourage, and inspire Catholic families.

Donna-Marie was invited by the Holy See to participate in an international Vatican congress for women. Her work has been featured in national and international media. She has written for *L'Osservatore Romano*, *Magnificat*, *National Catholic Register*, *Catholic World Report*, *Our Sunday Visitor*, and more. She is also a contributor and General Editor of the *Divine Mercy Catholic Bible* (2020) and writes and lectures frequently on Divine Mercy and the Eucharist. She is an authority on the life of St. Maria Faustina Kowalska.

Donna-Marie is a regular guest on national and international radio and has been profiled on many television shows.

Donna-Marie presents retreats and lectures throughout the world on topics relating to Catholic and Christian men and women; faith and family life; the Eucharist; and the saints, especially St. Faustina, and her friend Mother Teresa. She has received numerous awards for her writing and was blessed to enjoy a decade-long friendship with St. Mother Teresa of Calcutta. For many years, her spiritual director was Servant of God Fr. John A. Hardon, SJ, who also served as one of Mother Teresa's spiritual directors.

Donna-Marie is a photographer and jewelry designer who also dabbles in art. She lives with her family in rural New England, admiring God's creation. She can be reached on her website: www.donnacooperoboyle.com and her social media platforms.

NOTES

[1] Saint Maria Faustina Kowalska, *Divine Mercy in My Soul: The Diary of Saint Maria Kowalska Faustina* (Stockbridge, Massachusetts: Marian Press, 1987), 1318. Hereafter *Diary.*

[2] Ibid, 1775.

[3] Saint Teresa of Calcutta, letter to the author, August 28, 1993.

[4] Pope Francis, *Spes Non Confundit* (*Hope Does Not Disappoint*), May 9, 2024, 1. [www.vatican.va/content/francesco/en/bulls/documents/20240509_spes-non-confundit_bolla-giubileo2025.html]

[5] *Spes Non Confundit*, 24.

[6] Ibid.

[7] Ibid..

[8] See *Catechism of the Catholic Church* (hereafter *CCC*), no. 1655; also Acts 16:31 and Acts 11:14.

[9] Saint Louis de Montfort, *True Devotion to Mary: With Preparation for Total Consecration*, (London: Catholic Way Publishing, 2013), 55. [www.catholicwaypublishing.com/wp-content/uploads/2018/03/True-Devotion-to-Mary-With-Preparation-Saint-Louis-de-Montfort-5x8-Paperback-PDF-Edition.pdf]

[10] Ibid., 16.

[11] Brother Eliott, MIC, "In the spirit of Padre Pio, pray the Rosary, and pray it well," Marian.org, September 23, 2023. [https://marian.org/articles/spirit-padre-pio-pray-rosary-and-pray-it-well]

[12] Pope John Paul II, Homily, Holy Mass at the Cathedral of St. Matthew, Washington, DC, October 6, 1979. [www.vatican.va/content/john-paul-ii/en/homilies /1979/documents/hf_jp-ii_hom_19791006_washington-san-matteo.html]

[13] Pope Benedict XVI, *Spe Salvi* (*Saved in Hope*), November 30, 2007, 2, 35. [www.vatican.va/content/benedict-xvi/en/encyclicals/documents/hf_ben-xvi_enc_20071130_spe-salvi.html]

[14] Pope Francis, Homily, May 9, 2024. [www.vatican.va/content/francesco/en/homilies/2024/documents/20240509-indizione-giubileo.html]

[15] See "Norms for Proceeding in the Discernment of Alleged Supernatural Phenomena," Dicastery for the Doctrine of the Faith of the Holy See, May 17, 2024. [www.vatican.va/roman_curia/congregations/cfaith/documents/rc_ddf_doc_20240517_norme-fenomeni-soprannaturali_en.html]

[16] *CCC*, 67.

[17] *True Devotion to Mary*, 25.

[18] *Spe Salvi*, 50.

[19] Pope John Paul II, General audience, May 8 and 15, 1996, in *Theotokos: Woman, Mother, Disciple: A Catechesis on Mary,* vol. 5 (Pauline Books & Media, 1999), 88, 90.

[20] Saint Stanislaus Papczyński, *Saint Stanislaus Papczyński: Selected Writings* (Marian Press, 2022, Stockbridge, Massachusetts), 90. [https://images.marianweb.net/archives/flip/en/Selected_Writings/images.marianweb.net/archives/pdfs/papczynski/en/Selected_Writings.pdf]

[21] See Saint Ambrose, *De virginibus ad Marcellinam sororem sua libri tres* (*Three books concerning virgins*) II 2; PL 16, 220, 6–7.15. [https://www.documentacatholicaomnia.eu/03d/0339-0397,_Ambrosius,_De_Virginibus_Ad_Marcellinam_Sororem_Sua_Libri_Tres_[Schaff],_EN.pdf]

[22] See Second Vatican Ecumenical Council, *Dei Verbum* (*Dogmatic Constitution on Divine Revelation*), November 18, 1965, 5. [www.vatican.va/archive/hist_councils/ii_vatican_council/documents/vat-ii_const_19651118_dei-verbum_en.html]

[23] *Spe Salvi*, 49.

[24] Pope John Paul II, *Redemptoris Mater* (*The Mother of the Redeemer*), March 25, 1987, 36. [www.vatican.va/content/john-paul-ii/en/encyclicals/documents/hf_jp-ii_enc_25031987_redemptoris-mater.html]

[25] Pope John Paul II, *Ecclesia De Eucharistia* (*The Church from the Eucharist*), April 17, 2003, 55. [www.vatican.va/content/john-paul-ii/en/encyclicals/documents/hf_jp-ii_enc_20030417_eccl-de-euch.html]

[26] *Spe Salvi*, 50.

[27] Venerable Fulton Sheen, *The World's First Love* (1952). [www.catholictradition.org/Mary/cana.htm]

[28] Ibid.

[29] *Spe Salvi*, 50.

[30] Ibid.

[31] Ibid.

[32] *Redemptoris Mater*, 18.

[33] Margaret R. Bunson, editor, *John Paul II's Book of Mary* (*Our Sunday Visitor*, 1996), 139.

[34] Ibid, 138.

[35] *Saint Stanislaus Papczyński*, 92.

[36] "Our Lady of Guadalupe," *Nican Mopohua* translation, Catholic News Agency. [www.catholicnewsagency.com/ resource/55425/our-lady-of-guadalupe]

[37] "St. Juan Diego," EWTN website. [www.ewtn.com/catholicism/saints/juan-diego-658]

[38] Ibid.

[39] Cardinal Raymond Burke, *Studies in Honor of Our Lady of Guadalupe* (New Bedford, Massachusetts, Academy of the Immaculate, 2013), 8.

[40] "Raymond Leo Cardinal Burke," Shrine of Our Lady of Guadalupe website. [guadalupeshrine.org/raymond-leo-cardinal-burke]

[41] *Studies in Honor of Our Lady of Guadalupe*, 9.

[42] "Our Lady of Guadalupe."

[43] Donna-Marie Cooper O'Boyle, *30 Marian Eucharistic Visits: Adoring Jesus with His Mother* (Irondale, Alabama: EWTN Publishing, 2023), 38.

[44] *Studies in Honor of Our Lady of Guadalupe*, 13.

[45] Cardinal Raymond Burke, "Novena to Our Lady of Guadalupe." [https://novena.cardinalburke.com/ novena/reflections-library]

[46] Lucia dos Santos, *Fátima, in Lucia's Own Words: Sister Lucia's Memoirs* (Fátima Postulation Center, 1976), 161.

[47] Donna-Marie Cooper O'Boyle, *The Miraculous Medal: Stories, Prayers, and Devotions* (Cincinnati, Ohio, Servant Books, 2013), 31.

[48] The prayer commemorating the announcement of the Angel Gabriel to Mary that she would conceive of the Holy Spirit.

[49] *The Miraculous Medal*, 1.

[50] Ibid., 4. We know that Catherine did this because a household servant had been clandestinely watching.

[51] In 1969, the Feast of St. Vincent de Paul was moved from July 19 to September 27, the date of his death in 1660.

[52] *The Miraculous Medal,* 31.

[53] Father Joseph Dirvin, "Saint Catherine Labouré of the Miraculous Medal," EWTN website. [www.ewtn.com/catholicism/library/saint-catherine-laboure-of-the-miraculous-medal-5307]

[54] *The Miraculous Medal,* 70.

[55] Ibid.

[56] Pope Benedict XVI, General Audience, September17, 2008. [www.vatican.va/content/benedict-xvi/en/audiences/2008/documents/hf_ben-xvi_aud_20080917.html]

[57] Françoise Bouchard, *Bernadette: Her Story* (Paris, France, Salvator, 2007), 17.

[58] Ibid.

[59] Ibid., 75.

[60] Ibid., 76.

[61] Pope Benedict XVI, September 14, 2008.

[62] "Kibeho, Rwanda (1981–1989)," The Miracle Hunter website. [www.miraclehunter.com/marian_apparitions/ approved_apparitions/kibeho_rwanda/index.html]

[63] *Diary,* 429.

[64] Ibid., 635.

[65] "The Messages of Kibeho," The Miracle Hunter website. [www.miraclehunter.com/marian_apparitions/ messages/kibeho_messages.html]

[66] "June 29, 2001 – Declaration of the Bishop of Gikongoro, Rwanda," The Miracle Hunter website. [www.miraclehunter.com/marian_apparitions/statements/kibeho_statement_01.html]

[67] Ibid.

[68] Ibid.

[69] "Kibeho, Rwanda (1981-1989)."

[70] Pope Francis, "Address of Pope Francis to the Bishops of the Episcopal Conference of Rwanda on Their Ad Limina Visit," April. 3, 2014. [www.vatican.va/content/francesco/en/speeches/2014/april/documents/papa-francesco_20140403_ad-limina-rwanda.html]

[71] Immaculée Ilibagiza, "7 Sorrows Rosary Prayer." [www.immaculee.com/pages/7-sorrows-rosary-prayer]

[72] Marian Fathers of the Immaculate Conception, "The Chaplet of the Seven Sorrows," Marian.org. [www.marian.org/mary/prayers/chaplet-of-the-seven-sorrows] See also Joseph Pronechen, "Our Lady of Kibeho Calls for the Seven Sorrows Rosary," *National Catholic Register,* Lent 2024. [www.ncregister.com/blog/our-lady-of-kibeho-calls-for-the-seven-sorrows-rosary]

[73] *Diary,* 723.

[74] Pope John Paul II, *Dives in Misericordia* (*Rich in Mercy*), November 30, 1980, 9.

[www.vatican.va/content/john-paul-ii/en/encyclicals/documents/hf_jp-ii_enc_30111980_ dives-in-misericordia.html]

[75] Ibid.

[76] The Second Vatican Council, *Lumen Gentium*, November 21, 1964, 62. [https://www.vatican.va/archive/hist_councils/ii_vatican_council/documents/vat-ii_const_19641121_lumen-gentium_en.html]

[77] Pope John Paul II, *Veritatis Splendor* (*The Splendor of the Truth*), August 6, 1993, 118. [www.vatican.va/content/john-paul-ii/en/encyclicals/documents/hf_jp-ii_enc_06081993_veritatis-splendor.html]

[78] *Dives in Misericordia*, 9.

[79] *Saint Stanislaus Papczyński*, 93.

[80] *Veritatis Splendor*, 120.

[81] Ibid.

[82] *Diary*, 330.

[83] Ibid.

[84] Robert Stackpole, STD, "Why Do We Call Mary 'Mother Of Mercy'?"
TheDivineMercy.org, January 16, 2016. [www.thedivinemercy.org/articles/why-do-we-call-mary-mother-mercy]

[85] *Diary*, 1415.

[86] "Little Flower, Great Love," TheDivineMercy.org, October 1, 2021. [www.thedivinemercy.org/articles/little-flower-great-love]

[87] "Stop to Appreciate the 'Little Flower,'" TheDivineMercy.org, March 24, 2006. [www.thedivinemercy.org/articles/stop-appreciate-little-flower]

[88] Ibid.

[89] "The Life of St. Thérèse of Lisieux," St. Therese Church website, Alhambra, California. [www.sttheresechurchalhambra.org/?DivisionID=10357&DepartmentID=10676]

[90] St. Thérèse of Lisieux, *Story of A Soul,* Third Edition (Washington, D.C,, ICS Publications, 1996), 60.

[91] St. Thérèse of Lisieux, "Why do I Love You, O Mary!" v.18. [https://archives.carmeldelisieux.fr/en/archive/pn-54/]

[92] *Story of A Soul*, 63.

[93] Ibid., 62.

[94] Ibid., 65.

[95] Ibid., 64.

[96] Ibid., 63.

[97] Ibid., 65.

[98] Ibid.

[99] Ibid., 65, 66.

[100] Ibid.

[101] Ibid., 66.

[102] Ibid.

[103] Ibid.

[104] Ibid., 67.

[105] Ibid.

[106] Ibid., 15.

[107] Ibid., 247.

[108] Ibid.

[109] Ibid., 248.

[110] Ibid.

[111] Ibid., 271.

[112] "Little Flower, Great Love."

[113] Pope John Paul II, Homily, Holy Mass at the Cathedral of St. Matthew, Washington, DC, October 6, 1979. [www.vatican.va/content/john-paul-ii/en/homilies/1979/documents/hf_jp-ii_hom_19791006_washington-san-matteo.html]

[114] Pope John Paul II, Homily, Shrine of Merciful Love, Collevalenza, Italy, November 22, 1981. [www.thedivinemercy.org/message/john-paul-ii/homilies/1981-11-22]

[115] *Diary*, 260.

[116] *Diary*, 11

[117] Donna-Marie Cooper O'Boyle, *52 Weeks with Saint Faustina: A Year of Grace and Mercy* (Stockbridge, Massachusetts: Marian Press, 2018), 71, 72.

[118] *Spe Salvi*, 27. See also Jn 13:1 and Jn 19:30.

[119] Dan Barry, "New York homage for last surviving witness of Knock Apparition," *The Irish Times*, May 14, 2017. [www.irishtimes.com/news/social-affairs/religion-and-beliefs/new-york-homage-for-last-surviving-witness-of-knock-apparition-1.3082610]

[120] Father James, OFM Cap., "The Story of Knock," EWTN website. [www.ewtn.com/catholicism/library/story-of-knock-5600]

[121] "Knock, Ireland (1879)," The Miracle Hunter website. [www.miraclehunter.com/marian_apparitions/ approved_apparitions/knock/index.html]

[122] Ibid.

[123] "Official statement from Patrick Hill, Visionary from Knock," The Miracle Hunter website. [https://www.miraclehunter.com/marian_apparitions/approved_apparitions/knock/phill_statement.html]

[124] "The Story of Knock."

[125] *Diary*, 268.

[126] "The Story of Knock."

[127] "The Story of Knock," Knock Shrine website. [www.knockshrine.ie/history/]

[128] Dan Barry.

[129] Ibid.

[130] "Robinsonville (now Champion), WI, USA (1859)," The Miracle Hunter website. [www.miraclehunter.com/marian_apparitions/approved_apparitions/robinsonville/index.html]

[131] Bishop David Ricken, "The Decree on the Authenticity of the apparitions of 1859 at the Shrine of Our Lady of Good Help Diocese of Green Bay," December 8, 2010. [www.gbdioc.org/images/stories/Evangelization_Worship/Shrine/Documents/Shrine-of-Our-Lady-of-Good-Help.pdf]

[132] "Our Story," The National Shrine of Our Lady of Champion website. [championshrine.org/our-story/]

[133] Ibid.

[134] Ibid.

[135] Ibid.

[136] Ibid.

[137] Ibid.

[138] Ibid.

[139] Sister Pauline La Plante, OSF, "90 years at the Shrine of Our Lady of Champion." [www.gbfranciscans.org/ content/about/shrine-of-our-lady-of-good-help]

[140] "Our Story."

141 Mother Teresa, letter to the author, March 7, 1989.

142 Donna-Marie Cooper O'Boyle, "Mother Teresa Encourages Us to Be Loving Like Mary," *Catholic Exchange*, November 19, 2019. [catholicexchange.com/mother-teresa-encourages-us-to-be-loving-like-mary/]

143 *Diary*, 648.

144 Mother Teresa and Angelo Devananda Scolozzi, *Total Surrender*, rev. ed. (Ann Arbor, Michigan, Servant Publications, 1985), 102.

145 Mother Teresa, *Thirsting for God: Daily Meditations* (Cincinnati, Ohio, Servant Books, 2013), 17-18.

146 *Total Surrender*, 144.

147 Bob French, "Francis Xavier Nguyễn Văn Thuận, an Apostle of Hope," *The Word Among Us*, 2024. [https://wau.org/android_app/article/re_francis_xavier_nguyen_van_thuan_an_apostle_of_hope/?_key=8D23FA1C3FA5B6CF6494EDD83F8C5]

148 Cardinal Francis-Xavier Nguyễn Văn Thuận, "Ten Rules of Life of Cardinal Nguyễn Văn Thuận." [www.nguyenvanthuan.com/ten-rules-of-life.html]

149 Ibid.

150 Bob French.

151 Cardinal Nguyễn Văn Thuận.

152 Bob French.

153 Ibid.

154 Lucia dos Santos, *Fátima, in Lucia's Own Words: Sister Lucia's Memoirs* (Fátima Postulation Center, 1976), 62.

155 Ibid., 152.

156 Donna-Marie Cooper O'Boyle, *Our Lady's Message to Three Shepherd Children and the World* (Manchester, New Hampshire: Sophia Institute Press, 2017), 18.

157 Ibid., 33.

158 Joseph Pronechen, "Sister Lucia Explains Devotion to the Immaculate Heart of Mary Is a 'Must,'" *National Catholic Register*, June 20, 2020. [www.ncregister.com/blog/sister-lucia-explains-devotion-to-the-immaculate-heart-of-mary-is-a-must]

159 Mark Fellows, *Sister Lucia: Apostle of Mary's Immaculate Heart* (Buffalo, New York, Immaculate Heart Publications, 2007), 66. [https://fatima.org/wp-content/uploads/2018/05/Sister-Lucy-sm.pdf]

160 Donna-Marie Cooper O'Boyle, *Our Lady of Fátima: 100 Years of Stories, Prayers, and Devotions* (Cincinnati, Ohio, Servant Books, 2017), 83.

161 Joseph Pronechen.

162 "The Apparitions of Our Lady of Fátima," World Apostolate of Fátima, USA website. [www.bluearmy.com/the-story-of-Fátima/]

163 Cooper O'Boyle, *Our Lady of Fátima*, vii.

164 Ibid.

165 For Marian Consecration, I highly recommend *33 Days to Morning Glory: Group Retreat and Study Guide In Preparation for Marian Consecration* by Fr. Michael Gaitley, MIC (Stockbridge, Massachusetts: Marian Press, 2023).

166 "St. Finbarr's Oratory," Gougane Barra website. [gouganebarra.com/?page_id=80]

167 *Diary*, 742.

168 Saint Teresa of Calcutta, letter to the author, August 28, 1993.

[169] Pope John Paul II, World Youth Day, Toronto, July 2001. [www.vatican.va/content/john-paul-ii/en/messages/youth/documents/hf_jp-ii_mes_20010731_xvii-world-youth-day.html]

[170] Pope Francis, Homily, May 9, 2024. [www.vatican.va/content/francesco/en/homilies/2024/documents/20240509-indizione-giubileo.html]

[171] Saint Teresa of Calcutta, letter to the author, September 2, 1991.

[172] *Spe Salvi*, 31.

[173] Pope Benedict XVI, Act of Veneration to the Immaculate at the Spanish Steps, Dec. 8, 2007. [www.vatican.va/content/benedict-xvi/en/speeches/2007/december/documents/hf_ben-xvi_spe_20071208_immacolata.html]

[174] *Diary*, 79.

[175] Pope John Paul II, *Christifideles Laici* ("Christ's Faithful People"), December 30, 1988, 64. [www.vatican.va/content/john-paul-ii/en/apost_exhortations/documents/hf_jp-ii_exh_30121988_christifideles-laici.html]

[176] Pope John Paul II, *Evangelium Vitae* ("The Gospel of Life"), March 25, 1995, 105. [www.vatican.va/content/john-paul-ii/en/encyclicals/documents/hf_jp-ii_enc_25031995_evangelium-vitae.html]

[177] "The Message of Fatima," Congregation for the Doctrine of the Faith. [www.vatican.va/roman_curia/congregations/cfaith/documents/rc_con_cfaith_doc_20000626_message-fatima_en.html]

[178] *Fátima, in Lucia's Own Words*, 195.

[179] "John Paul II's Prayer to Our Lady of Guadalupe," www.usccb.org/issues-and-action/cultural-diversity/hispanic-latino/resources/upload/our-lady-of-guadalupe-jp-II-prayer.pdf

[180] Official prayer composed by Most Reverend David L. Ricken, D.D., J.C.L., Bishop of the Diocese of Green Bay. [championshrine.org/wp-content/uploads/2023/04/Our-Lady-of-Champion-Prayer.pdf]

[181] "Prayer of John Paul II," June 4, 1997. www.vatican.va/content/john-paul-ii/en/travels/1997/documents/hf_jp-ii_spe_04061997_prayer.html

More from Donna-Marie Cooper O'Boyle

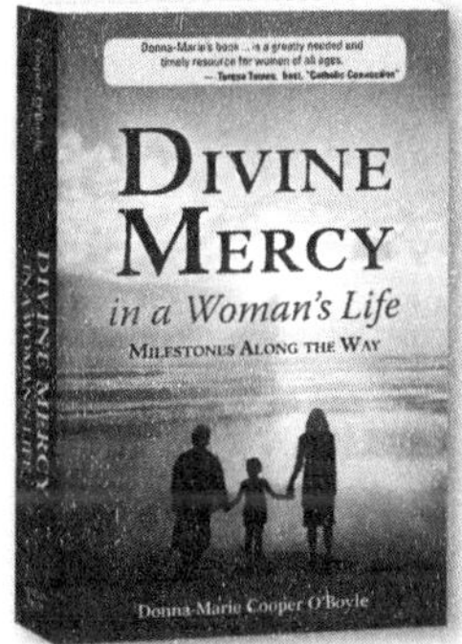

Divine Mercy in a Woman's Life: Milestones Along the Way

What does it mean for a woman to live according to Divine Mercy spirituality? In this loving look at life as lived by faithful female Catholics, popular author Donna-Marie Cooper O'Boyle has given modern women an important guide to letting the rays of Divine Mercy touch them, transform them, and flow through them to the world. Paperback. 416 pages. Y126-DMFW

52 Weeks with Saint Faustina: A Year of Grace and Mercy

Spend a year with St. Faustina! Perfect to begin any time of the year, this collection of weekly meditations and activities by EWTN TV host Donna-Marie Cooper O'Boyle, author of The Domestic Church: Room by Room, guides readers on a 52-week spiritual pilgrimage through the life and teachings of the Secretary and Apostle of Divine Mercy, St. Faustina Kowalska (1905-1938). Paperback. 390 pages. Y126-WEEKS

Diary of a Future Saint: Faustina's Incredible Journey

Diary of a Future Saint presents the authentic biography of St. Maria Faustina Kowalska for a new generation, told by master storyteller Donna-Marie Cooper O'Boyle. Designed for readers ages 10 and up, this lively and thought-provoking book tells the incredible journey of a simple peasant girl chosen by God to teach the world about His unfathomable Divine Mercy. Illustrated with scenes from St. Faustina's life. Paperback. 216 pages. Y126-UNST

Christmas Joy with Grandma!

Take an Advent journey with Joseph, Anne-Marie, and Grandmother! Together, you'll discover the story of Christmas and get ready to welcome Jesus into your own heart and home. Beautifully illustrated, this loving introduction to the true meaning of Christmas will become a beloved book and revisited each holiday season. Paperback, 40 pages. Y126-CHSB

For our complete line of books, prayer cards, pamphlets, Rosaries, and chaplets, visit ShopMercy.org or call 1-800-462-7426.

Join the

Association of Marian Helpers,

headquartered at the
National Shrine of The Divine Mercy,
and share in special blessings!

An invitation from
Fr. Joseph, MIC, the director

Marian Helpers is an Association of Christian faithful of the Congregation of Marian Fathers of the Immaculate Conception. By becoming a member, you share in the spiritual benefits of the daily Masses, prayers, and good works of the Marian priests and brothers.

This is a special offer of grace given to you by the Church through the Marians. Please consider this opportunity to share in these blessings, along with others whom you would wish to join into this spiritual communion.

The Marian Fathers of the Immaculate Conception of the Blessed Virgin Mary is a religious congregation of nearly 500 priests and brothers around the world.

Call 1-800-462-7426 or visit Marian.org

Give a Consoling Gift: *Prayer*

Enroll your loved ones in the Association of Marian Helpers, and they will participate in the graces from the daily Masses, prayers, good works, and merits of the Marian priests and brothers around the world.

1-800-462-7426

Marian.org/enrollments

Enrollments can be offered for the living or deceased. We offer a variety of enrollment cards: wedding, anniversary, First Holy Communion, birthday, get well, and more.

Request a Mass

to be offered by the Marian Fathers for your loved one

Individual Masses
(for the living or deceased)

Gregorian Masses
(30 days of consecutive Masses for the deceased)

1-800-462-7426
Marian.org/mass